IN THE VISUAL STUDIES SERIES

EDITED BY DOUGLAS HARPER

You Are My Darling Zita

Glenn Busch

TEMPLE UNIVERSITY PRESS
PHILADELPHIA

Temple University Press, Philadelphia 19122
Copyright © 1991 by Glenn Busch. All rights reserved
Published 1991
Printed in the United States of America

The paper used in this publication meets the minimum
requirements of American National Standard for Information
Sciences—Permanence of Paper for Printed Library
Materials, ANSI Z39.48-1984

Library of Congress Cataloging-in-Publication Data

Busch, Glenn.
You are my darling Zita / Glenn Busch.
p.   cm. — (Visual studies)
ISBN 0-87722-791-8 (alk. paper)
1. Aged—New Zealand—Biography. 2. Old age—New
Zealand—Case studies. I. Title. II. Series.
HQ1060.5.B87   1990
305.26'092—dc20   90-39060

ERRATUM

The photograph of Zita Edmunds on page
38 should appear on page 33. The photograph of Glenys Lewis with her father and
sister on page 33 should appear on page 38.

For Trish

Contents

Introduction

I was going to say it began with Alex, but really it started with Nana. My grandmother's name was Ida—the same as my mother's—but to me she was Nana; that is how I always knew her. When I was young she spent a great deal of time with us. The reason for that was my grandfather. At the time he liked to drink. Half-gallon jars of sweet sherry is one thing I remember, and when he drank too much Nana would leave him for a time and come to stay with us. In those days I was too young to have much of a feel for her troubles; all I knew was the excitement of seeing her walk round the corner of our street. I'd run then to meet her, eager as always to search inside the pockets of her coat for the jellybeans and peppermints I knew would be there.

The other thing about Nana in those days—apart from the lollies—was the stories she used to tell me. In the evenings, a little before bedtime, she'd take me up on her lap, cradle my head in her enormous bosom, and tell me stories I never got tired of hearing.

Nana told two types of stories and on a good night I'd get one of each. First there were the stories she invented—funny little stories that she made up as she went along. And then there were the stories she told me about our family. I liked them both, but it was the stories about our family, about real people, that I liked to hear best. Those were the ones I always asked for.

As for this collection of stories—this book—it started as a photographic project on coal mining. The day I met Alex it turned into something else.

I live in the port of Lyttelton, on the eastern side of the South Island of New Zealand. On the western side, across the Southern Alps, lies the province of Westland. Westland, known colloquially as "the Coast," is the major coal mining district of New Zealand, and was home to my father for the first eighteen years of his life.

"Coasters," he'd once told me, were tough, close, and very friendly once you got to know them. As I travelled about, many years later, they didn't seem to have changed much. By the time I had been there a couple of weeks, I'd talked to a lot of people but taken very few photographs. Most of my time seemed to be taken up indulging in "West Coast hospitality." By the time I came to return home, I didn't seem to have done much work. Perhaps the kindest thing you could say was that at least I'd made a start. The irony is that had I done more, I would probably never have stopped that day in Dobson.

Heading home, my mind busy with all the things I'd left undone two weeks before, and with trying to decide which of them should be attended to first, I was almost through Dobson before I even saw it. I had driven through the town a number of times on my trips around the area but never stopped—there really hadn't seemed much point. It's true there had once been a mine there, but it had closed down some years back. All that appeared to be left were the houses, and there weren't a lot of them. It was more of a village, really, than what you might think of as a town. A mile or so down the road I started to think again about how little I'd done in the last two weeks. It wouldn't hurt, I thought, slowing the car and turning it around, to take a quick look.

Set in close to the Grey River, Dobson once again straddled the main road in front of me. Rain had been falling through the night, and the morning was cold. The only sign of life, apart from the wisps of chimney smoke, was a sign on the door of the pub saying "Open." Inside there were no customers, just the barman getting ready for a slow day. It didn't seem to bother him that I wanted information rather than a drink; all the same, our conversation was brief. When I told him what I was doing, he simply said, "You'd better see Alex," and then he told me how I'd recognise the house.

I knocked on his door and got as far as my name before Alex interrupted. "No use standing here on the step, laddie. You'd better come in and have a cuppa tea." And then, because he wasn't feeling too strong that morning, he told me where I'd find the makings, directing me through the open kitchen door while he sat back in front of a well-banked coal fire.

A squat, once powerful man now weakened by illness, Alex had a voice still strong in both accent and volume. The last of his strength seemed to be carried in a gruffness bordering on the brusque. We must have talked for about three hours that first morning, or rather I listened, recording what he said about his childhood in Scotland—the parish of Beath. He recalled child-hood memories, rich in imagery and feelings about what he called "the war between the capitalist people and us slaves." He told of the beginnings of a lifetime spent hewing coal underground. And later, toward the end of that first meeting, he told me about his father, a craftsman jeweller who owned not one but two shops: a man of some standing in the community. A man who over time developed an awful thirst for whisky, eventually drinking away everything they had. "I could always tell when he was goin' out, and so could Mum. He'd get all shaved and poshed up. He had a wee moustache; it was waxed at the sides, and you'd see him wax-ing this bugger up. Then he'd take a teaspoonful of butter and put it down his mouth and let it melt. And Mum would say, 'He's on the whisky tonight.'"

I remember thinking about my own grandfather when I heard that. He'd done much the same thing with some property his father had left him. And it made me think again of Nana and the stories she used to tell.

She's dead now, Nana. She died some time back, when I was in my early twenties. She was—or so I had thought—the first old person I knew well. Listening to Alex, I began to think about just how little I had known her. Certainly I had never talked with her as I did with Alex. That is not to say I didn't love her. The day she died I knew, for the first time, what it felt like to grieve for another human being. Her death was unexpected. My mother rang me at work to tell me. I put the phone down and walked into the locker room looking for somewhere to be alone. I sat there on a wooden bench staring at the rubbish on the floor and thinking about my grandmother. Strange the little memories—tiny pieces of other people—we keep within ourselves, different for each. For me, a way she had with her eyes when she laughed, a kindness in her movements, but perhaps most of all a certain fragrance. An essence, almost physical, that belonged only to her. Cotton dresses, cheap talcum, the musk of her own body, mixed together in a wonderful bouquet as she held me close and told the stories of our family. Quite suddenly I began to cry. It was a long time before I could stop.

Leaving Alex's place that day, I rang my wife Trish to tell her I'd be a day late. That evening in a motel room, the volume turned up against torrential rain, I listened to the tapes I'd made only a few hours before. I wanted to think about some of the things Alex had said. Later still, lying in the dark, I kept seeing pictures of my grandmother's face and thinking of things that had not been said. It was true that I had loved her, but what struck me like a blow was to realise I'd never really known her. What's more, as we'd both grown older, I knew her less and less. Her old age was the part of her life I knew least about. The things I had wanted to know about, the things she had told me, were all from a time when she had been young. Never once in her old age did I extend to her the intimacy she'd so freely given me as a child. Not once did I tell her the truth of my life, nor ask the truth of hers. As I lay there thinking this, little snatches of Alex's conversation started to run through my mind. "A lot of people, they ignore the old. . . . The young today, they think you're something that's not worth talking to, an old dishcloth, finished with life. . . . The old can be used if society would use them. . . . There are things from the old that the young could learn." It was too late to ask my grandmother the things she might have told me, too late to learn the things she might have taught me. Not too late, I began to think as I drifted into sleep, to ask Alex. The next morning I rang Trish again. I would have to stay another week.

Alex felt better some days than others. Sometimes we were able to talk only for an hour or two. But for as long as was possible, over the next few days, he told me as much as he could about what old age was like for him.

GETTING HOME, I started to talk with other people—not old—about the idea of being old. As I did I became aware of a rather strange perception—a vague notion really—which was that time stands still. There were, it would seem, young people, middle-aged people, and old people, each isolated within their own stereotype. And that was the way it was. Well, that wasn't difficult to understand. I was approaching forty, the beginning, I supposed, of my middle years. I had now lived sufficiently long to have some concept of movement through time. And yet to actually imagine myself as "old" was very difficult. For the young I imagine it is almost impossible.

It seemed that the best and obvious way to gain an understanding of what it was like to be old was to ask the people who knew. And what I found when I listened to older people was that they did as Alex had. They told me about all their lives, not just the part they were living now. In order to know a part, you need access to the whole. To understand a person's perception of old age, it was necessary to place it in a context; that is what they seemed to be telling me.

A month or so later I went to see Alex again. I spent several more days with him taping our conversations. Occasionally when I asked him a question he would answer it directly. More often—and this was what I liked best—he would use the question as a point of departure for a leisurely exploration that ranged from one end of his life to the other, using up a ninety-minute tape in the process. On the last day he took a small box and from it produced a number of photographs. You could tell their importance by the way he handled them. He showed them to me carefully and with plenty of time between each one so that I could "take a good look."

It was not what you would call a comprehensive collection: a post-card of his hometown in Scotland, a few photos of himself with work mates, one with his wife in their middle years. Prompted by these, I asked if I might photograph him myself. He agreed.

Driving back that evening from the Coast, I listened to the tapes we had made, mentally taking note of the things I had yet to ask, things I would want to talk to him more about the next time. It was not long after this visit that my wife, reading over breakfast, came upon his death notice in the morning paper.

I had come to feel close to Alex. The intimacy with which we had talked made this happen a lot sooner than it might have otherwise. After reading his death notice, I spent the rest of that day going over the time I'd had with him, listening to the tapes we'd made and looking at the photographs I'd borrowed such a short time before. What had begun only a few months ago as an emotional quest, prompted by thoughts of my own grandmother, had become something more. A responsibility had been added. In some cultures there is a saying that suggests that if you save a person's life you become responsible for it. Alex was dead, but it seemed to me that on the tapes we had made, and in a handful of photographs, something of his life remained.

We had talked on my first visit about making what we were doing into a book. "Aye, laddie, that would be okay. I trust you to put it down right" was his answer. Putting it down right is the principle I have tried to observe, not only with Alex, but with all who trusted enough to become part of this book.

MEETING ALEX was unexpected. How I should go about finding other people willing to talk about what it means to be old was not immediately obvious. However, by the time I had transcribed the hours of tape and put together the first draft of the piece on Alex, I had a good idea of the format the book might take. I also had an idea of the size of the job I had taken on. It was apparent, by the fullness of Alex's story alone, that I would find it impossible to look at any more than a few experiences. Because of this I decided I would try—within the range of my own cultural experience—to find not only people interested in telling their stories, but people whose lives had been as diverse as possible.

Difference and age—over seventy seemed about right—were not, of course, the only things to look for. Interest in the idea was one thing, but more than that, I had to find people willing to talk about their lives in an extremely personal way. For this we needed time to get to know one another. Time for trust to develop. We had to decide that we liked each other enough to become friends. I didn't want an interviewer-subject relationship; the honesty I was asking for had to be reciprocal. That I now feel very close to all the people who appear in this book means a great deal to me.

Beatrice, after Alex, was the first person I met. She lives on a busy street in what was once a working-class district close to the inner city. Today the area has been taken over by small industry, and her house, sandwiched between factories, is one of only two dwellings left. I saw her by chance one afternoon as I drove past. With the aid of a walking stick, she was making her way slowly up the front path to the letter box. I stopped to talk with her, and after chatting for a while at the gate she invited me inside. By the end of the afternoon we had agreed to see each other on a regular basis.

After Beatrice came Zita, though it took me three months to find her. Living the last part of your life in an old people's home is not uncommon these days; I wanted to talk to somebody about what that felt like. A few days after I'd finished the piece on Beatrice, I was in a cafe having lunch with a friend. Across the road was an old people's home. It seemed like as good a place as any to start looking. The matron, after I'd explained to her what I was doing, was happy to let me spend a few hours there talking with the residents. By the end of the afternoon I had talked with a number of interesting people, but no one had felt quite right. I got ready to leave. "You really should see Mrs. Edmunds," the matron said. "She's out just now, but she'd be good to talk to." I was tired.

I had had a long day. I filed what she'd said under "maybe later," thanked her for her help, and went home.

For the next three months I spent a good part of most days talking to people in old people's homes. I began to wonder if I was ever going to find the right person, and doubts about the book ever getting finished began to creep in. Then one day I went back to the cafe I'd had lunch in three months earlier and remembered Mrs. Edmunds. Ten minutes later I was talking with her, and by the time I left I was wishing I'd paid more attention to the matron three months before.

Glenys Lewis is a woman who gave herself to God at an early age. This strong commitment to Christian beliefs affected her life in a profound way. I first met her briefly and by chance one afternoon while calling on a friend's aunt to discuss the project. Glenys had stopped in for five minutes to drop something off. We were introduced, and it was explained what I was doing there. My friend had thought her aunt might be a good candidate for the book, and indeed she was a delightful woman, but there was something about Glenys—difficult to put into words—that told me she was the one I was looking for. Later she told me she had felt the same thing. Before leaving she invited me to come and see her sometime. I went the next day.

Towards the end of this project John Morrison's name was mentioned a number of times by different friends aware of what I was doing. As he was then spending some time in the country, I wrote suggesting that we get together on his return. He telephoned a few days later to say he was interested in the idea and suggested a time and date. Right from the start it was obvious why people had suggested John, and I was very glad when he agreed to be involved. On our first meeting I also met his wife Muriel. Two or three more meetings followed. John and Muriel then came to my home for lunch. We had an enjoyable afternoon, and afterwards, talking with my wife about the way John's and Muriel's lives had been so intertwined, it became obvious that I should be talking not only with John, but with Muriel as well.

THERE IS A paradox of sorts in the making of a book of this kind. The premise of the book is that these are the words and feelings of real people. But this reality is reflected through the medium of a writer whose task has been to gather, select, arrange, and present the words that convey its essence.

As anyone who has read the literal transcription of a recorded discussion will know, the spoken word, unedited, simply doesn't read very well. While it's true that everybody has something of importance to say, something they can tell us and from which we can learn, the process of conversation is not often noted for its clarity. Mostly it comes out all over the place, a merry-go-round of remembered anecdotes and feelings in which false starts and half-completed sentences are common fare. Face to face we cope with this pretty well. By using indicators such as the tone of a person's voice and body language, we can mentally sort out a conversation as it goes along. On paper it is something else.

In preparation for this book I recorded some few million words. My task in sorting them out—transferring their essence to paper—was to make them as clear as possible while at the same time remaining faithful to what was originally said. From the out-set I decided to remove myself—in the form of my questions—altogether. My feeling is that the impression of a voice allowed to speak without interruption—a voice saying something in the most direct manner—communicates a far greater intimacy than a page intruded upon by questions. The order in which things were told to me has also been changed, though in this it was never my in-tention to alter the sense of what was said. Rather, it was to make more comprehensible what had been said, sometimes in the course of several conversations, over a long period of time. There were a few occasions when I found it necessary to add words of my own in order to connect and make things clear. There is, of course, a danger in this: the manner in which things are said originally, the words, character, may be changed. I have done my best to guard against this, and ultimately there was the safeguard that the people concerned would read and approve the finished piece. With the exception of Alex and Zita, who died before the work was finished, they did so.

For a long time now, using a camera and a tape recorder as passports, I have had the opportunity to enter other worlds, to meet, talk, and form friendships with people I would never normally have known. The insights offered here by people I have come to know over the last few years are reflected for me in the way my own life has changed by knowing them. That they have consented to explore and reveal parts of their emotional life, to show uncovered the private depths of their experience in a world more at ease with the superficial, is truly remarkable.

To Zita, Glenys, Alex, Beatrice, John, and Muriel—special people—my love and respect.

You Are My Darling Zita

Zita Edmunds

THAT NIGHT. Oh yes, I was in a state that night. I really was. I'd gone up to the gate—I went up to get the milk. I got the bottle out, and I got the papers out, and all of a sudden there was nothing, I had no power to move. It was just like all of a sudden I wasn't anybody or anything. There wasn't a soul in the street and I just stood there feeling like nothing at all. It was the most terrifying experience. Then all of a sudden I came back, and as I did I went straight down. My leg gave out and I just went straight down onto my knees. I've had falls before. I've fallen in the street and broken my wrist and had black eyes and all that sort of thing, but those sorts of falls were blackouts. I used to feel I had nowhere to put my feet and I would go down on my face. But this was different altogether, as if something came over me that took control—took control of me so that I couldn't move. I wasn't anybody, and it was an awful feeling. It was absolute despair. But then after a bit I got control, and I thought to myself, I've got to get out of here, I've got to get back, and I managed to get around onto my hands and knees. I could see that the light was on in the flat next to mine, and so I just crawled along until I got there. It was a long drive and I tore all my knees and stockings, but I never passed out.

She had the door locked because she was a widow and lived alone, but I tapped on the bottom of the door. Well, she opened it, she opened it and helped me in, and she said, "I'll ring your son." I said, "Please don't." I said, "I don't want you to ring them." "Oh," she said, "I think I should." And I said, "No, please don't." I said, "Look, I'll just sit here for a minute"—I was coming around to myself then—I said, "If you'll just help me back home and get me sat down." So she did, and I got her to get me a glass of brandy from the cupboard and some water to drink. She did all this for me but it was rather strange because I don't think she liked it. She didn't want to get involved, if you know what I mean.

Anyhow, I drank this brandy and I sat there in the chair for a long time. Then after a while I thought I'd better try and get into bed, and when I did I just sort of flopped, I went straight to sleep.

ZITA EDMUNDS

3

In the morning, when I woke up, all I had was a lot of skin off my knees—but I felt different in myself.

It had been a horrible, horrible feeling, and I began to think to myself, perhaps Myrna's right. Myrna had said to me before, "Nana, I really think we'll have to see about putting your name down for a home." And I thought, oh no, no, no, I don't want to go into a home. I don't want to. But you see it was old age. It was old age that was really coming on me. It was a horrible feeling, but that was the start of my downfall. I was going down. Now I'm in my eighty-sixth year, wearing out perhaps, but then that's old age—isn't it.

I WAS BORN on the thirtieth of June, 1900. Born in a little grocer shop my parents had at the time. I don't think they were expecting this baby to come along. When I came, they had to sell the shop. Then my father—he wasn't qualified for anything really— he started to work for the council. Just sweeping roads and that sort of thing. He did that practically right up until he died. He developed a lot of trouble, like men get, and he went into the hospital and he died. He was seventy.

He was a good father. He was strict, but he never chastised any of us. The only thing was—well,—he never got drunk, but he just sometimes got to be that little bit nasty, you know, what they get with drink. My mother was tolerant, much more tolerant than I could ever've been. But from then on I hated drink, and I made up my mind that if ever I got married, I would never marry a man that drank. And I didn't.

Really, I had a good childhood. I had a good home and good parents; we never wanted for food or anything like that. I was well looked after. But one thing that did have an effect on me— it was during the war—my father you see was a German and he was never naturalised. Because of that I had to put up with a bit of nonsense, and no one likes being teased. But what really did get me was that my mother had to report every week to a policeman that lived in the next street. Eleven o'clock every Saturday morn-

ing she had to report. I don't know if anyone saw my father, he never spoke about it, but my mother had to report, and I got very bitter about that. I didn't think it was fair. And I remember just before I left school, there was a boy, he was a telegraph boy, and he wanted me to go to the pictures with him. When I wouldn't go he said, "You'd better go, or I'll tell everyone your father's a German." Well, you've got no idea how that felt, how that worried me. People can be very hurtful, can't they—but I never mentioned it at home.

I was educated at the convent school and brought up a strict Catholic. I stayed there till I got my proficiency at just on fourteen. To my way of thinking now, there was so many—so many rotten, stupid things that they put into our heads. I was ten years old when Halley's comet came—1910—and the nuns said we might all die. It was going to wipe us out. This was the sort of thing they put in your mind, and of course we all had to pray. I was terrified. We lived near Mt. Eden, and I used to think if we all went up there, up the mountain and prayed, we could turn the comet away. When I look back and think about all the stupid little things we were told—the power of prayer, ha!—well, I've got my doubts. I've got my doubts about the hereafter too. Whether there is or whether there isn't, there's no one ever come back to tell us, has there. Oh well, whether I go up or down, I'll make friends wherever I go.

My mother wasn't strong. She had what they called a leaking valve in her heart. And my father had this idea—he'd say, "It's a poor household that can't afford one lady," meaning that I was to stay at home. And I did that till I was sixteen, but I was very unhappy about it for the fact that all my friends were working. See, my father was just a labourer, we were just ordinary working people, and I couldn't get the clothes and things that the other girls were getting. And oh, didn't I want them. In the end I asked my mother if she would talk Dad into letting me go to work, and she said yes, she would do that.

I didn't really know what I wanted to do, but there was a job advertised at Wilson and Horton's bindery. Well, I got that job and

I stayed there until I was married. I worked in what they called the cheque room, cheques that went to the bank. They were printed there, and they all had to be checked over before they were sent to the bank. Oh, I had several boyfriends too, you know, like girls do, but that's where I met my husband. At Wilson and Horton's. He was a paper ruler—now, that's a thing that's gone right out with the past. There was a big machine, and he used to set up all the pens, and the girls used to have to come and feed the paper through. Well, occasionally, if they were stuck for a girl, I would be brought out to help, and through that we got quite friendly. Then one night—there was a tramways strike on at the time— we all had to go back to get a job out. Afterwards, as it was so late and there were no trams on, he offered to walk home with me, which I accepted. Then when we were walking home he said to me, "What about going to His Majesty's Theatre on Saturday night? The Big Boys are on." It was a musical comedy thing called "The Big Boys." So I went with him and somehow it just blossomed forth and blossomed forth, and I eventually married him. So that's how it happened. And it turned out to be a good marriage too.

But I remember when we were first courting, the first time I met his family. I went there one night for tea, and you know what it's like, the whole family there, I felt a bit strange. Well, for a long time after that I never got invited again. I remember saying to my mother, "They were very nice," I said, "but I don't think they could have liked me." You see, at that particular time I was still going to church, I was still a practising Catholic, and I said to Mum, "It may be on account of the religion. They may not want Bert to get tied up with anybody like that."

Then I met his mother and sister shopping one time, and his mother said to me, "You haven't been around." I said "I've never been asked." "Oh," she said, "That's Bert." She said, "You know what he wants to do with you—he wants to take you on a desert island where no one else will have you or see you." So she said, "Will you come to tea on Sunday night?" Well, from then on it

ZITA EDMUNDS

7

was different altogether. I was taken into the family. The religious part of the thing never worried them at all. As it happened we got married in a Catholic church. Well, they didn't marry you in the church then—you had to go into what they called the vestry. They were very bitter against mixed marriages. Oh yes, the Catholic Church had some very strange things, as I've found out.

Being a mixed marriage—that was a sore point with my mother . . . well, not actually a sore point, but she would have liked me to marry in the Church. You see, married in the vestry I wasn't a bride. But I was perfectly happy about our wedding day and the way we went about it. I was very pleased and excited about it. Oh, I knew there would be a little bit of talk about it from the girls that I worked with—some of them had been brides and had big weddings—but that never worried me.

One time, many years later, we went to a wedding of one of the family, and Bert said to me then, he said, "You know, I often think I did you out of something when we got married. You would have made a beautiful bride." I said "Didn't you like the way I looked?" He said, "Yes, you looked beautiful." But he said, "You would have looked lovely as a—well—with a veil and all like that." So you see, he had thought about that. But it didn't worry me; if they didn't like it, well, I didn't care. I was perfectly satisfied. I had known right from the beginning that he wouldn't turn, that he had no religion.

When you are young and you are brought up in a religion, you take it all in. You take it all in because that's what you've been brought up to—you don't think for yourself. But, you see, later in life, when I met my husband—well, he had such terribly different ideas on those sorts of things, and that was a big help to me. I went to lectures and I learnt from him an awful lot. I started to think for myself, and I was able to voice my own opinion. I had never bothered to think so deeply till I was with my husband. He was really the greatest influence on my life—yes, I'm sure of that. And now I have a different outlook on life altogether. As I say, with

ZITA EDMUNDS

religion you don't think for yourself, but since then I have thought an awful lot—an awful lot.

WE WERE MARRIED about three and a half years when my son was born. We had a good marriage, and I don't suppose my confinement was any worse than anyone else's, but he said at the time, when he got me home, "You're never going through that again."

ZITA EDMUNDS

10

And I never did. That was up to him, it wasn't me. But then, in a way, I got selfish too. I had my son and I had Bert; I was perfectly happy. Nothing else mattered. Now perhaps, if I had my life over again, I might have more children, to have when you get older— and to have their children. See, it's alright when you've got your husband; even when your son grows up and gets married, you've still got your husband, or you've still got your wife. But then there comes a time when just you are left, and when that happens you can feel very alone.

I always used to think I was going to die first. I did. I don't know why, but I always thought that I would die first and leave

Bert. I never ever—never at any time—expected to live without him. But then I had to, and it was like part of you is gone. To lose someone that is so close and so good—I don't think you ever get over it. It'll be twenty-two years in June that I lost my husband . . . no, you don't ever get over it. Sometimes at night I look at his picture up there, and I think about him. I lie awake and look up there and think of the things we did—think of the things I should have said.

He is a lot in my memory of course—I have wonderful memories. We were very, very close. We did everything together, we went everywhere together. You know, he used to buy me little gifts, and in the morning he would put them under the pillow before I made the bed. He bought my cosmetics right up until he really took ill. I never bought any powder or anything. He was wonderful like that. But he only once, in all my married life, bought me flowers. I had the flu and he bought me a bunch of violets, and then he hid them in his overcoat pocket so no one would see them. He was funny about flowers . . . but oh yes, we had a good life. Of course we had our bad times too. I'm not going to say that we didn't have our little ups and downs like everyone else, but taking it all round, things seemed to go right for us.

You know, looking back, he always put me first. He did, he always put me first, and I just accepted it. After he died I thought perhaps I should have expressed more affection for him, perhaps I could have showed it more to him. Just little things like, but if I had it over again, I would show it more than I did. The fact is, though, you've lost them. Within yourself you wish you'd done more, but you didn't, and you can't get them back to tell them, can you. It's too late then.

In the beginning it was just a few backaches. He was always thin, but then he was getting thinner, and I was still thinking it was just backaches. I didn't realise he was going down to the extent that he was. Then one day, our doctor who was tending him, came and told me, he said, "He's got Hodgkin's disease," and he told me what was going to happen. That was a sad time. He got

really bad then and they put him in the hospital. They had to take his gland out—took his main gland away—and I knew then that he was going to die.

After that he had to keep going to the hospital and having all these treatments on the machine. I saw him suffer and it was

ZITA EDMUNDS

13

terrible. I hated to see him suffer like he did, but he was brave—he was very brave. Then one time they kept him in the hospital and gave him a transfusion, and he seemed so much better. He was only in hospital a week and a half, and he was so much better. Ha, the silly things you do. You see, he liked to sit on the settee in the kitchen, the fire going in the range. So I went out and bought a new carpet. I thought, he's going to be alright now, and I bought a bright new carpet for the kitchen—for him to come home to. But of course he wasn't alright, his own doctor said he wasn't, and they said the same at the hospital. I knew really, in my heart I knew, it was only a matter of time.

In those days I used to be a very restless person in the bed. If I could not sleep I would flounder all around. But those last few months of his life, when I knew how much he was suffering, I got to the stage where I just used to lie there, very still, and wait. I knew he was dying, and I would go to bed and wonder if we'd get through the night. Then the morning would come, and you'd be thinking, will we get through today? Will he last through the day? But then, I don't care how you are waiting for it—it is still the most awful shock when it comes.

He died at home—in the morning. I was sixty-three, and he was sixty-four, just a year older than me. That night he had haemorrhaged. My sister-in-law and I were at his bed when the blood came up. In the morning when the nurse came—she wasn't the usual nurse—I said, "He's dying, isn't he?" "I don't know," she snapped, "only God knows that." I felt like hitting her.

I sat on the bed and held his hand, and he said to me, "I'm going to die aren't I?" "Oh," I said, "we won't talk about that." "Yes," he said, "I am, and I don't want to leave you." Then he squeezed my hand, and I said, "Can you see me?" "Yes, of course," he said. "You're my darling Zita." Then he went unconscious, and at a quarter past eleven he was dead. You are my darling Zita—those were the last words he said to me.

At the crematorium, the day of the funeral, I don't think I heard or saw anything. When I came out it was all a blank. I just

ZITA EDMUNDS

14

wanted to get away home. Of course the people came, and they had to be fed. I had two good neighbours, and my sister, my elder sister, and they had arranged all the food. It was good of them, but I wanted to be on my own. I went into the front room and I just asked them to please leave me by myself. I didn't want anybody. My sister and others stayed on with me, but in the end I asked them to go too. I wanted to be alone—just alone—to do and say what I wanted. And I talked to him. Whether he heard it or not we'll never know, but that was the way—that is how it affected me. I missed him so terrible.

I had dreams then too. It was horrible really. They were always dreams that he was there. In the dreams he was always there with me, but then you'd wake up and you'd be all alone. I would kick out my legs to try to touch him, but I was always alone. I would just lie there then in a sweat, shaking and shivering. Eventually I moved into the spare room—I made up a bed in there, and that was my single room. I was better then. It might sound strange, but that's when the dreams sort of went.

The day that I burnt his things I called him for everything. I was howling and swearing at the same time. He was a very deep reader, my husband, and a terrible hoarder. We had a spare room in the house that he used for his books and things—a hoard room. After he'd died, and I came down to earth a bit, I thought, well, something has to be done about that. I went through some of his books and I got in touch with what they called the Progressive Book Shop, and I asked them to come and get them. After that, though, there was still a lot of stuff to be burnt. Well, I sort of broke down and I got very annoyed; I called him everything. I'm sure his ashes must have been turning over. Our next-door neighbour came in and she said, "Whatever is the matter?" I said, "I have just told Bert exactly what I thought of him and his damn room." She said, "Poor old Bert." She said, "Remember when he came back from hospital with his arm in a sling. He was going out, walking backwards and forwards to the incinerator, trying to burn up a lot of the rubbish himself." She said, "You remember

ZITA EDMUNDS

that, and don't go calling him those horrible names." But anyway
I did. I did that. I had quite a talk to him. And then I got on with
the burning.

THE LOSS of my husband was terrific, but I still had a son and
a daughter-in-law, and two grandchildren to live for. I still had
them to be going on for. But when Bert died, my son and his

ZITA EDMUNDS

wife—Myrna—they were living in England. Well, I wanted him then, I wanted my son very badly. And our family doctor—just a couple of days after the funeral—he came and saw me, and he said, "The best thing you can do now is go to Alan." He said, "The best thing—as soon as you get everything fixed up—is to get on a ship and go." He said, "Go on a ship, but don't go sitting in a corner and thinking you're the only person that's had any trouble." So that's what I did, I went to England. Bert died in June, and I went in November, the beginning of November.

The day I arrived in Southampton I expected Alan to meet me, but he wasn't there. I couldn't see him anywhere. Then all of a sudden I saw him, tearing down the road, his overcoat flying. He'd been trying to get a taxi in the town to bring down to the wharf, but he couldn't get one and he'd run all the way. That was the first time I'd seen him in three years. Of course I broke down, and so did he. However, we got over that, and we went and had a cuppa tea. That's when I thought to myself, I've made it—I had got there.

I had a wonderful time with Myrna and Alan, and I tried to think and do what the doctor had told me. To put things behind me and mix with other people. To try and lead a different life, which I did. Oh, I went to lots of places, and I did make the most of that trip. Going to see Alan and the family, going on that trip—I really think that's what saved me from getting too much into myself. It saved me from that. Even so, I was glad when it was the time for coming home. When the boat was getting nearer to Auckland, I was glad to be coming home. It was a strange feeling. When I got to the house there were quite a lot of friends there—everything had been arranged, and of course there was lots of excitement. But that night, after everyone had gone and I was alone in the house, I missed Bert then. I had been away all that time, I'd had all that experience and an awful lot to talk about, but he was gone. Like a part of me was gone. I did miss him then.

I suppose Bert going was just the start of old age creeping on me. Even before that, really, I'd started to have falls in the street.

ZITA EDMUNDS

Just momentary blackouts. Of course you think you are down a long time, but the doctor said, if you were down as long as you thought you were, you'd never get up again. He just said my blood pressure was too high, to take things easy, and not go rushing around. That was in my fifties, and it was quite a long time before I had another fall. It didn't worry me too much. I didn't lose any sleep about it. But you do realise that you're getting on, and you're not as bright as you used to be. Up to a point it did slow me down a little, but I didn't actually lose my nerve through it. It didn't stop me driving or anything. I suppose I just thought, I'll get over it. You know, you don't like to think that you're getting old—but I did—I did have the feeling that old age was starting to creep up on me.

WHEN I CAME back from England I settled back into my own life, and six months later my son and his family came back as well, to live in Christchurch. I went on living by myself in the old house in Auckland for many years, and I was happy enough. I could go down to Christchurch and see the family when I wanted, and my neighbours in Auckland—some were old people, and there was the young couple next door—we all got on well together. But then, without you realising it, there is something that is slowly coming on you. Gradually it comes on you, and each year you are losing a little more dash than you had the year before. You just think, well, I'm a year older, and you carry on. But, you see, my blood pressure was as high as ever and I was starting to have a lot more falls. Every year I seemed to get something, and so finally I decided to sell the house and move down to Christchurch. Be closer to the family.

After living in the same house for forty-nine years, leaving it, having to give it up—it was quite a break. But, you know, from the moment I bought the flat in Christchurch—before any furniture or anything had come—when I walked into that flat, I knew I was going to be happy there. The lounge was full of sunshine and

everything was so nice. Oh yes, I was very happy with it. And to me, I was going to be there until I died.

Actually when I first came down here I was still quite fit. I still did all my shopping and that. Oh yes, I'm a great window shopper, going up the road and talking to people—oh, I enjoyed all that. I used to walk for a very long way. But then there came a time—well, somehow it just seemed to be getting more difficult to go even a short distance without sitting down and resting. All the same I thought, I'm not going to let it stop me, and I still kept going. I just sat on the fences and all like that when I had to, but I suppose I did start to worry a little bit. Then a while later I got to the stage that I was finding it difficult even to get up to the shops,

ZITA EDMUNDS

and when that happened I started to worry a lot. Even walking to the mall from where I lived was becoming a terrible strain on me, and I was thinking, this is going to be awful. Soon I might not be able to get even this far.

I was having a few more falls too. And of course when you have these falls it shakes you up a bit. I started to think to myself that maybe I shouldn't go walking like that. That if I fall I could get hurt, and that's going to reflect on my family. On my son and daughter-in-law. All of a sudden it seemed to me I was old. I even said it to myself: "Zita, old age is definitely taking you over, and now you'll have to be very careful."

Then there came that night at the gate—at the milk box. When I had to crawl to the neighbour to get me back home. I felt so helpless—so alone. I wondered how I was ever going to get help for myself. I wasn't in any pain, if you can understand, I couldn't feel any pain physically, but mentally—well, I was sort of terrified. It was the most horrible experience. And even when I got home that night, after this lady had brought me home and I'd had my little drink of brandy, I sat for a long time before I had the courage to get up. Even to go as far as the bathroom. But then I did, and I got undressed and I lay in bed and I thought, I wonder what will happen to me, what will I be like when the end comes? What is it going to be like? And I'll tell you another thing that went through my mind. When my mother-in-law was ill and I was going up to the old home regularly, I used to think, oh wouldn't it be lovely if I didn't have to do this. And even after my mother-in-law died, there was still my father-in-law. We had him every Sunday night for tea, and sometimes you'd feel, oh I wish we could lead our own lives. I'm not saying that my own family thinks that; I'm only saying that's what I thought all those years ago. And that's what went through my mind.

That was the time really when old age finally did take me over. I never again made any attempt to walk to the shops myself. I just had to be taken. My daughter-in-law took me every Thursday to do my shopping, and it got to the stage where I was hanging onto the trolley to support myself. You see, it was creeping, really creeping on me. Then one day my daughter-in-law said, "Nana"—they call me Nana—"do you think you should have Meals on Wheels?" And I said, "No, no," I said, "I don't want Meals on Wheels." "Well," she said, "I'm just worried that you could have an accident at the stove or something." Well, a while later it did actually happen. I was putting in a big dish—you know, a big oven dish—and I let it fall. Now that gave me a fright. I never slept that night; I really and truly got worried. I realised then that I was actually going down, that something had come over me and my life was going to be different. But at the same time I never ever thought I was going to give up my home. I still thought I was going to be able to stay there and lead my own life.

That was a little bit of thinking you are better than you are. Nevertheless, I stayed there and stayed there. Time went on. I knew I was going down, and I used to think, what's going to become of me? And that's when the flu came. That's when I got that flu. I had the most awful cough, and I was so very shaky. And when the doctor came he said, "Look, Granny"—he always called me Granny—he said, "Look, I think we'll put you in hospital for a couple of days. To get over this flu."

I was there for two weeks, not quite two weeks, and then one morning they said I was going down to see the therapist. When I got down there she said to me, could I do something—could I make her a cup of tea? Well, I was on a walker, and I could hardly get about or reach across the bench, but I made a cuppa and we sat down and had it. Then, after I washed the dishes up, she said, "I don't really think you should go, but they are very short of beds here," and she said, "I think we will have to let you go." So I went out. I went to my son's place. I know there's lots of people, lots of patients, but I don't think they understand old people. I suppose they're sick of old age. See, I was taking up a bed where perhaps somebody else, a younger person, could have been given it. I was old. You're old and that's the end of it. Well, that's the feeling I got. That's the very feeling I got.

ZITA EDMUNDS

A few days later I tried to get out of bed to go to the bathroom, and I fell down. It was agony in my back, and when the doctor came they had an awful job getting me up. Then the next thing I'm in the ambulance going back to hospital. I was really ill then. I was going down to the extent that one night Alan and Myrna practically stayed there because they didn't think I was going to pull through. They said every time the doctor came out they thought he'd come out to say I'd gone. But, as I say, only the good die young, and I hung on, I came out of it. But I was very sick then, and I started to get very, very distressed. I had no power anywhere, I couldn't do anything, and I was thinking, is life worth living? It's a horrible feeling to know that you are losing your grip on things. Things that you've done all your life. In hospital I used to think, oh the flat, if only I could get back to the flat. But all the time the feeling is growing . . . you're feeling . . . I suppose you're feeling sort of useless. It's hard to describe the feeling that you're not going to be much use to yourself or anybody else.

Eventually I got through that. When I got into the ward I saw other people worse off than what I was, and I had to think to myself, it's no good going on like this. It's a silly way to go on. Some days I still got despondent—I went through a lot of pain—but then after a time I was beginning to feel much better. And walking—I had to use a frame, but I was walking again.

I went into the hospital in June. I had my eighty-fifth birthday there on the thirtieth of June. Apart from that short time out, I was there all that time until September. And that's when the crunch came. The doctor said, "I want to see your son and daughter-in-law. I don't think you're fit enough to go back to your own home." That's when the end of the world came. Never going back to my home. They said I'd have to sell the flat—oh, I thought the world had ended. Not being able to go back to that flat . . . I just felt that everything had sort of gone, and I wondered what was going to be. After eighty-five years leading your own life, when you are told you have to give up your home—oh Lord, it just feels like everything is being taken from you, and you are no use to your-

ZITA EDMUNDS

self or anybody else. Everything in that flat was so important to me. I used to buy little souvenirs from everywhere I went—all those little things—and my linen, all my linen, what was going to happen to everything like that? All those things go through your mind. And now they are gone. This meant a lot to me, but not to anybody else. Everything had to go, it had to be sold. I had nine years of happiness there. I was very happy, but that was all to go— that's all gone now. And I've never been back to see it. No, I don't want to go back and look at it.

THE FIRST DAY I came here to the home, when I came in that front door—well, I didn't know whether to cry, or laugh, or what to do. I'd never felt so alone or out of place in all my life. I didn't know what was going to happen to me. The matron came, and we talked and we had a drink, and then the matron said, "I think you'll be happy here." I said, "Have I been accepted?" "Oh yes,"

ZITA EDMUNDS

she said, and took me in to show me the bed—and she introduced me to the two ladies that shared the room. That was my first look at the place. It all seemed so—so different. I felt like an intruder, and I thought, I'm not going to be able to do it. That night I was very upset and I cried and wondered to myself how I could go on. You see, I just felt that all the life I'd once had was gone.

I suppose in that first week I gave them quite a bit of trouble. When they gave me my first meal I had to leave some of the food. I didn't actually refuse the food, but there was too much of it, I couldn't eat it. I was so tensed up I was sick. Sick to the point of vomiting. I tried to sit in the sun room—a lot of them were in there talking, but all I could think was, I can't stay here. I'm not going to be able to settle in. I went up to the lounge, and there were all these chairs. I didn't know if any particular chair was for me; I just sat down. Then the matron came in and she said to me, "Are you alright?" I said, "I think so," and then I started to shake. So she said, "Would you like to go and lie down?" Well, I came and lay down, and I thought to myself, I don't think I can settle in here—I don't care if I die now.

Later that night I lay on the bed, and my lip was trembling and carrying on, but I thought to myself, it's no use crying, there's no one here to sympathize with you. Then all during that night I kept wanting to get up to go to the toilet. Five times I went out. It seemed so stupid, but that's what I was doing. In the morning I woke very early. One of the women had a light on in the room, and I wondered if something was the matter. I didn't know what was happening, and I thought, what will I do? Will I get up? Will I get dressed? In the end I just lay there, still shaking and shivering. Then, after a while, I had to go to the toilet again. At that time I was still on the walker—the walking frame. By the time I had got up out of bed, standing there on the carpet—before I could get to the toilet—I felt my bowels move. That embarrassed me terribly. That was awful. And one of the women that works here had to clean it up. She must have thought, what sort of an old thing have we dragged in. Anyway, I struggled out to the toilet, and I was

ZITA EDMUNDS

sick. I vomited for a long time. It was nerves. It just got—well, it was just nerves. When I came back she had cleaned up. It wasn't a big thing to clean up, but it was a mess and it had to be cleaned. Actually she's a good friend now, but then she must have thought, oh glory, what have we got. Well, she didn't know what they'd got—I was still shaking like mad, and when some breakfast was brought to me I couldn't eat it. She said, "Oh go on, you've got to eat." So I had some Weetbix, I spooned down a bit of Weetbix, and I was sick again. I just brought it up. I was so unhappy. And later, there was something else—I had to be showered. I had to get undressed in front of somebody I didn't know. It's hard to explain, but getting undressed—there's nothing more undignified than an old person's body, and getting undressed in front of somebody I didn't know, I felt embarrassed. Of course you don't think about it now, but then it was my first time, my first experience, and it felt horrible. At the hospital I had said I would accept this place, but I thought then I could never do what I'd said. I would never accept this place. Then I was wishing I had died in the hospital. I really meant that.

When I got back to my room I looked out the window and I thought, if only I could just walk out of here. Just go and get right away from it all. But I couldn't. Anyway, when Myrna came I felt a little better seeing her. She was most understanding. She said, "Oh Nana, it will take a while." I said, "No, Myrna, I don't think I'm going to be able to settle in." But she said, "Look what you did for yourself up at the hospital—you'll settle in." And the thing is that as time went on, I did start to settle in. Of course you get moments when you think, this is no good, this is the end. But slowly I got more confidence, and I could talk more to the other ladies, perhaps about the television and things like that. Oh yes, I was starting to come round. Then one night when I got into bed I said, "Look, Zita, it's no good going on like this, this has got to be your home, perhaps for the rest of your life, so accept it and make the best of it." I thought again about what I had said to the doctor in the hospital, how I was going to make the most of it,

ZITA EDMUNDS

and I thought, well, that's what I will do. I will just go according to the rules, and I will make the most of it. That's what I've done, and I don't think I've looked back since. I'm not going to say that I'm a hundred percent happy; no, I wouldn't say I was satisfied, that's not the word for it, but I am lucky to have got as well as I have after being so ill. I am contented, if you know what I mean. And contentment is quite a good thing.

BREAKFAST IS brought in to us any time between twenty to seven and seven o'clock. That suits me 'cause I wake up early. Usually I'll get up and have it at the table beside the bed. Then I rinse my mouth out and go back to bed until five minutes to eight. At five minutes to eight I get up and get dressed. There are three of us in the room, and I always try to get out early so that the other two can have it to themselves. I get on well with the two ladies in my room, but there have been times when I wished I was by myself. Mind you, I think to have had a room by myself when I first came here, it would have been worse. You see, when I first came in they talked to me, and they tried to help me, which was kind of them. Oh yes, it would have been worse—it would have taken me longer to settle in without them. I was glad those two ladies were there. But on the other hand, having no privacy—well, there are times when you like a little privacy. When my niece died a little while ago, that was a time when I wanted to be by myself. I wished then just to be on my own, to work it all out. I knew she was going to die, I knew she was ill and suffering, so I didn't wish her back. But at the same time, to think I was never going to see her again—well, I was grieving. Of course I went into my room to lie down, but then you're all the time thinking someone will come in. You feel silly weeping, going on like a silly old woman, but you do need that time just for yourself. That's the only thing—and visitors— that can be a bit awkward. But then, on the other hand, I don't think I would like to be shut up by myself in a room, be all the time by myself—I wouldn't like that. No, no. Anyway, you can't have everything, and I like company, I've always liked company. I do try to get on with everybody.

Usually, if it's not a shower day, I go from my room into the lounge. There I will sit—perhaps read some of the magazines that are there. *Woman's Weekly*, anything like that. Matron usually brings the paper in about quarter past nine, and I have a glance over it. Of course you can't monopolise the paper, you have to pass it on. But you try to keep up with the times. You like to be able to discuss these things as normally as you can.

It is a different sort of life to what you lead at home. At home there was always something to do, but sometimes now I feel I'm a bit useless. Well, I am, aren't I. I'm not putting anything into life. I'm just living from day to day. When I was young it was the furtherest thing from my mind. Even when I was getting old, I never thought that sometime I was going to be useless. You see, when I first came in here I wasn't in the best of health. I could hardly walk about because I was in so much pain. I just sort of sat around, and then automatically it somehow becomes part of your day to do the same thing. You get into a groove, and none of us here—none of us—want to do anything. You just sit, and you read, and you go out when you get the chance. What I mean to say is, you're not giving anything to society, are you. You're just taking everything out.

It's surprising really how you get yourself into this way of doing nothing. Up at the hospital, one of the nurses—her and I got quite friendly—and if she had some time off we played euchre. Well, that would appeal to me, but as for wanting to do any knitting or anything like that, I've got no ambition. There's no ambition to do anything like that. It's gone. I did an awful lot of knitting in my time, even in the flat when I first came down here. I knitted jumpers and all for myself, but I'm not interested now. I am not interested at all. I have got so lazy I don't feel I could concentrate. I don't even know what I would want to do. There is only two ladies out of all the fourteen of us that do anything.

ZITA EDMUNDS

27

One does crochet, she does it all the time. And the other one—she's a bit deaf and wears a hearing aid, I think I'm the only one that talks to her—but she does knitting. Well, she does more pulling off than she does putting on; all the same, she is knitting. But that's only two out of the fourteen that do anything. No one else does anything. Ha, just old ladies, sitting around and looking at each other, and you get a bit tired of that at times.

Anyway, I sit there. Then, around about quarter to, or ten o'clock, morning tea comes. I always drink coffee, I don't drink tea. On Tuesdays a lady comes in and she reads the paper, you know, news and all that. Some of them go to sleep. But then she reads the life of the royalty. That's quite interesting. She's got a life story of the royal family and just at the moment she's on the Queen Mother. Then there's another lady that comes for singing sometimes. That is something I really and truly enjoy. I enjoyed her up at the hospital, and now she comes here. All the old songs we've had, from years back. Oh, I like that, that does get me. Yes, I suppose you could say there's a lot to be thankful for. The old lady here that is ninety-nine, she has the first choice of song, and she always chooses "Bless This House." That's her choice every time.

Some days, if the sun is shining, I will try to get out the back and sit for an hour or so. We've got a very nice backyard—you just sit out there in the sun, and you feel quite relieved. Then sometimes another woman comes out, and I sit with her in the chairs at the back of the garden. I listen to her telling me her life, but I don't try and tell her mine because she is confused. I just listen to her. You listen to other people's stories and the things that are happening to them. The people that don't have anybody seeing them, coming in and taking them out, you feel sorry for them.

If you are out in the yard, you come in at about quarter to twelve to go to the toilet, then you wait in the lounge to be called for lunch. Well, of course you've got to have some rules and regulations, but I remember that first day here, all sitting in the lounge, and they come and ask you if your bowels have moved. Oh glory, I didn't like that. I suppose that might sound silly. I mean, when you're old you've got to be thankful that someone is looking after you to some extent, but you do resent it up to a point. I know when I first came in and they said, "You had better go to the toilet," I didn't like that. Well, you feel like a child—I didn't like being told like a child. That's not very nice, but then, that is the rule and they've got to have some rules. Well, they have to tell some of them, otherwise they are going to have trouble. Anyway, I've got over that now. Now you just see that little book come out and you know what it is; you just say yes or no and that's it. Of course if I get out, if I go someplace that I have been familiar with prior to my illness—say taken to a friend's place for lunch or something like that—then I am my old self again and all that goes. It does, it doesn't hang around. You can be yourself again then. You can express yourself and get interested in things like you used to. It might only be for an hour or so, but you feel you are doing the things that you want to. Then when you come back—well, you're not exactly coming back to be told what to do, but you are coming back to abide by the rules of the rest home. You have got to. So you slip back into it.

I'm not really complaining, I am contented here. As far as this home is concerned, you couldn't get better. No, I'm very fortunate to have got here. But there is still a longing, I suppose you'd call it, to be on your own and doing for yourself. You sit there and look out the window and you see other elderly people going about, and yes, you are a little envious. You can't help that. You're not begrudging them, but you are envious for yourself. You see, you have got to rely on other people. You have lost your independence. Well, that's not very nice, not when you've been in the habit of having it. I suppose everyone here has felt the same. Having to give up their homes—I'm sure they all felt just the same. But then we come to the stage where we accept it. We've got to accept it, really, don't we? You don't have any choice.

Lunch is at twelve, and the food is always very good, a great variety. That's one of the best things, I suppose. You get to the stage during the day where you are looking forward to the meals.

ZITA EDMUNDS

29

In the afternoon you go back into the lounge. There might be a movie on television by then that you can watch. Some days, though, the time drags. You look at your watch—oh glory, it's only so and so, and you sit there wishing you could drop off to sleep like some of them do. But I cannot doze off to sleep in the day. I can't. So you just sit there. That's what you do. It's just boredom, really—I don't get frustrated or anything, no, I just accept it. I think I have got to the stage now that I don't want to do anything. You get into that groove. I think we've all got to that stage now, where we are just happy to sit around. Awful, isn't it, when you think about it. You just sit down. Passing time. Some days you get people coming in—other people's visitors—and they have got grandchildren with them. It's nice to see them all, and of course what I really look forward to is being taken out. That is the best thing that happens. I am very fortunate that I am able to get out and go to Myrna and Alan's—they are very good to me. There are others get taken out too, but some don't.

Sometimes we can go out on a trip. It only costs a dollar for about two and a half hours. We go for a drive and then somebody takes us to their house for afternoon tea, all for a dollar. It's the best dollar I've ever spent. When I first came here I couldn't go. I was still on the walker, and you can't take a walking frame on a mini-bus. I thought I would be on the walker for the rest of my life, but the matron was very kind to me, and she said, "Come on now, we'll try and get you on the walking stick." Thanks to her I was determined to straighten up my back and manage that stick, instead of being all arched over like I was. And now I've got to the stage where I can walk with just the stick—I never thought I was going to be able to do that. Now I can go on the trips. Yes, I've been on two trips and two concerts so far. One old lady here says going on these drives is just going over the same old ground. Well, I don't care, I'd go anywhere now. I wouldn't care if we went to the same place every time. The last time we went to that beach—what's it called? Sumner. Yes, Sumner. We just called in there and watched the waves rolling in, none of us got out, but that was lovely to me. I wouldn't care if we went to Sumner every time we went out. You know, it's just something—it's good to get out.

Most afternoons, though, I'm in the lounge, and so I might watch the movie, but then later on if they are watching something that I don't like—*Sesame Street* or something like that comes on— well, I can't stand that, so mostly I'll just go to my room and lie down. I stay there until about four o'clock, and then I clear out to make way for one of the other ladies to do her insulin injection. Either I go back into the lounge or I might have a bit of a wash before tea. After we have dinner you go back into the lounge to watch the television again. Of course we watch *The Young Doctors*, and then the news. Then you just sit there, and around about half-past eight, unless there is something I want to see that goes a bit longer, I come to bed. And that is my day here. That is a full day and you accept it. Of course many of them sleep a terrible lot—go to sleep in their chairs. It puts the time away for them.

Sometimes you don't think that you should be sitting there like that all the time. You get bored sitting round, and you just wish you could put your shoes on and go out, but you know you can't. There is one lady here, she is in her seventies. Now, she can go out. Any day she can go off walking into town. She goes to the thrift shops—she's got a nice lot of clothes for a small amount of money—and she goes into the square and to the ladies' rest rooms. She has a nice walk round. I would love to be able to do that, but I can't. I envy her for that. Not that I'm thinking she shouldn't—I wish her all the best. I just wish I could too. In one way she's really the best off of anybody, of any of us here, yet she has nobody. She has got family somewhere, but they have never bothered about her. She doesn't talk about it much, but she must think about it sometimes. If I get feeling down I think about that. Yes . . . I have a lot to be thankful for. I have a good family. I am not neglected. It's them that have no one, it's them I feel sad for.

OLD AGE IS something that you think is never going to come upon you. It's like a disease, it creeps on you. It creeps and creeps and then all of a sudden it comes upon you with a rush. It's got you and you have no choice except to be stuck with it. You can't do anything about it. You can't turn back the clock. What will happen, how long you'll live, you don't know. My wish, my ambition, would be to go back to my flat. Go back to my flat and just live the rest of my life there. Just to walk down that driveway again, and be able to go to the shops and things like I did before—oh, would I love that. That would be my wish. But I don't think I will ever get it. No, that's not to be. There's not a hope in the world of going back now. And that is the horrible thing. That time is gone, and you can't do things for yourself any more. Everything you want, and everything you do, you have to rely on somebody else. You lose your independence. That's something you don't think about when you're young, we don't cherish it enough. But you do when you are old, you miss it then.

Still, it's no good thinking about what you'd like to have done. You have to be satisfied with what you can do, and if you can do that, you make life much more pleasant for everyone. Old age is not the best thing that could happen to you, but then it's not the worst thing either. You do get some days—I wouldn't call it depression—but you get the feeling, you know, that it shouldn't be happening to you. Then I've got to think, well, I'm lucky. I am still able to eat and sleep and enjoy the sunshine. My family are very good to me. I can go out and look around, and I can think for myself. I could be a lot worse off. At eighty-six that's a lot to be thankful for. Now it's a matter of acceptance. The time comes on us all—and now it has happened to me.

I suppose I should say I am contented with what I have now. When I look back I seem to have got a lot out of life. Oh, you think of lots of things you should have done, and lots of things you could have said, but at the same time I don't regret any part of my life. How I will finish, what will happen, how long I will live, I don't know. Sometimes I think I don't want to live like the dear old soul that's in her hundredth year. You think, no, I wouldn't like to live to that age. But I suppose if I do, life'll be having

something to give me, or I'll be giving something to it. Sometime, though, the end has got to come. And how it's going to come—how that's working out—I don't know. But it's no good worrying about it—we've all got to face it. Ha, that's the only thing in life we are sure of.

Some nights I lie in bed and wonder what it's going to be like. When the end comes, what will it be like? I've often thought that. Will I be here at the home, or will I be transferred back to the hospital? It's a strange feeling. I don't know if I want to die in this bed or not. It makes you wonder, death. I don't feel as though I'm frightened; if I die, I die, and that's all about it. But what will I feel like actually—when I come to it? I don't think about where I'm going or anything, but I just wonder how it's going to affect me. How's it going to come on me—it's got to come on you, you know that. Like a good book, you can't go on forever.

ZITA EDMUNDS

33

Of course a lot of old people go back to religion. I think it's because of fear. Ninety-nine percent of the people that go like that, they're frightened of the hereafter. They have a minister who comes here. He's very jovial, but same as at the hospital when one came there, I'm just not interested. I told them, don't stop on my account—I wouldn't be nasty to anyone—but don't let them try and force it down my throat. I may be wrong, but I think we are just like the animals—we live and we die, and that is the end of it. That time when I was really ill, up at the hospital there, Myrna said to me, she said, "Nana, don't be afraid to say if you would like a priest to come and see you." "No, Myrna," I said. "I came in here as a free thinker, and I will go out of here as a free thinker." That's my feelings. When I die I will be cremated. There will be some ashes and they can do what they like with them. As for this business of the hereafter—well, I'll just have to take pot luck about that. That's how I feel about it all.

ZITA EDMUNDS

Glenys Lewis

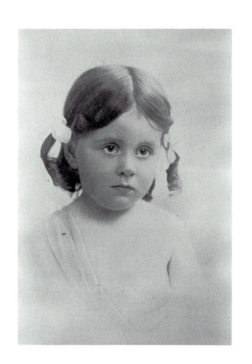

IT WAS EVENING. An evening in Cardiff when my father came to tell me my mummy was dead. My own mother. Such a shock it must have been, such a terrible shock. So hard to look back.

I had been sent to my aunt's; my aunt Dege. I remember my father in the front room there, his arm around me . . . such sadness in the telling. Then I was alone. Put into a great feather bed, sort of sinking down into the centre of it. And I can only just remember, just vaguely, a most terrible feeling. I don't know what word one could use . . . I don't know—it was just horrid. An aloneness, I remember that. Yes, somewhere in it was the most terrific sense of being lost. Devastating. Even more than I realised, I think. That was her death. That was how it felt. And even though one's life is kind of under control—I do believe that—still, I remember her, all dressed up and looking so beautiful, and I can't help thinking that my life would have been totally different if she had lived. I feel now that her death has had the most extraordinary effect on the whole of my life. I wanted so much to be like her, you see. I used to pray to be like her. Time goes on though, and when you get to my age you know a little better. You know that in the end your life must be your own. Now, I must accept that my life has been what my life has been. That is the truth of it. As to the bits and pieces of what I remember—what I have felt—and what I now feel . . . yes, I will try to tell you some of that.

FIRST THERE IS my father. I don't know what you'd call it. Middle class—upper middle class, I suppose—anyway, he was really very much a man about town. He lived quite a gay bachelor type of life it seems, and he was going with a woman who was what they called in the snobbish world of the time "county." You wouldn't call county "aristocracy," but, you know, pretty wealthy kind of thing. Not exactly top drawer, but certainly second drawer. Of course all this is before my time. I heard it later from people who had known my father.

My father had a brother who had got what they called in those days rapid paralysis—creeping paralysis—and a nurse had to be

GLENYS LEWIS

brought into the family home to look after him. It was not a large family. Grandpa was very religious, an ardent Baptist. Daddy and his sister, Aunt Addaline, were the only two children apart from the one who was dying. And so there they all were, Grandpa religious, and Grandma anything but. And Daddy having this kind of wild, gay—well, not so wild, but, I gather, very gay life.

And then something happened. My uncle, whose paralysis was quite far advanced, could not speak. But one day, while my father was with him, he suddenly asked for the Bible, and this had an enormous effect on my father. A kind of sudden conversion. And during this religious process he got to know his brother's nurse—fell in love with her in fact, and married her. I don't think his mother would have been very pleased—she was an utter snob, she would have wanted him to marry this county woman, not a Welsh-speaking nurse. Oh no, my mother would have been very much third drawer. Anyhow, he marries her and becomes a Baptist along with Grandpa. And Mummy, who was I think a Welsh Methodist, becomes Baptist with Daddy. After that Daddy didn't drink, and we were brought up in a really religious household. He became the rock. Always he was there, standing behind you. Undemonstrative, and yet one always knew that he loved you dearly and would do anything for you. You knew it, you see—if ever you were in trouble, he was there. A rock, a solid rock. That is where I came from.

MY MOTHER DIED of tuberculosis, and she was buried in the Lewis plot. In those days you used to have a kind of family plot—at least you did if you could afford it, I suppose. We had this Lewis plot in the cemetery in Cardiff where my grandparents were buried, and where my mother was buried, and where my father would be buried too. Personally I never went to the cemetery. Not on my own initiative. Not even when Dad died; I never thought it was a good idea. I don't believe they're there you see. Their carcasses are there, but I've always had this very strong belief that they themselves are alive and well. So what was the point then in going to cry over a bit of land where the bones were rotting? To me it seemed nonsense.

Her funeral, my mother's funeral, passed in a sort of daze. I remember a service of some sort in the front room of my aunt's house. Then the men all going off to the cemetery, to the grave. The women, they didn't go, they just kind of grieved quietly. It was hard for me to think of my mother dead. I can remember thinking that I ought to cry, that it would be the done thing to cry. I can't remember if I did or not, but I remember thinking that I should. That, and the terrible sense of loss in my bed the night Daddy told me, that is all I remember. I think I must have gone into a kind of cold storage. What happened to me then—between mother's death and going to live in Porthcawl—is a blank. I never went back to our home in Penarth after that. I have no recollection of ever going back to the house. What happened to all of us at

GLENYS LEWIS

39

that time—my older sister, who was having scarlet fever when my
mother died, and my younger sister, who would have been only a
tiny baby—has gone from my mind. All I know is that somehow,
eventually, we arrived in Porthcawl.

Porthcawl was a seaside town, and in the summer months
there I was set free. This was because I was such a sickly child and

my father so anxious in those days of tuberculosis. In the summer months, when the weather was nice, I was always being taken out of school. He was adamant that I be out in the fresh air. And so I would play all summer long on the beach and the rocks, jumping one to the other. Ha, these days I've lost all sense of balance, I can't walk on a rock at all. But those summers back then—oh, we were everywhere. Following-the-leader, jumping from rock to rock over what seemed at the time such great caverns—oh yes, taking risks and feeling very brave.

After my mother's death her sister had come to help look after us. It was an arrangement that worked extremely well, and in the course of time we all grew to love her very much. And then eventually, when she and my father decided to marry, we were overjoyed. Oh yes. When they told us we jumped all over them, we were so happy. Going to their wedding we were all dolled up in pretty dresses, and pretty hats, absolutely loving it. You know, I still have this vision of them in my mind. A remembrance of sorts. I am at the top of the stairs, and Daddy has just come home for the evening. I've got this lovely picture of them in each other's arms—he must have loved her so, you could see how happy they were together. Oh yes, Porthcawl was a very happy place in my childhood.

Later they had a child, a girl, and we became four sisters instead of three. I suppose you could say it was the place where we once more became happy, the place in which we once again became a family. Such happy years . . . full of joy. And then it started to happen again, just as it had happened before; it suddenly went all wrong. There was so little protection in those days from tuberculosis, and now our second mother had it too. We had been so very happy . . . to go through it all again so soon, so desperately soon . . . it brought great tragedy back into our lives. We left Porthcawl not long after—away to Cardiff. I think Daddy thought she might get better treatment there, but still she died. She died that Christmas.

The strange thing now is that, looking back . . . well, in some ways it's just a blank. I try to separate the two deaths, but I sometimes get them mixed up. I can't actually picture it at all. I think I must have been getting very good at blanking things out by that time. Perhaps it was nature's way of coping with something that is not copable-with. I know that we all felt badly for my dad, my older sister and I particularly. He had so much sadness. And I know how happy we had been with Mum, my second mum, and how much we had loved her. Really, I think the fact of her dying must have been more than we all could cope with. All this taking away of security and love at that age, we must have been so hurt. To have lost our first mother, and then to have found love again, that must have been so wonderful. But then to lose it all again so quickly, it must have made me wary, it must have. Looking back into such a time, one sees perhaps how I became afraid of love, inhibited in the giving of love. Yes, slowly you begin to see where all these things stem from.

CERTAINLY in the beginning we had been a demonstrative family, before our mother died, but after that I don't recall us ever doing much in the way of embracing. No, after that we didn't get much in the way of cuddles, and I think that's a big lack in any child's life. We kissed Dad, we kissed him goodnight and that kind of thing—I mean, we did love him—but there was no kind of emotion, which is always so important. And that, I think—that obviously had an effect on us. You could say perhaps there was a dearth, a dearth of the demonstration of love really. And Daddy, after Mummy died, he shut himself away rather a lot. He didn't want to be hurt any more; no thank you very much.

There was only once in that time that my father tried to hug me, just once, and when he did I fought him like a wildcat. It was down in Porthcawl, when my father knew that his second wife was going to die. She was upstairs in bed, and we were together down in the drawing room. He must have been so sad. He must have

been feeling absolutely ghastly, and he sort of tried to draw me up onto his lap, to give me a hug. He must have just wanted to give me a little hug—he wasn't telling me of his sorrows, I think he just wanted a bit of company, but for some reason I wouldn't go near him. I fought him like a wildcat. I could not bear him to touch me. I didn't know why I was like that, not at the time, not consciously, but it must have hurt him very much. I have looked back on that many times since, and I think perhaps I must have known something was wrong with Mother. Subconsciously I must have known that things were not going right and associated it with my first mother's death. Whatever happened, it started something inside me that has affected anybody trying to get near me for the rest of my life.

That is part of what happened to me. Just what those times must have done to my father I cannot begin to think. That the human spirit can cope with such devastating things . . . how my father coped at all, I don't know. All I do know is that it shut him away from us emotionally. It shut him away for keeps. Certainly he never tried to hug me ever again.

You MISS your parents when they are gone. Always with my father you had this strength of feeling . . . a solidness that was always there. I think we all had this. We knew that he loved us. And even as an old man—wherever we were—he would write to us regularly. And I remember how his writing slowly changed. I used to think, poor old Dad, his handwriting is getting so shaky. Ha, now I've got to the stage where my own writing gets shaky now and again. Perhaps I will have been doing a lot of physical work and then I'll go to write something down and it's all over the shop. Oh, most peculiar . . . quite all over the place. And then I'll always think of seeing dad's writing, thinking, the poor old darling, he's getting old—then I think, poor old darling, you're getting old yourself! But you know, I don't feel it. I mean I don't act old, and I don't dress like an old person either. Just in the handwriting sometimes, and a few other things . . . it's there to see.

GLENYS LEWIS

HER NAME WAS Miss Shepstone—later we came to call her Aunty. I don't think we ever got to know the full story—she had something to do with a school, was the message we got—but other people said that Daddy knew her from a shop in Cardiff. It doesn't really matter; she came into our lives. My father was a very attractive man, you see—and he was a man who needed a woman. The thing was, we used to go down to Cornwall for the summer holidays. We'd take a house for a month or so, that kind of thing. Well, she came down with us, it was said, to help Daddy look after us. Four young girls we were then. I suppose my older sister and I would have been about thirteen or fourteen, and the two little ones quite a bit younger. It was alright at first—I think we were too innocent to know what was going on—but there must have

GLENYS LEWIS

45

been some sort of goings-on because suddenly she was ensconced at home. After only a month's holiday in Cornwall she came back with us to the house. Oh, he must have told us that she would come back and look after us, be our housekeeper—he must have told us that. But we didn't expect that she would move into the best bedroom. That she would have the best bedroom with the balcony, and everything that goes with the best bedroom. We saw her then as an intruder. I don't know that we even realised it was a sexual thing. We were just outraged at this woman coming into our mother's room and wearing our mother's clothes as she started to do. I suppose in a way we kind of accepted things, but we hated her wearing those clothes. Hated it. And my sister and I were quite horrid to her. Looking back I don't know how my father could do it. It's extraordinary what men can do, isn't it? He must have been quite struck by her to be able to do that. I think he must have. Yes, but then, when you think of it, he must have been so sad, and meeting this woman who was young and very attractive—yes, I think really he must have been very lonely. But to us it seemed that our whole life had been disrupted by her coming. Of course at the same time we all had a great love for our father. I loved him dearly. And I think my older sister and I had a feeling of trying to protect him as well. We tried to guard him from our unhappiness with this woman. But we hated her for what she had done to our home. And she was such a parsimonious person too. We found out later that her father was a drunkard, really, and her mother had run a butcher's shop to keep them. So money was very important to her; she thought that she had to kind of look after the pennies. Anyhow, that was our life at the time . . . we really did dislike her very much.

Five years later my father married her. My older sister heard them quite by chance one morning after breakfast, Daddy and Aunty discussing their marriage. She was just standing in the hall, by the hall table, and she overheard this extraordinary conversation. And so she went in, straight in, and she said, "What are you two talking about? Are you planning to get married?" Just like that, you see. And then of course Daddy was in the apple cart, poor darling, because we were terribly against it. Well, he said to us, he said, "Your happiness must come first, and so if you can't accept this marriage, I won't marry." Well, that put us on the spot, didn't it. Oh yes, because no way could we have stood against our father's happiness. We said yes to it, and she became our steppie. It was not, however, a happy occasion, not by any means. Not for me.

An extraordinary childhood, when you look back on it. I think you do accept an awful lot—children do. Quite extraordinary, really. So many people these days say a person's life can be ruined because of their childhood. But I think, for us, we had our father's love, and I think that was a tremendous bulwark really from the kind of trauma that a lot of children get when families split up. They are kind of cut in half in a way in which we were not. For while we had all this trauma, still, we had in my father a man of substance, and that, I think, did help us. It must have helped. Although, interestingly enough, the three that were really caught up in this trauma, the three older sisters—we never married. Only the youngest married. I don't say that's the reason, but it's interesting, isn't it.

I WAS ATTRACTIVE to men. I was quite aware of that. You can't help being aware—I mean, it's silly to beat about the bush. Actually I seemed to be attractive to older men a lot. Though, somehow . . . I don't know—somehow I was not always able to give easily. Looking back on my life I would say I was very handicapped inside. I wasn't able to be free with men at all. I was very shy with them and just didn't know how to treat them really. You see we were . . . sex . . . it was so little talked about when I was young. I mean, you didn't talk about sex at all. Not people who had been "nicely" brought up, don't you know. I remember a girl at school once—I can see her now, laughing at me—she asked me if I knew what a French letter was. I looked at her absolutely blankly and said that I supposed it was a letter written by a Frenchman and

with a French postmark. She was expelled shortly after for playing around with the village boys. But you see this kind of innocence I had. I didn't even know what she meant until years later. I didn't think about sex. I mean, when I saw boys I didn't really know anything about their sexual side. I had never seen a boy naked or anything like that, whereas if I'd had brothers, you see, I would have. And my father was very careful to always have his dressing gown on, always. Whereas fathers today would be more likely to go around the house naked sort of thing. And of course one must remember that in those times people did very little in the way of embracing, very little touching at all. It was very much that you kept your emotions hidden. Well, you can imagine what things were like. But there was one thing I think that probably did me more damage than anything else. It's always been with me. This incident with Aunt Addaline, my father's sister.

She really was such a terrific snob. I mean, it was all so antediluvian, so Victorian, not the sort of thing that would happen today at all. So silly looking back . . . this trauma of being sent away as a kind of punishment. Not knowing, yet feeling that I had done something wrong in just talking with three young men. "Come with me, Glenys," she said. I mean, they weren't embracing me, they weren't kissing me, they weren't touching me. They weren't doing anything at all to me. We were so innocent. You look at youngsters today . . . well, we were just so innocent.

The thing was, I had this friend, Valerie, she was a swimmer—actually she became an Olympic swimmer—but anyway, she and I were buddies and I think I must have met these boys through her. I don't think we just picked them up. Anyhow, we met them somehow and we were friends. We just enjoyed each other's company. We cycled, we rowed, we swam, we did all these quite innocuous things together. I mean they weren't . . . they were very nice boys . . . they were nothing. They weren't swank—perhaps that's why she did it—they were nothing. Just three boys.

We had known them quite a while by then, but on this particular day the five of us were down by the park when Valerie said, "Look, I must go back to the house," back to her home, which was just nearby. She said that she had to go back to get something, or do something, I don't know, but she left me there at the gates to the park with our bicycles and the three boys. And so there was Glenys having a great time, more or less—I mean, we were chatting and laughing together, and I was quite free with them. I didn't feel any inhibitions at all, I was just enjoying them. Then all of a sudden there was this aunt walking up the road and coming straight towards us. And I remember that just seeing her I felt as if I had done something wrong. Well, the fact that my reaction when I saw her coming was "Hide me, boys" must say something. But, at any rate, it was too late. She had spied her niece talking to three boys at the park gates. She walked straight through us and said, "Glenys, come with me." And in her voice was something that put a kind of disgrace in me. Something that I perhaps then connected with men—because I was talking to men, to boys. Had I been talking with three girls she would probably not have said a thing, you see. But the snob in her did not approve of her niece talking to three young men on the street. I mean, were they suitable to be talking to her niece? And did my father know?

Of course I knew them quite well, but she didn't know that. And somehow she made me feel slightly unclean. Perhaps if I'd been a little older . . . a little more assured. I don't know if fear is really the right word for what I felt at the time—perhaps not. But she had got herself a pretty wealthy and ferocious husband, and she was—what would you call her?—rather regal. Oh, I don't know, somehow she affected me. I mean, I wasn't afraid of most people, but there was something about her that took me off with my tail between my legs. I remember—after this had happened—I remember going out with her. I was still, it seemed, in disgrace, for I was made to sit up front with the chauffeur. In those days you had these kind of cars where the chauffeur part was separated from the people who owned the car. And while my sister and cousin sat in the back with my aunt, I was put to sit in the front with the driver. All of which gave me a feeling of guilt of course, even though I did not know what the guilt was for.

I think I would have had—well, I must have had feelings for the boys, but it was completely unsexual at that time. We didn't do anything. Not like they would today. There was no petting or anything like that. Actually I still went on seeing them, but I had got to be a little nervous of it all. And one time when we went up into what they called the wild part—there was a shelter there with partitions—and Valerie and her boy went in and kissed, but Ken and I . . . I couldn't kiss him. And I don't know if he could have kissed me. I probably had my barriers up too much. It would only have been a kiss. There was none of this what they do today. We were innocent . . . very innocent. And yet I think perhaps this is the time when I became afraid of young men. Because of this ridiculous business with my aunt . . . and being sent off a little while later to boarding school, more or less in disgrace. It was bound to have an effect on me. I was only about thirteen, and you can't be treated like that—not without it having some kind of effect on you.

I think I had been quite free with young boys my own age until that happened. I don't remember being afraid until that time. But then there was this period in school—three years when I did not meet any boys. Even during the holidays. We had no brother, you see, so there were no boys brought home that we could have met. I think that sort of thing, coupled with what had happened with my aunt that time—it pushed me into a box. A box I could not freely get out of. By now I did not know how to treat boys. I just didn't know how to behave when I met them. You know, when you think of these things—when you think back—well, perhaps it's little wonder I've never married.

THERE WAS A bishop once who was very . . . well, he was a widower, and I could have married him if I'd made the slightest gesture. I really could. I mean, although I was very involved with my work, at the same time I used to kind of spark with men, you know, as one does—male and female—that kind of thing. Yes, I could have had him like that, but again, you see, there was this inhibition in me . . . I was inhibited and I could not bring myself to move. Well, one sees how much women do the running in so many cases. You read these books, or you see films . . . the woman does a lot . . . goes more than half-way. Anyway, there was this time in the library of a retreat house where he gave me this absolute opener. He was kind of asking me, but he was so inhibited himself. It was a question of our hands being just that distance away from one another—but he could not speak it. And I knew, I knew what he was feeling because I liked him too, even though he was a much older man. I was attracted to him but still I could not do it. I couldn't bring myself to make that gesture towards his hand, something he was obviously asking me to do. It was an extraordinary experience. To be so close to a different life, yet both so inhibited. I don't know that I can describe it really. I just couldn't do it. I turned and left the room, and as I was closing the door I heard him groan . . . still, I didn't go back. There he was, so very attracted to me—thought I was absolutely the cat's whiskers—and, as I say, I liked him too, but something made me run away. I went out of the room, and that was the end of it.

I THINK I was caught by Jesus when I was a very tiny child. I have this memory of my mother singing over our beds—perhaps it was that that did it. I don't know. I just have this love of Jesus, and I can't go back into my life without being aware of it. There were always things happening that made him so real to me. Like the fire. The time of the fire, when we lived in Porthcawl. I must have been around ten or eleven, I suppose. For a time my sister and I shared a room at the top of the house, and the maids lived on the same floor at the back. Then, when my sister went away to school, I was alone in the room. I think I must have been rather nervous about sleeping there by myself. I would see all sorts of things in the dark. And one night, lying there by myself, I became aware of this terrific kind of red glare coming in through the window. I got up and looked out, and there was this great fire across the street, which seemed to me to be coming closer and closer to us. I was very frightened, and I knelt on my bed, eyes shut tight, and I said, "Please, Jesus, please make it rain." About five minutes later it did. It poured with rain, and I got into bed and went to sleep. Well, looking back at that, at how real he must have been to me then, I see that I have belonged to him now for a very long time.

The only time I can think of when I did not have him—a time when my feeling for Jesus seemed to just go out of the window— was the time I spent at boarding school. We had to go to this dead little church which was part of the school complex, and it was also the village church as well. Oh gawd, the vicar—he was such a deadly bore. Nobody took any notice. We all just seemed to muck about and have great fun. I wouldn't call it unbelief, simply that we didn't think much about it. I seemed to have no feelings at all about religion. And then all of a sudden I was brought back in a rather dramatic way. I had of course been dedicated in the Baptist

Church as a child. That is how you are done as a child. And then, when you feel the call to become a follower of Jesus, you are baptized in toto. It is the adult baptism in the Baptist Church. You do it when you feel you can offer your life to Christ. Very much a believer's baptism.

As it happened—it was right about the time I finished my

schooling—my sister had decided to go forward for baptism. And without thinking about it at all, I just said, "Oh well, I might as well be done at the same time." Oh boy, did I get it in the neck. "How dare you!" she said. How dare I think of it in those terms. I got this absolute telling off from her. And it must have had a great effect on me, because a while later when I was standing there, waiting to go in and see Mr. Haggard, the minister, I suddenly burst into tears. It was the most strange experience. This great feeling of what was happening came over me, and I realised then that I was ready for it. I was ready to be baptized. It was a very emotional experience which obviously had great impact. I was ready to give myself to Jesus. Well, as much as one can at that age; I knew that I wanted to serve him. I decided I would become a nurse like my mother, and go to China as a medical missionary. Of course everybody laughed when they heard this. In those days I would faint if I saw anybody in pain, and of course I was always in such bad health myself. Even so, I did it. I got my SRN—state registered nurse—and then my father thought it would be good if I could complete the thing by becoming a certified midwife. He was such a darling, he paid for me to go to Bristol as a student and do it, so I could do it in six months instead of the usual twelve.

My father was always concerned for me, right from babyhood. I mean, not that you'd think so now from looking at me, but I was a frail child. Even then in my twenties I was still not good. I became ill there in Bristol before I finished my training. My lung, which had always been bad, really started to pack up. The lung, you understand, is like a leaf; it has all these little veins going through that take up the oxygen. Well, mine, I'm afraid, began to break down. The veins become like bunches of grapes and they collect sputum, which you cough up in great volume. Unfortunately one of mine worked in a way that it would bleed and I would cough up blood. Bristol is where I had my first haemorrhage.

Bronchiectasis they decided it was, and I was sent down to Weston-super-Mare, a place by the coast, to recuperate. That's where I met my friend Bud. She was recovering from something or other, and we were put into the same room, just the two of us, and somehow we just seemed to click. We laughed such a lot together, and we became in the end very good friends. I suppose we must have been friends now for over fifty years—not that we've seen each other in such a long time. But back then, after our time at Weston-super-Mare, we saw a lot of each other. She would stay with me or I with her. In fact it was while staying with Bud that I had one of my great flashes. Something that's very difficult to describe. I've just had these kinds of things happen in my life. Indescribable really. No words. It's not a voice. Just an inner certainty of some kind. It's what I would think of as the Holy Spirit working in one. And it was telling me I had to join the Church of England. Somehow I suddenly knew that I had to join the Church.

All this of course was some time after we had first met. I'd had two operations since then, and they had taken out one of my lungs. The second operation must have been about 1942–43. Yes, because I can remember lying in bed and hearing the bomber formations flying overhead and thinking how glad I was that they were ours going to Germany and not the other way around. Anyway, I was staying with Bud, and it must have been a Monday morning, because we'd been to church, she and I, the day before. Whenever I stayed with Bud we went to this Anglican church nearby. And the next morning, the Monday, Bud brought me breakfast in bed before she went to work, and that's when it happened. Suddenly, like a flash. Bud was a bit bowled over and said, "What are you talking about?" "Well," I said, "I don't know, but I've just had this sort of big push inside me, I've been told that I've got to be an Anglican." After that I didn't pause to think of anything, I just knew what I'd got to do. I rang the vicar—actually he was an archdeacon, we always called him the Ven—and he was so good about it all. He told me he'd been expecting it for some time and that if I would come and see him every night that week I could be confirmed the following Sunday.

This whole thing of course had a big effect on my father. I had been a Baptist with my father all this time, and now I had become an Anglican. And in that time it was not like it is today. In that period there was this terrific division. Either you were Church of England or you were Nonconformist, and never the twain should meet. He was furious with me. He was desperate about me becoming an Anglican. I mean, to him the Church of England meant nothing. It was absolutely dead as far as he was concerned, and he was horrified that I would do this. Oh yes, it really did something to him. And I know that a little while later, when I had decided that I would go to St. Christopher's Theological College, it was like a stab in his very heart. Even so, even then, he was marvellous. He had once said to us, my sisters and I, that he would give us a dowry of three hundred pounds if ever we should marry. And when I asked him if he would give me this to go to college, he said that he would. Even though it hurt him to do this, he gave me the money, and that is how I did my training. What a neck I had to ask him that, but he was a special dad. He really was.

ABANDONMENT IS perhaps too strong a word, but there are times when you feel . . . what? . . . a bit out on a limb, shall we say. Definitely there is this old age situation where, unless you are involved in things, you're of no great interest to others. The other day I was buying something from a shop that I go to quite often when I'm in town. The man behind the counter and I were talking—it was about the weather—and I said the great advantage in being retired sort of thing was that you can be out in the sun—something like that. And he said, "What is it like being retired and on your own?" We'd talked before, you see, and so I said, "Oh, it's great." He said, "Well, I live on my own, and I don't always find it great." I thought about that afterwards. I thought to myself, if you hadn't got what I have got in the way of belief—of not being alone when you are on your own—it must be very lonely. And yes, I suppose there are times when I am a little lonely too. I don't claim to be perfect yet. There are times when I have very much wanted to have a friend, someone close by to do things with. Like the cinema, or go off in the car to picnics or the beach. Someone to go bathing in the sea with. A "buddy." But I haven't met a buddy here yet. A buddy you can't manufacture. You either find a buddy or you don't find a buddy. Some people do. One of my neighbours who is retired also—she's a lovely person, and she's found a buddy. They have two units next to each other, and they do things and go places together . . . they have lots of fun. If somebody like that came along for me I should be delighted, but it is not the sort of thing that you can make happen. It does or it doesn't. In the meantime, if you have not got that kind of deep belief or realisation of an unseen presence . . . well, then you could be very lonely. There must be a lot of people—people who live alone in their old age—who are very lonely indeed. As for myself . . . the word "acceptance" is very strong in my mind. I have been learning these last few years the need to accept what has happened in my life. In many ways it has been an interesting and exciting life, but whatever has happened I have got to accept the result of that. Not grizzle about it, or be miserable about it . . . or shout to God about it . . . or go for him, which I have done. "Acceptance" is a great word. To accept what my life has been, what God has wanted of me. To accept what my life is now . . . yes, that is the thing.

WHEN I WAS young I used to think that I would marry. I used to say that I should marry at about twenty-eight. I wasn't going to marry a poor man. No, I should have to marry well because I was to have four children, and I would want lots of space. Ha, all that kind of balderdash. Well, I don't suppose it was balderdash, it was a very normal thing for a young woman to think. But then twenty-eight came and went, and really I don't think I thought a lot about it. I didn't go in for a lot of introspection, I just got on with my life. I mean, perhaps there would have been some sort of picture in my mind . . . yes . . . I suppose I could still draw up a kind of picture—as far as I ever do visualise anything—a kind of picture that would be Mr. Right for me. Still, I've yet to meet him. It's hard to put into words. I remember having this strong vocation to be a medical missionary in China—something that didn't happen.

GLENYS LEWIS

57

How much that vocation had to do with the way I related to men is a moot point, but the fact remains I did have this vocation. Now, I sometimes wonder what would have happened to my vocational thoughts if I'd met Mr. Right at that time. Would they have gone out the window? I don't know—who knows? Certainly I never did meet him. I might see a man in the street sometimes that I thought, oh yes, you're a bit like the kind of person—a bit like the kind of man that would appeal to me. I still do today . . . funny, isn't it? Actually I don't think . . . even if I meet Mr. Right, I don't know that I could honestly live with anybody now. No, not now, I would never marry now.

The thing is, I have this total belief in my Lord, that he is the one who is really in control of my life. No doubt there are people who would say that my work has been a substitute for relationships I might have had, for marriage, but I don't think so. Perhaps it sounds frightfully arrogant to say it, but I feel my life has been kind of planned and I've just gone along, I really do. And so perhaps yes, there will be people who feel I have sought substitutes, but I can't say yes to that. No, I don't think so.

NEITHER FISH nor fowl nor good red herring—we used to say that in the early days, back in Guildford, when I first became a deaconess. And it was absolutely true. You weren't laity, you weren't the clergy, you were some peculiar creature in between. Somehow you didn't belong. You belonged only to the deaconesses, and they were pretty thin on the ground. Yes, looking back to that time, to the work, you were in a way set apart . . . lonely. You were different, you see. And of course I was unmarried, so you had to cope with this spinster business as well. The embarrassment of being a spinster. Yes, people used to feel you hadn't really arrived unless you were married. It was like you'd failed in some way, you hadn't made the grade. You hadn't succeeded in getting a man sort of thing. I used to feel rather self-conscious that I hadn't got a ring on this finger. There was always the feeling of wanting to cover up your hand—the nakedness of this finger. It was quite something to cope with at times.

It's alright for men, they're Mister all their life, but we're Miss and then we're Mrs. That was the kind of Victorian environment in which I was brought up. Well, *post*-Victorian era, I suppose—but not all *that* post. It did loosen up of course as I got older, but it does make a difference being a Miss—you miss out, miss out on a lot of social life. Whereas a man, a bachelor, is very popular at parties. But a woman, oh gosh—you'll have to find someone to

The Bishop of Guildford has appointed Elinor Glenys Lewis to the office of head deaconess in the Diocese of Guildford and secretary to the Council for Woman's Church Work. The new deaconess is a trained secretary and has done her theological training at St. Christopher's College, Blackheath, where she took the certificate of the Central Council for Woman's Church Work in Theology and Education. She has been doing parochial work in Marylebone, and asked for ordination as a deaconess about two years ago. She was accepted by the Deaconess Selection Committee, but remained in the parish where she was working till 1948. Since January she has been doing six months final training for ordination, together with gaining additional experience in pastoral work at Gilmour House, Clapham Common. She will spend the five weeks prior to her ordination by the Bishop in Holy Trinity Church on September 21st, at the Central Deaconess House, Hindhead, in devotional preparation.

[Newspaper article, September 3, 1949]

partner her kind of business. There's a lot of that. And widows find it a very bitter pill to swallow when they lose their husbands. A lot of them are dropped socially when the husband dies. They just don't get invited out. I've heard it over and over again. You drop out of social life as a single.

It's not the sort of thing you think about a lot, though I suppose it's always been there right through. Something I've grown up with. Ingrained, I suppose you'd say. Not the sort of thing you can throw away all that easily. I expect it affects a lot of women. Perhaps I've been lucky in that my job has been my work *and* my recreation. Fortunate really that it's been so engrossing. I haven't missed the social wining and dining kind of thing as much as one would in a nine to five job. Had that been the case, who knows?—I might have lived a totally different life. One might

have done all sorts of things. Perhaps even written to one of these groups—agency kind of place—that find you somebody to go out with. Heaven knows what one might have done had my life been different.

Certainly I've missed men since I retired. Having always worked with men, I enjoy their company. When you retire, though, you find your whole life seems to be spent mostly with women. It is, I think, the way our society tends to do things. You're either paired off—male and female—or it's all men or all women sort of thing. It is a very real aspect of being single. Quite frankly I've never been able to understand it. Naturally at times you wonder if the fault is in you. I'm really quite an outgoing, friendly type of person. Whether it is that . . . whether I'm too friendly and people find that too much, I don't know. But defi-

GLENYS LEWIS

nitely there is this thing between couples and singles . . . I don't know that it's jealousy—more a kind of nervousness perhaps. In some curious kind of way, people seem to feel some sort of subconscious danger. And strangely enough, it is often men who are nervous of single women. Well, heavens above, you'd think that people would be past worrying about this sort of thing at our age. You'd think so, but let me give you a little illustration. I was at the home of some people I'd met—this was some years ago—and I suppose there must have been four or five women there, as well as this woman's husband. We were all just talking sort of socially in the sitting room. Then, at some point, the other women got up and went into another room to do something or other and I was left talking—we were discussing something, the husband and I. I mean, I was feeling quite leisurely about it, I wasn't frightened to be left with him or anything. But suddenly he said, "Oh, the others have gone, I'd better go." Well, it made me so mad. I said, "Yes, and I will have to be going too." I was frightfully kind of cool to him, and I'm sure he got the message. I was so mad. I thought, damn you, here I am at my age, and you can't even treat me as a normal human being. It was just so rude. We were just talking of something, and suddenly he says, "I'd better go." Unbelievable. I mean, I don't suppose he meant to be deliberately rude . . . probably it was quite subconscious. But it has happened so many times in my life—I mustn't be seen alone with her sort of thing—as though you are some sort of vulture.

I DON'T KNOW that I've had an awful lot of happiness as such in my life. Contentment I think would probably be nearer to it. Happiness . . . I don't altogether know about this word. How does one describe happiness? To me it has always been something ephemeral. Here one minute and gone the next. There are some mornings that I feel full of joy, and even though it may not last for long, I think "joy" is perhaps a word I prefer to "happiness." Happiness to me . . . well, perhaps if I'm honest . . . perhaps I relate happiness to sex. I don't know why, I'm just thinking aloud really. When does

one say one has had a happy day? Years ago down in Cornwall there was this little group I got caught up in—what did they call themselves? Anyhow, they were very religious, very fundamentalist, and they built a ship on the beach there with a little organ on it. They would sing this old doggerel, this chorus: "I am H-A-P-P-Y, I am H-A-P-P-Y, I know I am, I'm sure I am, I am H-A-P-P-Y." Ha, I don't know, perhaps I think of happiness as a more superficial thing. Yes, perhaps that is what it is. Perhaps it is not sex, just superficial. Whereas joy—I love the word "joy"—you can have joy in your heart, deep in your heart, even when you are in turmoil. Joy is a kind of serenity of mind, whereas happiness to me is something *pwht!* . . . like the wind. Yes, that's a good way of describing it. Oh, you do have happy days of course, but I think it would be true to say that you don't get as many happy days as you get older. Nor joy for that matter. You just can't call on joy to emerge. It is something that comes, but not something that you should expect.

GLENYS LEWIS

63

What you can expect are quite a lot of arid times in between. So now . . . now I think perhaps contentment is far more important than either happiness or even joy. Joy and happiness both come and go, whereas contentment . . . well, you can feel ruddy awful one day, moaning away, and then you look around your little house and you think to yourself, aren't I fortunate. That's contentment.

THE THINGS you miss most in old age are not always easy to put into words. Certainly it is not material things. Perhaps the thing one feels most is the loss of a sense of worth. For me now that has to be met by my religion. That God thinks I'm worthwhile, therefore I must believe that I am of worth. What you don't get, what we all need, is the support of other people's sense of your worth. We all need that. Yet as you get older . . . well, somehow it seems that you get it less and less. People are very kind of course, and loving, and friendly, but that is not the same thing. Not the same as when you are young. Nowadays you find yourself being very grateful to younger people who offer you their friendship. I did a tape just the other day for a couple who have been so caring, and I put a little note with it which said, "With thanks for your caring friendship which I value." Now that is something I would never have done—I just thought to myself later, I would never have written that when I was young. I would never have thought of writing that. I would just have accepted the friendship—almost as my due.

SOMETIMES PEOPLE say to you, would you like to have it all again? Would you like to have your life back over? A lot of people say they would like to, but not me. I have no desire at all to go through all that again. There has been too much trauma in my life, too much illness, and really, apart from the spiritual side of my life— my work—there has been no great fulfilment. So no, I can't see any point in wanting to go through it all again. If I think of it, I sometimes think it's sad that I never met an eligible man that I really went for. I never met the man that I'd go over the moon for,

and yet I know that somewhere, somewhere he must exist. Yes, I do believe that—people who are your kind of true mates, that there is a true mate knocking around somewhere. I just never got to meet him.

In a way, we never had a terrible lot of chance, being four girls in the house. There were no brothers to be bringing boys home,

GLENYS LEWIS

65

and we didn't do a lot of entertaining, so there wasn't great opportunity. Of course I suppose there was when I went nursing, but by that time I had this chip on my shoulder or whatever you'd call it. By then I was a bit of a prude. Actually I was very prudish— I didn't really know what to do with boys. I didn't know how to cope at all. Probably I think things would have been very different if my mother had lived. I should think my life would have turned out very different. Even so, things like relationships and sex were very little talked about in those days. I remember a friend of mine who when she got married—the night before she married—her mother took her aside and said, "Now, darling, you'd better put one of these"—a menstrual pad—"you'd better put one of these in your case. You might need it." And that was all she said. That was all that girl knew of what was going to happen on her wedding night. And her intended didn't know much more. He was as innocent as she was. Now that is monstrous, absolutely monstrous.

It was the same sort of thing for us in our home. I remember my sister and I asking our steppie about how things happened when people had sex. She would not tell us. I remember we went into the drawing room and sat her down and we demanded to know, but still she would not tell us. I think probably she was too shy to tell us. I suppose I would have been about eighteen by then, and I doubt if at that time we even knew of coitus. We knew very little of anything like this. But she would tell us nothing. She wouldn't open up at all. She just shut herself off. Strange, wasn't it . . . a different kind of world. Who knows, perhaps we lived in a time when we didn't need to know.

BEING WHERE I am now, at the other end of my life, I have to face the fact that no relationship I have ever had has reached fulfilment. It would seem that all of this kind of love to me has been a painful experience, never fulfilling. Interesting, isn't it, that it's always been cut off like that. Actually I remember reading somewhere, I don't remember the words exactly, but I thought, well, that's me.

GLENYS LEWIS

66

Somebody who had had a painful experience in loving as a child. And right through their lives after that—their love experiences after that—they were never able to be fulfilled. And when I read that I thought, well, that is true of me, that is my experience also.

Of course it's not an easy thing to talk about, but yes, I suppose any woman—and I imagine any man—who has not had an emotionally fulfilled sexual life would regret that. I regret it, and I would be an abnormal woman, I should think, if I didn't. Certainly it seems to me a normal thing to feel that way, particularly as I read such a terrific lot, and you know how much sex is in books these days. You can hardly get away from it. And so, yes, I do, I do feel that part of my life has been starved. At the same time I feel that I have been compensated, that my life has been, in a sense, directed. In a queer kind of way I don't think I've had a lot of say in the way things have gone. In a way it's all part of a kind of pattern, right from after that trauma in the park where my aunt treated me almost as if I was a leper—closing me in to the giving out of love. All part of becoming so inhibited, as I did when I was young. Ha, I remember I became terribly pious at one stage, and in fact, to be honest, I think I became bitter. I simply didn't know how to cope with myself. Oh gosh, when I look back on it . . .

As I got older of course I had one or two things happen—emotional involvements—which were not right, but which were probably inevitable. I can't really see how any kind of normal woman or man can go through life without being emotionally involved at some time with the opposite sex. I can't see how it couldn't happen. A long time ago there was a man I cared for; I loved him very much, but he was already married to a woman I knew. It was not a good marriage, he was very unhappy, but in no way could I be responsible for breaking up a marriage. That was something I could not do. Later they had a child, and that was that, I was out in the cold. But still, I loved him for years.

It started during a visit—his wife was out of the room, and we were just sitting there, he in one chair and I in another. Very simply he put out his hand, and took my hand, and he said he loved

me. That was how it started. I was not even consciously caring for him at that time, but that was how it started, and my feelings for him after that went on for a long time. His need was so great, and when he said he loved me . . . well, I suppose I responded because I was pretty starved for affection too. There was me, somebody who was a pretty affectionate kind of person, loving, and equally in need of being loved. We all need to give love, and we all need to receive it. And I was in an age group, a time, when one naturally yearns for the expression of emotion. No doubt I would have been a happier woman if I had not got emotionally involved, but human nature being what it is, I don't know how I could have survived my life without any emotion in it at all. In the end, though, such emotion is a costly thing. It was for me. A dead end. An unsatisfactory thing with no future.

GLENYS LEWIS

In the beginning of course, you are too taken up with it all to look into the future. It is very nice to be attracted to somebody . . . and to have somebody attracted to you. You don't bother at that stage to count the cost. And it does cost. Particularly for the woman, for the odd one out. Because the man goes home, he lives his other life, and the woman is never able to say, "This is my man, this is the man I love," which is something I think we all like to do. Not that I ever felt I was being used, so to speak—emotionally we were both caught up in it. No, it was give and take on both sides, so I never felt anything like that. What I did feel was the denigration and frustration of it all. The denigration inherent in keeping such things secret, of never being able to do or say anything in public. And frustration . . . well, there was frustration all the way through for us. Because of my work in the church, because of my faith and very deep feelings for the Lord, I was never able to have what you might call a total relationship. To have done so with a married man would have been terribly disloyal, though in truth it was all I could do to fight off the genuine affection that we had for one another. Wanting to see one another, wanting to be with one another . . . it was very hard.

You know, I can remember a time not long after all this started—I was so frustrated that I was literally down on my knees and more or less shouting at God. I had invited this man to a meal. And when he came I was so very tempted . . . tempted to tempt him. In the end I was able to resist the temptation, but when he was gone I was absolutely mad. Mad with God. Mad as hops. I was frustrated and angry, all of those things, and I was down on my knees shouting to God. It would have been so easy to have gone ahead and tempted this man, so easy, and yet I didn't do it. I had stopped myself. And in a sense it was a kind of triumph, but it was not a triumph that pleased me. I had resisted because I loved God and I had thought of the man and his position, all those things. I had resisted, but in that resistance I was very angry, angry with myself, and with God. And I suppose too I was angry with the frustration of not being able to love somebody I felt close to.

GLENYS LEWIS

69

We all need to be loved, but I had stopped myself from doing this thing. I felt that I should not do this thing that would have been so easy to do. And when he left—I can see myself now—I was down on the floor and this anger just kind of poured out of me. I can't remember the words I used exactly, but I was shouting at God, really shouting at him. Then somehow I remembered something I had once been told, that if one offered one's pain to God—one's temptations or sorrows or any of those kinds of emotional things—then he could take them and use them to help somebody else. Somebody who did not know how to pray. Someone who did not have this contact with God. And so I offered it totally. I mean, I was still mad. I said, "Take it!" I just kind of threw it at him. I was not at all in a lovely mood. "Damn well take it!" I said. "Use it for somebody if you think you can. If there's anyone going through what I'm going through, use it for them." And suddenly it was gone. Suddenly I had this sensation of peace and tranquillity that was remarkable, that was in such contrast to the way I had been only moments before. I could only believe that God had been able to take this pain from me and use it to help someone else.

That was in the beginning, and had I been able to stop it there my life would have been a lot easier. That, however, was not the way it worked out. This whole frustrating thing went on for quite some time, and it was, as I say, all we could do to fight off this great affection we had for one another, this wanting to be with each other. I could not seem to get away from it, and in the end it began to feel like I was digging myself deeper and deeper into some great ditch. One gets into a kind of rut, and there is no way out. In the end I didn't seem to be able to cope with it myself, and I started to pray to be released from it. "I will run the way of thy commandments when thou has set my heart at liberty." I used to pray that madly. "I will run the way of thy commandments when thou has set my heart at liberty." And that is what I longed for, to find a way out of what seemed like a kind of blindness to me. It was a terrible thing that I wouldn't want anyone to go through, and yet it seems a lot of single women do. It is perhaps an almost inevitable thing of being single.

Just as inevitable perhaps is the fact that single women always get the blame for any misconduct of the husband, any deviation of his love to somebody else. It is always the woman who is the fiend because that is the easiest way out. Well, one thing I have learnt—not only out of my own experience but also from the many confidences that I have received—is that in marriage there is no right or wrong; there is no one person who is innocent. Of course, in my own situation, not only was there this triangle type of business, but there was the whole religious thing as well.

In my work at the time I did a lot of public speaking, which meant I was well known to a lot of people. Well . . . I did not want to let the Lord down. I loved God, and I did not want to make a mockery of his teachings. Nor did I want people going round saying, what a hypocrite she is. I used to feel a bit of a hypocrite, of course one does, and guilt too, I felt that. It was a totally dead-end situation because neither of us would go any further kind of business, and that was that. We had the guilt and the frustration, we had that alright, but without what you might call any of the joy. No, it was grim . . . grim. And that is why I was praying that prayer. "I will run the way of thy commandments when thou has set my heart at liberty." I used to pray that madly because I could not seem to get away from it. I prayed to be released from it, and in the end New Zealand—going to New Zealand—was the answer. That severed it totally. It also took me into a deep freeze. Saying goodbye to my sisters, everybody, I couldn't feel a thing. I think now that I simply had to, I had to go into a deep freeze to survive. The funny thing was that when a friend of mine first suggested I might be needed for work in New Zealand, I laughed her to scorn. Eight months later I was on the ship coming out. There are times when what happens in life seems inexplicable. Now I feel that I was picked up and "put" in the most extraordinary way. Certainly having my emotions frozen as they were was a real life-

saver . . . and thank God I have not been emotionally involved like that since.

It may be in some sense true that your life is shaped by the things that have happened to you. I don't often think a lot about the past—I don't know really that it is good to look too much into your past. One of course is sorry if one caused anybody any pain—in all things—as one would be. But no, you can't really put the self of today back into the past. It's true I did go through a rather difficult period just after I retired. A time when work stopped being my life. It was hard to realise that my work had been my life so fully, so completely, so entirely, that there had seemed at the time not much room for anything else. But when it stopped, that was a time when I started to rebel against God for not letting me have this other side of life. That side of life which had not been fulfilled in me. I did go through a time of feeling that something was missing, a time of negative thinking, a sort of blackness, but I came through that and I realised that if things had been different I would not have been fulfilled in the way I have. I would not have done what I felt was God's call for me to do.

Basically now I am content. Yes, I think I can say that with all honesty. It's true one has days when one does not feel that way, but then that's true of anybody. Overall I'm contented with my lot. I'm also enormously grateful for my extraordinary health in this last bit of my life. I've had such shocking ill health most of my life that to have the ability now at seventy-five to cut my own lawn when other people are talking about getting their grandsons to do it—that's something. Not that I enjoy doing it, it's just that I'm thankful I can. That may sound a bit Irish, but no, life for me now is full of gratitude. I am a happy person with a tremendous belief in the love of God—and in my love for him—which is even more powerful and more real after having come through such a bad time. Such a vale of darkness.

In the end we must all come to terms with our lives. God gave us free will, and we are all free to say yes or no to any of the things

GLENYS LEWIS

he might suggest. Of course, if you're not in touch with him you are not going to hear his still small voice pushing you one way or the other. I suppose I could have said, to hell with it, I'm going to find a man that can bear to marry me and I'm going to go holus bolus in that direction. But I can't see myself doing that. Not if I was the same person. I have always believed in commitment to God and in his guidance. I feel he has put me where he wants me to be, where I can serve him most. And that is how I've always seen my life, as a kind of a plan. All of those things that happened in my life, all those little chance things, I don't call them chance any more. I believe it is all part of being open to his love and guidance. To some people, I suppose, there's no sense in it . . . but to me there is.

Now I am seventy-five. Seventy-five is three-quarters of a hundred, so by years I'm old. By all that living I'm supposed to be an old woman. The thing is, I just don't feel old. I remember seeing a woman once down at the beach. If she was even sixty I'd be very surprised, but she was very podgy and she walked like an old woman. There was a little step there, in front of a cafe, where you walked down onto the sand. It was a very small step, but she had to have her husband's hand, she took his arm and did it as though she was a hundred plus. Well, I thought to myself, there is an old woman. That is what I think of as old age. Certainly it is an attitude of mind, plus it helps to have a fairly active and agile body. Yes, the body side of it is terribly important. I had a lot of illness when I was young, and so I know how this affects your mind. It's a two-way thing—your body affects your mind and your mind affects your body.

Perhaps one of the things you learn when you're getting old is not to fash too much with the funny aches and pains you get. When it first started I would go off to the doctor with any little thing. Poor darling, I'm sure he used to think, oh yes, here comes another one sort of thing. The thing is, you do get all sorts of little aches and pains. Don't ask me where . . . everywhere, I suppose, at some time or other. It's all part of the aging process really, something you learn to live with.

I am aware of course of some difference. In particular, I would say, when I'm in the garden, and also walking. Walking, I suppose, is where I'm most aware of it. The fact that I now walk slightly unsteadily, that I don't feel frightfully secure on my pins, is not a good feeling. It's a question of balance really, just a little bit, but enough to make me use my stick whenever I go on one of my longer walks. Probably the time will come when I use my stick just to go to the supermarket, which is, well, a bit disconcerting. It seems to be my balance that's affected. If I'm walking and I look up at anything, I tend to go over a little to one side. It's not enough to trouble me too much—some people get it very badly as they get older—it's just that I find I can't wear high heels any more, things like that. It's a shame because I've got some really nice shoes which I don't get to wear now. And that's a bit . . . well, they're so much smarter, you feel more dressed in them—nicer somehow.

I suppose in a way we still have this hangover from the Victorian era, haven't we? These expectations of how a woman should look. I mean, you've only got to look at television or at a magazine to see these beautiful women everywhere. We talk about women being liberated, but there is still a tremendous hangover that women have to be feminine and attractive, and men have to be strong and all this kind of thing. We still tend to do this. Even at my age I still like to look as nice as I can. Certainly I have a pride in my appearance. I have never been one who slops around in a dressing gown. When I get up in the morning I get dressed and then I put my face on—which is a great blessing, I don't mind telling you. You take a look at your face in the morning, and I must say it's good to be able to stick some stuff on that makes you look a bit younger. I always do this before I leave my bedroom. I don't know what it is, something I've always done. I just like to look as nice as I can, and not merely for other people, although other people are important—I do the same thing whether I am spending the day by myself or not.

GLENYS LEWIS

75

The whole aging process in this regard of course is not a very kind one. I always remember when I first saw that my arms had gone all horrid. My upper arms had kind of flopped, as it were. Ha, the first time I saw that I thought, oh gudge, how horrid. It was all so . . . flappy. Oh no, I didn't like that. I think I minded that much more than my neck—my neck went much earlier on. I remember a little girl saying to me at the time—this was years ago—she said, "Oooh, Aunty Glen, you have got a funny neck, it's like a chicken's." Ha ha ha, gorgeous, isn't it. Oh yes. Still, physical appearance is quite important to a woman, I think. And then you sometimes get these people—you know, you might have a grumble about all the lines you're getting, and they'll say to you, "Oh, you mustn't talk like that, your lines are a sign of your character." Well, I think to myself, ha, if they're the sign of my character, I could do without one.

Of course if you have to be old, well, then, I suppose it's marvellous to be old in this time when you can do as you like and dress as you like and not feel that you are doing something quite dreadful. Imagine if you lived in nineteen—say nineteen twenty. At my age now I would be dressed in black. I would probably have a little lace cap on the top of my head—I'm thinking of my grandmother—little white curls down the side of my face. She would wear a very high collar, black, so as not to show her scrawny neck—like Queen Mary. Her arms would be covered, and oh, to go without stockings, that would be utterly the end. And as for putting makeup on my face, I would be a scarlet woman. What a change. It's funny, isn't it, but in my lifetime . . . what a change.

QUITE FRANKLY I never thought about old age. I mean, I knew that one day I would get old, but life was too busy and too full somehow to really think about it. So I can't honestly say that I did. Of course there's this great business today where you plan your retirement. That you get hobbies and things all ready for your retirement, this kind of thing. Well, I never—I never even gave it a passing thought. I always lived very much in the present, and I

PIONEER DEACONESS TO RETIRE

After 25 years devoted to church work, Deaconess Glenys Lewis, head deaconess of the Auckland Anglican diocese and warden of the Anglican hostel in Remuera, will retire at the end of the year.

Originally from Wales, Deaconess Lewis trained in England as a nurse and midwife with the hope of becoming a medical missionary. When her health did not permit this she decided to become a deaconess.

Her training was completed after 3 years, and in 1950 she was appointed head deaconess of the Guildford diocese, and she was there for 10 years.

In 1960 she came to New Zealand and took up hospital chaplaincy work in Christchurch for 3 years.

"Following this," she said, "I travelled throughout the country for 18 months preaching and speaking on women's ministry in the Church.

"In 1963 I spoke to the members of St John's College in Meadowbank and was invited to lunch by the warden. He told me I was probably the first woman to attend an official meal in the refectory and was therefore seeing history made. Today," she added, "women residents are accepted at St John's and this act is so ordinary that no one thinks twice about it."

After her 18 months of travelling, Miss Lewis was asked to supervise the deaconess training house in Parnell, and for four years organised the training programme.

"I feel," she said, "that it is an advantage if one has had some experience with people before entering this service. It can be invaluable when dealing with personal problems."

Last year, when St John's College decided to accept women residents, the Parnell house no longer served its purpose. It was shortly after this that Miss Lewis became warden at the Remuera hostel where she has had charge of 25 girls.

[Newspaper article, November 19, 1971]

just didn't think about it. And the thing was that my work was so totally involving as well. My work was my life. My life was my work. Then one day I retired—and suddenly I was kind of chopped off. The phone didn't go, the letters didn't arrive, engagements didn't happen. Suddenly the responsibilities had all been handed over to somebody else, and there was just an absolute kind of void. Dreadful. So dreadful. It is very hard to describe what that first year was like.

Certainly it was an extraordinary experience. I was sixty, and I was very strained, very overstressed. I had worked so hard— I was asked to do these things and I did them without question. Then nothing . . . retirement . . . well, I didn't find it easy. It was not easy. I felt so suddenly dropped, suddenly abandoned and lost somehow . . . so hard to put it into words. You see, along with the fact that they don't rely on you any more goes the fact that you are no longer important, you are no longer needed. And you get to thinking, well, here I am, I have done all these things, and your image—your inflated self—gets very bashed about until you fall back into seeing what you really are. I'm not minimising what I have done, I believe that I did have a call, a vocation, and that therefore it must have been of value. But I also had to realise that a lot of the—well, not adulation, but a lot of the wanting me, was due to the fact that I was Head Deaconess of the Auckland diocese type of thing, and not just Glenys. That was hard, particularly when you have been very much in the public eye and having, I suppose, a sort of fuss made of you. I remember I had this book with all sorts of newspaper cuttings about myself, and I'd be on the radio, and I'd be on television. And I would speak in synods and things where women had never spoken before. All that, and so you get to feel in yourself a little bit important. And then—very suddenly—you simply stop being important. I had been a deaconess for over twenty years. Right from the start I had been given very responsible jobs, right from scratch. Naturally I thought I was quite important. Not just the deaconess, but me. Oh, I was still Glenys, but Glenys, I think, got hidden under this attention

GLENYS LEWIS

she received—got a bit above herself probably. I think perhaps I
thought I was more important than I really was. I don't know. The
job, you see, was important . . . and I had created this job—in a
sense I was the job. But then when I retired it was all gone from
me, the Head Deaconess was dead. Dropped and buried, and who
was left? I had to find out who Glenys really was. I had to find me.
And it took quite some time.

GLENYS LEWIS

79

I was very nervously exhausted. I had overstretched myself, and now somehow it seemed that I could only see the negative side of myself. I began to think less of myself, that I was a pretty lousy kind of person. I had a very poor image, my self-confidence, everything, seemed to go. It took me a long time to get it back. I don't suppose it will ever be the same, I'm sure it won't, and perhaps that's a good thing. I was a bit of a bulldozer at times; in a sense I had to be—kind of forced into it, being in these positions and having to get on and do it. The Deaconess House job towards the end was pretty traumatic in so far as I had students who were all strong characters—dynamite—and learning this new theology, God is dead kind of business at the Theological College. Then they'd come back to an old square like me. We had some quite difficult times together, and I think this is what really more or less finished me off.

I had been told by a priest a couple of years before I retired that I was in for a serious time, and that's what happened. My work was gone, and all I had left was what people today call a nervous breakdown. I had quite a gruelling time of it really. I couldn't even seem to talk with people. I would get this terrible physical reaction in my body—kind of jumping nerves. My finger tips would be absolutely jumping. Mostly people wouldn't notice it, but my nerve ends would be just absolutely screaming. Stress. And when stress like that goes beyond a certain point, you need help. I was too alone—too alone for too long—and I got mad at God again. I went through this period of being really mad with God because I thought he had given me a pretty raw deal somehow. I could no longer see that I had done anything good in my life. In my own mind I was just a loss, a total loss. It was a time when I really didn't like myself at all. I could not seem to give myself one good attribute. I sat there in bed one day with a piece of paper in front of me, trying to find out if I had any good qualities at all. I put this line down the centre of the page and listed all my negative qualities to one side. Then I tried to put the positive qualities, and I couldn't find one. That's when I got pretty mad with God. It

GLENYS LEWIS

was all part of the illness, of course. To think that I could only see bad things in my life, that I hadn't done anything of worth . . . well, I'm glad that has more or less gone from my life now. I do get flickers of it still, but I make a concerted effort to shut it out because it's nonsense really. I mean, of course I've done things that I am sorry for, and things that I don't admire myself for, but on the other hand I would not get fifty Christmas cards from all over the world and I wouldn't have just had such a wonderful seventy-fifth birthday if all my life had been wasted. No, it's nonsense to think these things . . . it's the devil really. I don't know if people believe in the devil these days, but there is certainly a side to one that wants to put oneself down. That, I think, is not good. You can't be contented and happy if you think you are a worm. Ha. The worm has to turn from time to time. But this, of course, is how I feel now. It was a very different thing when it was happening. Things were so far out of kilter then, and nobody really understands what that's like. I remember a woman years ago in England saying to me, "You will never know unless you've been there yourself. It was like being," she said, "in a pit. All I could see at the top were the faces of my friends and I hung on to that." She was not far wrong. You have to experience something to know it. I don't think a lot of people really understand that. It's strange, isn't it—if you get a boil on the end of your nose you get a lot of sympathy, but if it's something unseen, more hidden, that's a different thing.

We all need to be needed, and that, I think, is a very true fact of life. You see it in the young ones today—the ones who can't get work—feeling so denigrated and so unnecessary. Life ceases to have a purpose for them. And you see it in the old. Yes, you see the old having to cope with it too. There are, I think, a lot of lonely people like that. People who feel that they have ceased to be of any worth—they just kind of see their days out. I went through all those feelings of uselessness and despair. There were even times when I felt resentful, that this woman who had done so much was being allowed to be forgotten, was unwanted. There was a sense of diminishment . . . yes, I should think most people who have this experience lose a sense of their worth . . . their self-confidence. You have to build that all back up again.

BECOMING A PRIEST, it was very unexpected. I had never dreamt that it would come in my lifetime. Back in 1963, when I was travelling around the country talking about the woman's ministry, people used to ask about it—this whole question of woman priests—but I didn't even discuss it. It all seemed so remote, you see.

I suppose I must have been retired for four or five years when the bishop asked me whether I'd like to be ordained into the priesthood. I had been through that very bad spell and was just starting to come out of it. Not that I had been miserable all the time, but I'd had to come up from quite a deep level. I was glad that general synod had passed the idea of women joining the priesthood, but I never thought of considering myself in that role. I felt that I had been retired too long. When he approached me my reaction was, oh, gosh no sort of thing—I really thought I had finished my ministry. A while later though, I started to have what I call my little pushes, inside.

My time as a deaconess was enormously fulfilling, and yet it's true I always carried with me the knowledge that what I did was not complete. We could go so far, but some of the vital things we couldn't do. Celebrating the sacrament, giving the sacrament of absolution, the blessing, these sorts of things that complete the ministry—we couldn't do that. And that was something that was always there—with others as well as myself. We were not laity, we were not clergy, we were something in the middle, and you carried that with you throughout. It was something you were always aware of. Anyway, the bishop had asked me to think about it, and some months later, when he asked me again, I said yes. Yes, I would do it. I felt somehow that I must.

When you are ordained a priest, you are at the same time licensed to work. I could not just receive it and do nothing—it is a gift to minister—and so I started working again. And physically I was able to do it, I felt great. It was a wonderful renewal really. My retirement had been such a grim period, and from being so down in the depths to really being accepted in this way—it was wonderful. One had a sense of worth, obviously, from the amount of joyful acceptance by other people of what I was doing. And certainly it was lovely to celebrate the sacrament. The actual ability to administer the sacrament—I had very strong feelings about that, I still do. It is a wonderful privilege, the greatest privilege of my life, I think, and a culmination of all my years in the ministry. Yes . . . the work I did then—it was a special time for me, what you might call a rounding off.

I had three or four years, I suppose, before it was time to stop again. I'd used up my personal strength, I really had, but this time it felt good. I was seventy years old. I had my seventieth birthday while I was at my own church. In the Sunday main service—they stopped the early part of the service and presented me with the most beautiful bouquet of flowers. That was in August, and I retired then at the end of September. And this time I was ready for it. I thought it a good and proper time to stop. I was given a licence then to minister within the diocese—this is what they do with retired priests. I could go to any parish to take a service of communion or that kind of thing. Funerals—I did quite a bit of that—any priestly functions I can fill in for. It's got less and less, though, and I've been happy for it to be less and less. Yes, a good rounding off.

LACK OF VITALITY. It's ludicrous and irritating and maddening, but when you're old, it's true, you don't have the vitality you would like to have. It's just a fact that one's body is aging, and nothing can stop that. It is a thing that one accepts because there is no point in not accepting it. It is a fact. Everything takes longer when you've not got the energy. It takes more out of you. I cut the lawn—that takes a lot out of me. I ought to do the edges and all that kind of thing, but I can never do the edges after I've cut the lawn. I've got to do them another day, and then I forget to do them, so they don't get done until next time. And weeding. Weeding is an anathema. I used to enjoy it, I used to spend hours on my knees weeding, but I don't now. If I kneel now I have to have something to hang on to to get up, and that is very humiliating. To feel your old body getting so . . . well, "humiliating" is the wrong word. One just doesn't like one's body slowing up, I suppose.

My great joy until I was about sixty was the sea. In the sea, under the sea, on the sea. Oh yes, the sea has been a great love. I loved to splash around—bathing, swimming, boating, yes, I even yachted once or twice and got my bottom beautifully wet. Adored it, but I don't do much of that now. I do have the advantage of a pool which I can use. I use it quite a lot. Funny, you know, I used to think it a frightfully bad show to jump into the pool and not dive. Well, of course the time came when I didn't dive, I jumped. Ha—now I don't even jump, I just walk down the steps. It's called progressive old age.

It's hard to put a date on such things of course—when does it all first start to happen?—but nowadays, as I say, if I'm out weeding I take my bucket, and I hang on to it. I hang on to it just to get up. Actually I fought rather hard against that. I used to really pressure myself because I did not want to acknowledge it. Even now if I was to kneel on the ground I think I could probably get up without hanging on to anything, just out of sheer dogged determination. Ha, ha—no, probably I'd fall over. All a question of acceptance, I expect. In the end you just have to accept it and try not to feel . . . to feel self-pitying. My pleasures now are much simpler than they used to be. I get enormous pleasure, for instance, when my roses are in bloom. Or sitting here at the window with a glass of sherry before dinner . . . just enjoying the beautiful view. And mixed up with that somewhere is gratitude. I am so enormously grateful to end up my life in a spot like this. When I think of some of the places I've lived in, it seems wonderful to have a home like this for the latter part of my life. Oh yes.

GLENYS LEWIS

WOMEN ARE SUPPOSED to mind terribly when people know their age, but I tell everyone I'm seventy-five. I don't mind, you see; I've never had that hangup. I've never minded people knowing how old I was. And then of course there are some benefits to being this sort of age. You have, I think, a certain wisdom that comes with experience. You don't get into quite the same kind of tizzies that you used to get into. You don't get these emotional involvements that one tends to get when one is young. It is a more tranquil time, I suppose. Not that you become perfect of course. One still tends to have these silly concerns—whether you've upset someone or done something wrong—you know what I mean, the way everyone does. No, you don't exactly lose all that, but as I say, life somehow seems to become a more tranquil business. There are some people, I suppose, who would like to live their life over again, but not I. I should hate to. To go through all that trauma again—no thank you. No, I've come into calmer waters now, and I'm very happy to be in them. But then, you see, I have my beliefs. I don't think of myself as a candle that will just go out when I die. I don't ever feel that I must make the most of it because I am coming to the end. I suppose in a way I just feel closer to God. It would be a sad thing to feel otherwise.

NOW I'LL TELL YOU a strange thing, shall I? Only once in my life have I ever remembered a dream, and that wasn't until I was into my sixties. Yes, I would have been in my sixties, and I had this most vivid dream. It was strange in that I had been talking to this woman, and she obviously had some sort of extra perception or whatever you would call it. She said to me, if you want to know your dreams, you must tell yourself you will remember them. She said to say this to myself just before I went to sleep. Well, I did it that night, and I had this very, very vivid dream which woke me up with a jolt. It was a dream which I've never forgotten, and it relates right back to the time my father came to tell me that Mummy had died.

GLENYS LEWIS

85

In the dream I am on a little boat going down a stream, and I am as happy as Larry because my Mummy and Daddy were in a little boat behind me. And then suddenly my little boat meets a powerful current going across in front of me. Suddenly I'm cut off and I'm kind of drowning, and my father from the other side comes and rescues me. You see what I mean. I'm coming down the river and I'm kind of broken—chopped off there—and then my father sort of rescues me. And there's something frightening in his rescue. I'm quite terrified. So terrified that I actually woke up. And the strange thing is that the horror I feel when my father rescues me is definitely a physical horror. I don't know why—I won't ever know—but somehow I felt that certain inhibitions I've had all my life were rooted there in this thing. That the boat sinking is linked with my mother's death . . . my father drawing me to him again when my second mother was dying . . . and me being so scared of the physical. Perhaps it all sounds farfetched, but it does in a way explain this very real inhibition which I have. And that was in my sixties, that dream, so you see one never knows what goes on in the mind of a child, or how long things stay there.

I suppose the strange thing about my life when I was younger—when I was working—was that I didn't really think about it. Not very much. I never asked questions as to what was the purpose of it all, what was I doing. I just kind of did it, if you can understand that. I had within me a very strong prayer life, and prayer was my substance, so to speak. I never bothered much about what life was for, I just got on with what was waiting to be done. When things came to me, I did them. When people asked me to speak, I spoke. When I was asked to preach, I preached. I considered that this was what God wanted me to do. So I did it.

Now I have become old. I am here in what has been called the shadows of later life. That is where I am. I am conscious now of the fact that there are limitations. There are things that ten years ago would have been nothing . . . nowadays the body gets more feeble. Now there are times when you feel you have done your stint—when you don't feel so terribly useful or valuable any more. I have lived . . . I feel I have lived my life. There's the sense that no further horizons lie ahead—that takes a bit of accepting. You get older and there are times—not all the time of course—but there are times when you wonder what in the world you have done. Just what you have achieved with your life. Naturally there are other times when you think of all you have done. But certainly that big balloon I used to have—of what a wonderful woman I was—that balloon has been pricked. And the way I accept it all now is to know that my horizons are no longer in this dimension.

At different times we feel different things, and lately there have been times in my life when I have felt I would like to die. You see, I have this very strong belief in life after death, that there is something infinitely better waiting for me to go to, and I will be happy to go. But for now I am still here, I go on. God, it seems, must still have some purpose in me yet. I have always been available to him, for whatever he has wanted me to do. I have always tried to be sensitive to his will. But I think we all of us find it difficult to do nothing. To do nothing and yet to believe there is a purpose in doing nothing. That is not easy, I think. I have tried. For a time there I rushed around trying to get involved in different things, and always I seemed to come up against the closed door, the stone wall. I had to stop, to think to myself, this is not right. Always before, the doors had been open—wide—without me even asking. Now they are not. So were you to ask me what my purpose is . . . well, I honestly don't really know what my purpose is now. Except I know this, that I am still in his loving hands.

It is something I have to look forward to—going on, discovering Christ Omega. The end point. The culmination of what I call the process of homogenization, where personal and universal meet in supra-personal. The concept of another dimension, which I have entered into more and more. It is a lovely feeling—the vastness of it all. A dimension that I believe is very close but which we cannot see. As St. Paul says, "Our eyes are holden that we cannot see." He was the only one given the opportunity of seeing this other dimension, and his eyes were blinded for three days when he saw the risen Christ. I believe that. I am not a fundamentalist, but there are certain things in the Bible that to me are authentic.

Just imagine if you were standing by a pool, and the pool is teeming with life. Well, that life is completely contained, it knows nothing else. And were I to stand there, beside that pool, there is no way in which that life could see me and comprehend me. It could not imagine me moving from there and, say, getting on a plane and flying to America. That would be totally beyond its comprehension. The pool, you might say, is one dimension. We live in another. And beyond that I believe there is yet another dimension that can look at us in the same way. A dimension in which things would be as mind-boggling to us as our way of being is to the life in that pool. Mind-boggling indeed, but I am fortunate, I think, to have this belief. Were I to think otherwise—well, I'd be nothing, just a speck, something of no account. No, I'm grateful for my belief. It is why I have no worries about getting older, getting feeble.

Of course I'm not saying that I like the idea that I can't ride a bicycle any more, that I can't wear high heels, that I'm getting slower. But imagine if you felt that you had nobody outside of yourself. Nobody that you felt was in charge of you, and you felt feeble . . . you would start worrying then. So you see, I'm not worrying too much now—I live each day as it comes and try to keep away from negative attitudes which rather tend to pull you down. I can't even say that time seems more precious to me now. Although I love the day and the beauty of things, I don't, on the other hand, care a button when I die. Whether that would change were I suddenly to get "old" . . . I don't know. I hope in the end I just go out like a light. I think most of us would like to do that, but of course you can't pick and choose. What I do hope and pray is that I don't become a cabbage. I have seen so many of these people, physically and mentally incapacitated, not moving, can't even go to the loo for themselves. Calling out as people rush by,

and nobody taking any notice of them . . . so pathetic . . . so sad. Those are things which I do hope will not be my lot.

All that happens, though, is part of life. And to me dying is just one more thing—part of the pattern of the wholeness of life, but it doesn't end there. That is not the whole of life. I don't think I could believe in God if I thought this was the whole of life. Not that I dwell on these things—I don't. But every now and again one naturally thinks about it. It's not easy to put into words really, just that one's mind kind of meanders around those things now and again. There was a night a little while back—I was getting ready for bed, I'd put the cat out, and I was walking back through the lounge in the dark, and there was the moon shining right in. The curtains were open, and I just stood there and thought, gosh, aren't you lovely. And then I opened the door and went out there, stood outside there on the concrete, and I looked up, and the heavens were just a blaze of stars. This vast cosmos. And I was thinking how fantastic it is. To know that there is something out there to which I am going. Oh, I know it would be quite easy to have doubts about this belief of mine, the reality of it—you can understand people not being able to believe in it. But for myself, I am still able to believe, and I should hate not to. I think I would be frightened . . . no, perhaps not frightened, that's the wrong word, but I wouldn't want to die so much. Not if I felt I was just going to snuff out like a candle. That the real me would just be ended. No, I believe the real me—whatever is me—is eternal. Well, if it wasn't, it would be so unfair. Monstrously unfair. When you think of people in Africa and all those places . . . such rotten things happening—oh, it would be crazy. I mean, life . . . well, it would be a bit absurd, don't you think?

GLENYS LEWIS

Alex Coutts

COUTTS, Alexander Hodge
On April 27th, 1985, at Greymouth,
dearly loved husband of the late
Thelma Elizabeth Coutts, Main Road
Dobson. Loved father and father-in-law,
and a loved granddad and great-granddad;
in his 77th year. The funeral service
will be held in our chapel, 134 Tainui
Street. This day (Monday) at 3 p.m., then
interment at the Karoro Cemetery.

END OF THE PENNY SECTION

I WAS YOUNG and then I was old. It was like passing through a screen, a ray or something. Old age is a thing that didn't creep up on me, it hit me—bang. Before that happened I was always going like hell. Speed was everything to me. If I did anything, I did it fast. Think fast, talk fast, run fast, play fast, everything was fast, until this. And that's what hurts me most of anything, to be so slow. My old age come on just like shuttin' the door. I'd gone through a door, and that's when I come out an old man. See, I was clinically dead. The doctor explained it to me. My heart had stopped, there'd been a blockage in there somewhere, and I was clinically dead. But when I fell and hit the floor it started working again.

My ear was all cut, all that side of my face was busted up, and four of my ribs was broke. When I started to come conscious, my head was on the floor, and I'm trying to get up. I tried to push up; I was always fairly strong, but I couldn't push up. I was pinned to the floor. I couldna get myself off that floor. I was starting to get into a panic. I was wanting to get somebody for help. That's all that was in my head. Get assistance, get assistance. Christ, I was bellowing it out like a bull. I wanted to get to the phone, to ring my neighbours next door, but I couldna budge. I couldna crawl. I couldna even crawl to the phone. I was helpless. I just felt, this is the last, you know, you're buggered. You've had it. I was thumpin' the floor and my lungs were burstin'—crying for help—anybody!

All this I'm saying is according to what I think, but later the doctor was asking me these questions. He says, "Did you do it, or did you just think you did it?" That's what he kept asking me, the old doctor at the hospital. Christ, he's older than me. He kept saying, "Are you sure you did that?" I said, "Are you callin' me a liar?" Well, that's what he's asking, he's practically saying I'm a liar. I says, "I'm telling you the bloody truth man, I'm not telling you lies, I'm not a bloody liar." "I'm not sayin' you're a liar," he said, "I'm trying to find out if you really did these things, or if

ALEX COUTTS

93

you just thought you did them. That's what I'm after." "Well," I said, "I'm sorry then, but I thought you were disputin' me, that's what it seemed to me. I thought you were callin' me a liar, and I'm not one of them." "No," he says. "But it could have been a picture in your mind, laddie, and that's what I'm trying to find out, so I know where to start on you. You could've been thinking you was roaring out and you were nae makin' a bloody sound."

Anyway, I must've been up and fell and knocked everything over; then sometime later I got over to the other chair by the bookcase and managed to struggle up between them and got myself sat down. How the hell I got round—I can remember struggling to get around—but oh, what a bloody relief when I sat down. My clothes were soaking, I was sweatin' like a turkey. The bloody sweat was pouring out of me. Well, I sat there for five or ten minutes, maybe more. Then I got a grip on the table and got myself up to the phone. I couldn't let go, my legs were shaking like hell, but I phoned next door, and Jesus, they were not long in coming. They were over here in their nightgowns and picked me up—he's a big, strong bugger—and put me to my bed. Up until that time I was as well as anybody. Och, I wouldnae call the king my uncle. But from that time everything went dead slow—yeah, from there on. Now that's a terrible shock, to anyone.

When the doctor came she put the old stethoscope on me, blood pressure and what have you, and then it was into hospital. And Jesus, I didn't like that—that was a prison, not a hospital. The food they feed you—it wouldn't ground a bloody sparrow the tucker they gave ya. No, and I told them too. I wasn't frightened to talk out. That's one thing I've always been in the habit of doing, talking straight from the shoulder. There was one sister there, "I'm in charge of the ward," she says. I said, "I don't care if you're in charge of the bloody Ark, you're not speaking to me like a dog." Cause I bellow out like a bull—you know, when I'm wild. They must've heard me all over the ward. She was not well liked anyway. All the nurses were clapping their hands—by Christ, she was a tartar. And all because I went and asked her for a cup and saucer

ALEX COUTTS

to get a cup of tea. It was about one or two in the morning, and she went me like a bloody turkey. "What are you doing up!" So I just turned on her, like a turkey cock, a gobbler. Jeez, I ticked her off. I says, "You should have been in the Belsen camps, you'd have made a bloody good Hitler," and I gave her the two up sign when she went. Anyway, after she buggered off, this other wee nurse come down with me cup of tea, and she said, "Good on you, Jock, she's always knocking people down, you give her the works."

Oh, but all the fussing about, you know, getting somebody fussing around you like that. I can stand it for so long and no more. Bloody nurses—I'd tell them to bugger off if they were fussing too much. And this bloody cardiogram thing, you're like a wireless set. It's round your ankles, and round your neck and round your chest, it's true—you're like a bloody radio. And every day they were taking blood away. I'd say, you're like Dracula, you buggers, what are you doing down there, making black puddin's? I was always pulling their leg, see. Every day I'd get a new nurse, they all wanted to nurse me. That's what they said when I left, "We're all gonna miss you, Alex." Even the patients did too.

There was this old guy across from me in the ward, he's an old Italian. Day and bloody night he's going ohhhhhhhh, ohhhhhhh, and through the night it's worse. I never used to let on I heard him like—you try to block it off. You can up to a point, but then, you know, it gets to you—after a while it does. One morning I woke up, and he was moaning like usual, and so I said, "Buon giorno." Well, he looks at me, and then he says, "Come stai." So I said, "Bene, molto bene." Oh, a good big grin on his face, so now I knew, I'd worked out what was wrong with the man. He needed someone that knew Italian; I only knew a wee bit of it through the Italians down the pit. I was just keeping an eye on him, watching him. Yeah, he'd lie there quiet as one thing and all of a sudden he'd start again. I said, that bugger's got something on his mind, it's mind over matter with him. Well, one night the family was in there and I called the daughter over. I said, "You know, there's something wrong, there's something troublin' your father and it's all up here, it's all up in his head." I says, "What have you been doing to him, has somebody been ill-treating him or something?" "No," she said. "He wants to go home—to his own home, but Mama wants to put him in an old people's home." I said, "Well, you get the old woman's mind changed and he'll come right. You get her to change her bloody mind and take him home." "Oh no, no, Mama's the boss, she's the boss." I said, "You get around her, the whole bloody lot of youse, and give her the works. Don't torment the old man or he's going to go mental. There's nothin' wrong with him, it's all in his mind."

Christ, one night they put the oxygen on him and gave him the needle. Shoved a great long needle into his ticker and pumped this stuff in. But it wasnae the hospital he was afraid of, it was the bloody old people's home. Yeah, he was frightened of the old people's home. Now, to an Italian that's terrible. It's like these Godfathers, you know, these Mafia. Once they've put the spot on you, you've had it. You might as well go and commit suicide. I know what I'm saying because I've been to visit people in these places. I seen one guy there—I had a mate with me too, we both went down and had a look at him. He was quite happy when we were there, speaking to him, but he was lying on his bed and you could see he was losin'. I sort of picked it. I said I'll give him two weeks, three at the most. Well, it was under two weeks he was dead.

WHEN I FIRST saw the doctor there at the hospital I asked him straight out. "Come on, I'm not frightened," I said. "What's wrong with me, is my ticker gone or what?" "Well," he said, "you've had a big shock to the system and now you've got to fight back." "Oh, I'll fight the bugger," I said. And so he said, "If you keep going steady and do what you're told, take your tablets, there's nothin' to stop you getting back to where you were." Well, Christ, I was always full of humour, you know, wit. Every pub, every hotel I've gone to, they always remember me. Dancing and acting the bloody goat. Nothin' for me to get up and sing a song or two for them. Keep the company going when it's in a dirty mood, five minutes and I'll change it. They never beat old Couttsie, full of fun.

So the doctor, he's pumping all these tablets and pills into me, and I said to him, "Do you have any humour pills?" "What do you mean?" he said. I says, "You been asking me questions all the time, now this is my time to ask you the bloody questions. What did I have, a stroke, a blackout, or what? All you've done is pump pills into me, one for m'heart, one for m'water, one for sleeping, one for puttin' under my tongue when I get a bumpin' in the heart, and that's bloody poison too. By Christ, it gives me a sore head. Now," I said, "Have you got any humour pills?" "Never heard tell of them," he said. "Well," I says, "I'm starting to lose my humour and I don't want to. I want the pill that will keep me going." He said, "You've never lost your humour, lad," and that's when he told me I was clinically dead. He said, "It must have been a clot in the vessels," and he said, "Whatever happened, when you fell

ALEX COUTTS

97

it must of cleared itself, so your ticker could go again." And the nurse said, "Aren't you a lucky boy." I said, "I don't know. If I'm going to be like this all the time I'd be better off bloody dead."

Not being able to do what you used to do, that is very frustrating. Oh Christ, it makes you wild. It's a retardate, a hold back. I hate it. I bloody hate it. It's retarded me to where I'm just like a bloody Womble now. You get wild because you know you've done it before, but now you're getting held back all the time. You want to go ahead but you canna do it. Well, it's bloody awful. It's like puttin' a horse in a dray and then tying it up to the bloody wall. That's what it feels like to me. Just like puttin' you up against a big brick wall and saying, now, go ya bugger, if you can. If I walk up the road what I used to do, I have to stop seven times before I get to the pub or the post office. Now I can hardly go out to my mail box or over to my shed, which used to be regular. Yeah, I used to cut my own lawns and hedges, everything. I can't do these things now. It's like they cut off your hands and feet. Now you can think. That's all you can do; oh, you can eat, or you can up and put a bit of coal on the fire, but me next-door neighbours have got to cart it all in, and take the ashes out. They're like fairy godmothers to me, the two of them. But now it's got that I have to rely on everybody, see, and that's a bloody awful feeling.

It's like a defeat. The strength part of it, the way your strength goes, you feel defeated. Even silly little things—because you can't do them, it makes you defeated. It's holding you back, you know it is, and until you get that back, it will never be the same. You want to, you want to get back like before, but you can't, the bloody strength's not there. I'm as weak as a kitten—look at these legs. I went from eleven stone to nine stone two. My bowels got all blocked up, it was like shaking concrete bricks—oh, terrible. It was so bloody painful that it held you back from going anywhere, in case it attacked you. Even when I went into town there to see the doctor—well, I was plottin' out me toilets before I hit town, where I could go in case it attacked me. It was terrible, I took everything, medicated paraffin oil, Epsom salts, God knows what—everything. Then I seen the doctor and he gave me a wee bottle. What a horrible bloody taste, but all bad medicine is hard to take. Take five millilitres—well, that's only a teaspoon, ten is a dessert spoon. I'm starting into the new millilitres and millimetres and all that bloody jazz. Now that was a dirty thing to put on the old people. They're not used to it, they don't know what it means. Anyway, now I've got to build this energy up again. With the shock—the system got such a shock—I've lost all my energy, and I've got to build it back up again. But the doctor, he says it won't come quick. It won't be a quick job. I've got to be patient.

Yeah, all of a sudden I'm an old man. I wasn't old before I fell, I was a young fella, chasing round, doin' this and that, fit as a rabbit. But ever since I took that turn I can't do a thing. I know it's senile decay, I know that, but this thing brought it on faster. It's too sudden. It shoulda grown on me like when I was growing up, shoulda grown and deteriorated the same way. I know you should get old, but you should get old like growing up. See, you don't grow into a man straight away, no, you've got to work your way up there. Then when you get to your zenith, that's when you work your way back down to the six-by-four. It's as simple as that. But you've got to prepare yourself for that in the mind, otherwise it's just bloody hopeless. Oh yes, you'll not tell me any different. I know life comes slowly, goes slowly, you grow into it. I know it goes the other way after you get to the zenith, you go down the hill the same bloody way. But see, I went through too quick, too sudden. And what they say now is, I've got to be patient. Very patient. Well, I still feel I can do what I used to do, if only I could get the strength back.

MY LEGS, they're comin' down now, but jeez they swell up to buggery, just like a woman's when she's gonna have a baby. It's water. I've got to keep an eye on them. You know, I asked the doctor, does a man have a change of life same as a woman? "Oh yes," he says. "Some of them have it pretty bad too." "Well," I says, "I think that's what's happening to me. I think it's happening

ALEX COUTTS

99

all at once." "That's quite possible, old son," he said. "You've had a hell of a shock, you know, and you've got a long way to come back." I said, "Christ man, you're not tellin' me anything there." Everywhere I go—so many steps and I've got to sit down. I'm short of breath, short of energy, short of everything. And my legs in the mornin', they won't hold me up properly, I'm like a wee baby. I grovel like a wee baby. And it's frustrating because you've still got your mind. As a man your mind's developed, that doesn't weaken, it's just you can't get about the same. The physical part of it, that's the main thing.

Christ, you don't even feel like having a girl friend—anything like that. That's all gone in the past—senile decay. The wife and I, we were quite happy that way. But I mean, once the wife was gone—well, I was free to go where I liked, and play with who I liked. See, I had no obligations because Mum wasn't there, and you can't go on living in the past. No, it's still the old people's privilege to do that—it's their life, isn't it? What the young thinks the old people should do—well, it's not their business. They do it, why shouldn't we? After all, it's our life, not theirs, when all's said and done. And if I can meet up with an old girl—which I did— and we meet up and have a beer together, and if I put my hand on her leg or anything like that, it's just, well, it's only what you'd call a dry romance. Yeah, it's touching but not doing nothin'. But they still get that feeling. They get the same feeling as you do. You know, he likes me a lot. I give her a squeeze on the legs or a nip on the bum, things like that. Nothin' else. I think it's a kind of loving. It's two people come together, they've never met be- fore, and they're sort of looking for a sweetheart. Looking to find one that's compatible. Then between the two of youse you get to know how far you can go. I've seen me put my hand on her leg, and she'll hit me hand, you know, naughty naughty. Of course that's in public; what might happen if we were in private—well, that might be a different thing. It's a different thing altogether. But then, have you got the ability, that's the story. The thing is, if you can't do it, don't start, you'll only be making a fool of yourself, you really will. See, if you take a girl out and she's willin' and you're willin', and you can't get an erection, you're just making yourself look stupid for attempting it. You should have enough sense, be old enough to know where to draw the line. Verbally, okay; talk, that's okay, you can keep your end up there, but at the bottom end you can't. You'd be coming to a dead end there. Anything sexual is out. You've lost the whole bloody idea. Takes you all your time to point it at the pan when you want to make water. Yeah, just a lump of skin now. Well, it comes with this bloody turn, see. Oh, you still get the mental—bloody oath, you'd like to have a go—but you find you bloody can't.

Sometimes I often think back and say how many girls have I lain with, you know, right from the start, just to see how good the old memory is. Testing it out. Sometimes you think, I shouldn't have done that, or I shouldn't have done this, but it's only human nature. There's nothing to condemn yourself for. Every boy will have a go at a girl if he can get a chance. I've only felt guilty for what I've done wrong. Certainly, for instance, I've been with other women; even when I was married I've lain out with other women. That's guilt. But that shouldn't prick your mind. You've done it and it's past and that's it. You can't rectify that, 'cause it's done, it's happened. I just chuck it to the side and say, they were good old days, they're gone. See, it's like your senile capacity has gone, so that part of the mind goes with it.

Really there's no crime there. It's a game. We play it when we're young. But then when you're married and you do it, that's bad. You get the odd one, you get the odd fling here and there. But you don't take much notice of that, that's under the carpet sort of thing. Sneaked, stolen. Seems to be sweeter. It's like stolen fruit. And as they say, the grass on the other side of the fence is always greener. But I don't know, you think you're clever. Say you've got a married woman—you've got a crack at her. Well, it's sort of, Jesus, I did it. Because, you see, they're supposed to be very resistant. Married women are supposed to be the depender, you know, dependable—don't come over my place. But eventually you get

ALEX COUTTS

your foot in, and you've had a victory. It's like playing a game of football or something like that, when you score a winning goal. Same thing—it's a victory you've got. What you shouldnae really get, but you've got it, you've got your goal, your ambition. It just flies into your head and then you have a go. Then you've got to try and keep it from the wife for as long as you can. It's a sort of a game, be caught or not be caught. But you shouldnae be doing games like that, because if you do get caught it causes a lot of worry and trouble. It's a risky caper if you want happiness. Yeah, it's something you shouldnae be doing, but then you get a victory and it's a lift, it makes you feel great. Well, a bit of forbidden fruit is good at any time, whether it's apples, plums, or any damn thing. The only thing—although you've got a victory, all you can do then is think about it. It's just a thought—really it should be wiped away. But going back in memory like this, I like doing it, it makes me feel younger again. It takes me back when I was young, what I did when I was young, and if I had the chance, yes, I'd do it all again. But I'd rectify, I'd rectify some of the things that was really bad. I'd step over them and walk on.

Now THERE's an emptiness in me. From the day I left the mine, when you lose your work, there's an emptiness. The days are long, they become terribly long because there's nothing to do. Well, you had a few hours at the boozer, and then your spare time was doing bits around the place. Then it was bedtime, and so it goes on. And as it got on, it got slower. You got that way that you didn't give a damn for doing this or that or the next thing. You kept your lawns and hedges trimmed, you painted the house. You did those odd jobs, and it stretched it out. You've got to stretch it out. The time is still twelve o'clock to twelve o'clock. Thing is, you see, when you're working for a firm, the firm's got you. You've got to be there at nine o'clock, you've got to be there at eight o'clock, you've got to be there at six o'clock. Whether it's a.m. or p.m. The clock, the timepiece, is the thing. It's not like the birds and bees—go to bed when the sun sets and get up when it rises. Oh no, that wee thing that goes tick tock, it controls you, it controls your life. Then, after that, when they take the firm away from you and you're free, you can do what you like in that day. Twenty-four hours, it's all yours. The thing is, you have your freedom, but you don't have the mates, the company. Just like I am now, I haven't got the wife. I've got no company. Well, I had the pub to get my company, and I do the same now. But it's not the same, not really the same.

Every man that gets married should be taught to cook. Because nine times out of ten, if it's the wife that goes first and the man's left, then he's buggered. He's eatin' all the rubbish he can get his hands on. He's buyin' pies and stuff like that that's no good to him, and then he starts to deteriorate. Oh yes, making your bed, electroluxing, washing dishes, things you've never done. Well, that helps to pass away time for a bit, it kept me busy and kept my mind off things, but then it started to get monotonous. And gradually it got away a bit, and I'd say, oh, I'll do it tomorrow. And then tomorrow comes, och, I'll do it the next day. You get lazy then. The bloody dust piles up, and it brings you onto being a lazy man, which I'm not. You're used to cleanliness, but you see it piling up all around you. There's always something you want to do. You never stop wanting to do something, but you lose your strength and your days come quicker and the years come faster. Everything seems to go faster away from you. You've lost it. But I'm a lot luckier off than old people that's got to go into homes. I'm fortunate because I've got the lady next door. She comes over, she's done all my rooms. She's washed all the blankets, she takes my curtains down and washes them, and the windows. She does everything. She's like a fairy godmother. I tell you she's sent from heaven, that woman.

A lot of people, they ignore the old, they just think, oh, the old fogy. But what has that old fogy done before they were born? I used to load twenty ton, twenty tons of coal a day for four and sixpence. And that's a lot of coal. If you seen it piled up in the yard there you wouldnae believe it. The young today, they think you're

ALEX COUTTS

something that's not worth talking to. You know, you're old, and what the hell's the good of telling you anything. You haven't got long to last. It's a waste of time for them, and that's how their attitude is today. One time it wasn't. You'd go up and speak to the old people, give them a bit of chat, something fresh. Not today. They're more like to take the nap out of you, make fun of you instead. That's not right. The young should have more time for the old. Be more pleasant, more placid with them. Don't throw them to the side like they're an old dishcloth. They're not finished with life. Even though they're old, they're still useful. It would do them a lot of good to come and speak to old people, get their advice. They'd be different people if they did. But you're too old to ask questions of, he's an old fogy, don't talk, don't take any notice of him. That's their attitude. But the old can be used, if society would use them. There used to be an old song, "Don't forget the old folks when they're turning down the brae"—well, that's my motto. Don't forget the old folks when they're tottling down the road, don't make them think they're in the way. Make room for them, make a place for them. Remember it's the wise old owl that knows the story. Well, that's only natural, you've been living with yourself for near on seventy-seven years, so you must, you must gain knowledge. You see, you don't just make a decision on the spur of the moment, you think it over, and that makes you like the old world, cunning and wise. Oh yeah, you get wiser. And the more they want to learn, the more they should talk to the old, because it's from the old that the young can learn.

THE MOST I'm thinking about now is my sickness. It's on my mind a lot of the time, and I know I shouldn't be doing that, it's like holding me back, retarding me. I know that. Well, it's mind over matter. The more I think I'm crook, the crooker I get. Some mornings I rise up and say, jeez she's going to be a great day today, and then I'll drop away back into that bloody abyss again. Take pity on myself, which I shouldnae do. No strength you see, the physical's gone. Just this bloody September, the twenty-ninth of

ALEX COUTTS

last September, and it's three years September that I lost my wife. Put her death notice up on the wall there. Everything's happened in this dirty month September. Sometimes I have a wee bubble, you know, a wee cry, but boy, if you start pitying yourself too much you've had it. So now I break these things up, small units instead of big lumps. You can swallow a small thing, but you can't swallow a bloody mountain. Soon as I start thinking that way now I go and do something to take my mind away off it. I'll get a book or some bloody thing. Well, then you're occupied, so you're not losing anything, you're not worrying. You've got the mind away out of it. I read a lot now, and whenever I feel stuck for company I'll get a book, then I'm in company. I'm travellin' with the company.

I still keep to the old clocks too. I still like fixing the old clocks. But my hands are getting that bloody shaky, I tell ya, they shake like grass in a strong wind. I can't get the pivots into the pivot holes half the time. I lean my forearms on the table now to get them steady. Oh aye, I've got to improvise for myself from now on. Still, as long as your mind is occupied and you're doing something, well, you're using up time, time is passing on and you're going easier through the day. Course, if you've got nobody to talk to, chances are you'd just be sitting here blinkin' away at the old telly. The old gas box. But that's not company, I'll tell you that. An awful lot of them say, oh, you've got the telly for company. Well, that's not company. They're speaking—on the picture they're speaking—but they're not speaking to you personally. You can't make conversation with the telly. It's doing all the yackin' and you're doing all the listening. That's right. But boy, when I get somebody in the house they're bloody lucky they ever get out again.

Solitary confinement, that's the worst torture in the world. It is, you know, it's the loneliest part in the world being on your own. You start yackin' to yourself and you start seeing things, and that's when your imagination—well, if you can't control that, you're buggered. I didn't realise how bloody crook and sad I was going to be after the wife died. It wasn't so bad when they were all here, the family, but when they'd all gone and I'm sitting here every day, that's when my mind started to go into things. Well, that's no good to you. It's no good lying there in your mind. You've got to put it out of your head. Bust it. It's a bad balloon.

Every night I pray—I've done it for years. I pray to the Lord—the father, not the son—and after I've finished speaking to the Lord, I speak to my spiritual guides. Oh aye, I've been a spiritualist for as far back as I can remember. That's a belief I have, and it helps me a lot. The wife's passed over but she's watching me and the family, everybody. She's got her interest down here as well as up there, you know. She's not just floating through, she's keeping her eye on the kids and the grandchildren, and me too. She'll be wanting to tell me things—well, she's powerless to do that unless she gets permission, but I know she's there and that gives me a big help. She can't ask me any questions either, so I can't give her the answers she might want. But if I keep on yacking long enough, she'll get them in between. I'm soon bound to say something she's after. Actually the house could be surrounded with bloody spirit souls, and they could all be listening in, they're entitled to. Even when I swear, they'll say tut tut, but I can't hear them. It's maybe a bad mark against me, but that I won't know until I'm put in a coffin and face it for myself. Sometimes I wonder about that, the way the health is—I wonder if I'm getting hit over the knuckles for being such a bad boy. Teach you a lesson sort of thing. Well, you've got to repent some way or other. You've got to suffer for it somewhere.

TIME—I don't know, it's dragging both sides now. It's not that I want to die, nobody does. Not even Christ, he didn't want to die, but he did it for a purpose. I don't have to do it for a purpose, so I want to get as long as I can in this world. That was my mission, to go for a hundred. It's quite possible I could do it yet. The thing is, though, it's what I take away with me that counts. If I

ALEX COUTTS

can make it good and clean—the cleaner the better—I'll feel good. And I won't be frightened of death. I'm not frightened of death anyway, I just don't want to leave this planet too early. I should be wanting to get away. I've been told what it's like over there, and I'm a wee bit curious to see if it comes up to what I've been told. That's curiosity more than anything. I've no fear, but I still don't want to leave this planet. I don't know why, it's so beautiful over there, I should be bustin' to get away. But you hang on, you hang on to life to the last struggle.

There's some times I sit here and look back in years. I say, well, it's fifty-nine years ago I came here to this country. That's a long space in between, but it doesn't seem that long. No. Sometimes I say it's impossible. To have done so many things in such a time. And yet, it's silly, I turn around and say I should have done a lot more. It's a thing you can't fathom. You can only sort of guess at it. It's like guessing something, but there's no given point at each end. See, if I knew what day I was going to die, I could know what to do before I did. At the moment I've just got to take things as peacefully as I can. And die, just finish off like a piece of old rag burning, smoldering away. That's what it looks like today. Preparing you for the day. Feels like I'll be gradually smoldering away till it comes to the end of the rag. Then it's kaput. Well, time's slowly preparing everybody if they only sat down and thought about it.

Peacefully, that's how I'd like to die. Just to go to sleep and away. But there's different styles of death, different ways of passing over. Some people just drop, and that's it. Other people can suffer a lot of pain. I hate pain, pain is a penalty, a penance. Each night when I go to bed I say my prayers. I say, this could be the night. Well, that's okay, please give me smooth passage. That's me asking the last thing from him—physical thing. See, if you don't seek—that's what he said—you'll never receive. If he'd just let me finish my life in strength, back to where I was before I took that turn, that's all I want. I want to be mobile again, that's the way I'd like people to remember me. Full of fun and bloody nonsense.

ALEX COUTTS

The way I am now, it's a handicap. When you want to do a thing you canna do, that's worse than choking you. Taking your bloody life from you. That's no good.

Peaple say, how are you, Alex, how're you feeling? Well, it's one day I'm okay and the next I'm not, it's hard to tell. I'm like a fiddler's elbow, it goes up and down and so do I. But since the wife passed over and I had this bloody turn, I wouldnae say it's a good thing to be old. Not if you've become a spent force, gone into deterioration like. See, it's alright to be nice and old, mobile and all that. But when you start to lose your powers, your strength and your mobility, then you become a drag. You cannae keep up with the pace. You'd love to, but you see, it's senile decay. It's a way in the chemicals, the genes are dying off. You don't feel the same, and you don't act the same. The most active thing, the only thing in your body, is the mind, your brain. And if anything affects that, then you're puckarooed. You've had it. A silly willy. Saying silly things and doing silly things. No, I'd sooner be dead than be stupid, than be an idiot.

As it is now, I've got tablets to make me go to the toilet, make me widdle. I've got tablets to keep the heart pumpin'. I've got tablets to put under my tongue if I have a seizure. Tablets for everything. Well, you're not living on your own, you're living on chemicals. You're becoming a mechanical toy really, you're like a motor car without gas. It won't go. And then they say, do exercises. Well, exercises are alright, but you can't do it if you haven't got the strength. See, it's not them. They don't feel like you feel. They tell you what to do—that's okay, it's easy to tell you, but it's awfully hard to do. But they don't understand that. I tell the doctor there, I say, "It's all right for you yackin' away there, you're as fit as a fiddle, but here's me struggling to take every step." "Oh," he said, "come on, it's not as bad as all that." "Don't you bloody think so!" I said. "You want to swap places and see for a while." I reckon myself I need something to bring the muscles back to what they were, physiotherapy or whatever they call it. But they can't, you see, they're worn out. It's like these old clocks I fix. I've got to put new pieces in, like they do with hearts and all this. You see, it's just time. Yeah, time. You're wearing away and nobody can stop it. It's like a sandglass. You turn it up and the sand goes through, then you turn it up and it goes through again and again until you haven't got the energy to turn it over. Then it will stop, and so will you. Then it's your turn, end of the penny section. Well, your spirit life goes on, but the body, it's worn out. It's like an old gramophone or something, machinery. Yeah, it's a machine, that's all it is. It's a machine encasing the soul, and when the soul goes, motion goes. Then you're in the box and they screw you down and put you in the hole. That's the end of the body, it's manure, that's all it is. In fact, it's better below a tree where it can fertilize and do some good. There's too much—too much of this sadness at death. It's not death, it's only the body that's passed away. Well, it's no use any more. It's just like an old cardy—when you finish with it, you throw it away. It's done its life, it's done its spell, and that's it. Yeah—just like an old cardy.

GARDEN OF EDEN

When god made the garden of Eden, he created Adam, who was his own image. But he made birds and bees and fishes and every-thing with a male and female species, trees, plants, everything—all bar Adam, and Adam wasnae happy. And when God has been looking down on him for a week, he says, "I wonder what's wrong with Adam. He's not happy and he should be, he's got everything." And then suddenly the penny drops: oh, I didn't make a female of his species. So he puts Adam to sleep below the big tree, puts him in a trance, and he took a rib out of his side, and that's why they call the woman today the spirit of man. He created Eve out of that rib. When Adam came out of that trance, there's Eve stand-ing below the tree, and she said to Adam, "Come to me," so he did and they had two sons, Cain and Abel. Now Cain killed Abel and he's branded on the forehead and sent out in the desert. He come back with a family. Where did he get his wife? Now, there's

ALEX COUTTS

109

a conundrum for you, that's why the Bible's not telling the truth, see. Why does the Irish worship Mary? And not God or Christ? She wasn't raped, she wasn't conceived, and yet she had Christ. There's an awful lot of explaining to be done. I think somebody's sneaked under her tent myself.

WE HAD the three girls, three daughters, then the boy came next, and that was going to be the end. No more. I started gettin' rubbers, you know, to stop us gettin' children, stop from conceiving. But then, you know how it is, you come home on a Saturday night and you get into bed a bit tiddled and then you find you havena got one. But still you get a bit silly and you cuddle up and bang, the deed is done again. She says to me one morning, "I'm afraid you've done it again." Yeah, we was gonna have another baby, but that was the boy we lost.

That thing you dry your clothes on out in the kitchen, a rack, it's on a pulley like, but instead of letting it down, she got up on a chair and onto the table. That's when she fell, and she hit her head on the stove. Jesus Christ, the baby's about to be born and she's lying there, ohhhhhh. Well, I got her up on the couch, and she seemed to come right, you know. She had a bloody lump on the back of her head, it was a beauty, like a bloody ostrich egg, and I says, "That's what you get for climbing when you shouldn't be. Your climbing days are all past, you do that when you're in knickerbockers, not when you're an old married woman." I told her off a treat, I was that—well, she could've broke her bloody neck. Then the next thing that night—I was up doing the bar, I used to help out there part time like—and they said to me, Alex, your girl's at the back door, you'd better go and see, she's in a hell of a state. And when I got to her, she told me that her mummy was bleeding.

By the time I got there, the doctor was with her in the bedroom. There was the lady next door, and the wife's twin sister was with her too. I went in. Oh Christ, blood. Jesus, it was like a butcher's shop in there, it's all over the place. And the doctor, he

ALEX COUTTS

said, "Get out of here." I had to get out and walk around, I couldna bloody concentrate, I couldna sit, I was . . . I was wantin' to know what was going on. I wanted to see it, but he wouldn't let me in. Somebody run up and phoned for the ambulance. Her sister and I went with her in the ambulance to the hospital, and when we were going the doctor gave me this paper parcel. He said, take that to the hospital and give it to them when you go in. He never said it was the baby. It just went straight into the furnace at the hospi-

ALEX COUTTS

tal. They do that with these things. I didn't know what it was—I didn't know it was my own bloody son I was carrying. No. He didn't tell me I was carrying my own little child to the furnace.

So we lost that child, and I couldn't do much about it. We had his name picked—Duncan—but he was dead. That bloody thump on the stove, it killed him. They said he was a perfect boy in every way and I felt terrible angry, but then it was worse for my wife than for me, so I had to ease up, to give her pity, to help her on. I said, "It wasn't your fault, love, the only mistake you made is climbing up on the table instead of letting the pulley down, you won't do that again." She said, "There'll be no more again." And that was it from then on, she wouldnae let me near her unless I had a cover on, no bloody show. "I'm not going through that again," she said. And I said, "I don't want you to."

So NOW I'm seventy-six, seventy-seven in May. Same with my old girl. I wanted her to live till the golden wedding—she was only eighteen months off it, and I says, hang on to it, lassie, hang on. Only eighteen months to go. Bloody hell, on the Sunday morning she's dead.

She was a schoolgirl, going to the technical high school in Greymouth. She was sitting on the river bank when we passed down the road, me and this Jimmy boy. "I'll have her," he said. "You bloody well won't," I said, "I'll see that you don't." And I did everything I could to stop him doing what he said. I didnae like the way he was, not like that, not straight. But it was hard to convince her—he had some charm. Course in the finish, when I did get tangled up with her and going out with her, he stopped admiring her. Well, he daren't. I'da had his nose in with my fist, and he knew it too. He was not a bad peg himself, but I had something that gave me determination. That's the thing, make your mind up, have it, or leave it alone. Don't touch it at all. That's the way to get on in the world. Your life decisions have got to be made by yourself, nobody else. And once you've made it up, keep it going, don't you flicker, don't you weaken.

ALEX COUTTS

We were married at the back of the church. She was gonna have a baby. The old story, you leave it dipped too long, you make a mistake. But to be in love, oh boy, that was bloody nice. Oh yeah, when we first kissed and cuddled, that was the binder, that was the thing. But at the wedding only her old auntie came, and the minister's wife. I had no money and had to borrow five pounds off the auntie to get the licence and pay the minister. I did everything with that five pound. And I gave him a tip too, to get a beer with. Gave him ten bob, that's all I could afford. Her father and mother, they never came. He was of German descent and she came off the Norwegians, an old Norwegian—they were stubborn buggers, no liberties there. That hurt me badly, but still it was a happy moment. You make it that way. The contract was signed, and from there on we became one in our life. We were united before, but that was the day, that made it authentic. And you couldna ask for a handier friend—well, she was more than a friend, she was my second half.

Being together, that was the thing. We became a unit, just the yes-and-no's was the difference, that's all. Getting settled down was the big thing, getting to know one another's ways. What to do and what not to do, it's terribly important. Sometimes we used to get to arguing, and I'd just walk away out the back to the shed or someplace. If she wanted something done and kept nagging me, I'd do the opposite, it was just my way of paying her back. Well, every family has that, I don't give a bugger how close they are. Mind, there was one day she did the wrong thing at the wrong time and, bang, I hit her. I hit the wife. Christ, I wouldn't hurt her in all the world, but I'd done it. I coulda cut my bloody hand off. Never ever did it again—apologised and apologised, but that didn't make it right. I did the wrong thing, so I couldna do enough for her after that. Everything she said, I gave her her own way. No, it's not easy for you to have harmony between two people. You're not made of the same chemicals, for a start. Your likes and dislikes are not her likes and dislikes. You've got to cross the road somewhere, it's not possible to keep on parallel lines all the time, there's got to be some friction. But then a bit of friction can make a tighter love. It unites you, it doesn't part you. As long as it doesn't come to the physicals. As long as you can sit and talk about it. You have your tiffs, but you sit down and talk it out, you get closer and closer, then you come to a conclusion, and finish. That's harmony.

Ah, but her old mother, she was the old Norwegian breed, and right from when we was married she held it against me—nearly to the end. She never forgave me until when she was sick one time and I brought her down home. She was like me now, a spent force, ready for the old hooks. She said to me, "You know, I think you've turned out one of the best of them." I said, "You've got to give everyone a chance, Mum. Just because the donkey does the wrong thing, you don't kick it to death."

THE WIFE, she started to lose her sight before she died. We had a wee black and white T.V. here, and she used to sit away up close so she could see the pictures. I said, "Can you nae *see?*"—you know, I'm very abrupt when I speak. Sort of like a commander. It's just my way—you'd think I was moaning, but I'm not. It's just the way I speak. So I rang up the shop, and I said, "Bring out the biggest bloody machine you've got, colour too." Well, they brought over one that had a twenty-two-inch or twenty-three-inch screen. I said, "No, I want the biggest bugger you've got." "Oh," they said, "well, that's a different model to the one you want." I said, "Bugger the model—it's the screen I want man, for my wife, she's going blind." He says, "I've got a Phillips, a brand new one in the van." "Well, get it in here," I says, "and put the other bugger back." Then, as soon as I got it going, I said, "Come on, Mum, come and have a look," and she could see it sitting in her chair. That was the difference, see. She's happy. She loved the telly.

Oh, but it was hard when she went. Yeah, I was grievin', but I was grievin' inside, I didna make any emotional scenes. I'd like to have . . . but, well, you know, it's not so much the first few days, it's when everybody's away and you're on your pat, that's when it sinks in. You start to think, and the mind's a ter-

ALEX COUTTS

114

rible thing if it goes astray. That's half the time my trouble, and if you dwell on it, it gets worse. You know, I sit and look at her chair, but she's nae longer there. Many's the time we've sat in these chairs and debated about married life. What should be done and what shouldn't. How a married life is formed. We contracted our marriage to live together and to share everything, and that's how we kept going so smoothly. She was a very understanding lassie. Good-hearted bugger too. She wouldnae see a dog or a beggar go past this place. It didna matter who it was, the kettle was always going. A lot of folks used to come in, and no sooner'd they got their bums on the chair than away the kettle was on. That was her nature. Everything friendly like. Oh yes, she's a lovely woman. Yet still she had to suffer when her time was up, when she was taken away. I didna like that, I don't like sufferin', that's like getting penalised for something you've done bad. Well, she didna deserve that. Were it me, I'd say, yes, I deserve all I get. But not her. She was too good.

Of course being a spiritualist I was sort of prepared for it at the end. Well, I thought I would be, but at first I couldna make it out. I was stunned. There was a wantingness. That means you don't know what to do—*wantingness*, there's a want somewhere. I felt that straight away. Then after the people and all the kids went home, that's when I felt in despair. I didn't have my partner, and life for me . . . well, you sit and think, and then you have a wee bubble to yourself. But it's no good sittin' and cryin' like a baby all the time, you've got to get over that. You've got to say to yourself over and over, she's not here, she's not here, she's not in this place. You can talk to her, and she can hear you, but you canna hear her, and you canna see her either. But I don't forget she's still there, and I often talk to her. She's a spirit I'm speaking to, but I speak out in the open and it's for her benefit. I say, well, love, I may look daft, and I may sound daft to anyone come in and caught me yackin' away, but I know you can hear me. I know I'm conversing with the spirit world. And I just speak to her as if she was there natural. Just as if she was sitting in her chair.

ALEX COUTTS

SAD, OH YES, sad. Many's a time you get sad. When my brother died, and even the folks at home, a long way from them, I still felt sad. But I will see them again, I believe now I will. I've read a hell of a lot about it. The leading medium in the world—I've got all her books here, and if I feel anything, anything I want to query, I go and read these books, and it soothes me down. Settles me down. Cause the day is coming, and I don't want to suffer. I hate suffering. My brother suffered, poor bugger. He was only thirty-four, thirty-five. He died with the spinal meningitis. Great religious man he was, like Christ, he'd wash the feet of the bloody swaggies when they came through the village. Take'm home and give'm a feed, all that stuff. He was too good for here. He would-nae drink. No. You were lucky if you got him to drink a port wine, and I could never help more than one of those down. "No," he'd say, "I'm sorry, I can't go for that. I'd like to have a drink with you, but no, it's no good to me." "Alright," I'd say. "You please yourself, you get away home to your bairns," and he would, he'd paddle off. Oh, but he was good, too good to live.

His wife and I went with him in the ambulance. He was sort of unconscious, but if you touched him at all he'd moan like hell. You couldna touch him or turn him—he was getting paralysed. At the hospital we sat there. They took the tests on his spine with a needle, a big needle. Shove it in and pull the fluid out and test it. We sat to get the results. When the doctor came back, he said, "Mrs. Coutts, you are his wife, aren't you?" I said, "Yeah, that's right, that's his wife and I'm his brother." He said, "I've got some bad news for you, Mrs. Coutts, he's got spinal meningitis, and it's well under way." The next time I went to see him I told the sister who I was, but she wouldn't let me into the room—the bugs were spewin' out of him, see, these spinal meningitis bugs. She explained it all to me, she said, "I'll open the door and pull the curtains back and let you have a look." He was arched away up, his head and heels away back. "Oh, that's enough," I said. "How will you get him in the coffin? When he dies—when he passes away." "He'll just flatten out like a pancake," she said. "And," she says,

ALEX COUTTS

116

"he'll have to be put in a lead coffin. A lead-lined coffin to stop the bugs from gettin' out." But when he died you should have seen, it was the biggest funeral's ever been here. I forget how many buses—must have been eight or nine buses at least, and cars, he was so well liked, see. That's where you get respect, when they turn out in droves. He must've been a good man. But that didna bring him back.

I've lost all my family on my side now. There's only the wife's family, just her sisters and that left. There was a big family on my side, all those relations from home. But when they started going over the hill, going to live in Christchurch and other places, well, then it became a time when the village was empty to me in a way. Oh, other people were friends, but they weren't family. You couldna walk into a house and say, here I am, like family, like you could do then. Actually I think I could if I tried it. I'm well liked, don't worry about that. As a matter of fact, I just carry on the same as I always did, young or old, it's just the same. I've carried right through the same pattern, like me or don't. And that's how I've made friends—I'll speak to a dead stranger, "Hello mate, how are ya." Make them feel welcome to come to you, and they like that. That's West Coast hospitality; well, I've always been that way. I wouldn't let a man stand in the bar on his own. Even when I was doing the bar, I'd team him up with somebody else. Let a man drink on his own and he'll turn and walk away, but you team him up and he'll stay. That's good for business. And it's good for him too.

Thing is now, I know when I go over the other side there'll be a hell of a gathering up there, they'll all be waiting on me coming. See, I was always the clown. I'll brighten'm up—I suppose I'll carry that with me. I hope so, anyway. I hope I do.

IN MY DAY, when I was a young fella, we respected old age. Today they don't. We were all taught to respect, it was in the bringing up. Anybody that was over a certain age was classed as an old person, and they were helped, not hurt. Today, instead of helping

ALEX COUTTS

ya they make fun of ya. And if the old fella's not quick enough, or good enough to catch'm up, he's got to take the brunt of it. Tell you what, they'd never do that with old Couttsie. Oh no, too bloody soon for that, and they know it. Even the kids, from when they go to kindergarten and up, they know how old I am and how to respect me too. I am respected. Doesn't matter where I go, everybody knows me. It's "Hello, Couttsie, how are you, how are you feeling, how are you keepin'?" If there's other old people who aren't strong, well, I always feel sorry for them. Because that's the thing you need when you're getting older—strength. Yeah, so you can cope with these young buggers. If not in the body, then strength in the mind, and in the tongue especially. Because, you see, a simple answer can knock them back on their arse, just like that.

Like this bloody income tax joker they've got on my bike

now. Yeah, the bloody Inland Revenue—I'm fightin' them at the present time. That's what I get for saving up. It was a two-year investment, and they sent me an assessment thing and said, write why you didn't—what do you call it?—you know, why didn't you put this much in? So I went and seen them, this joker there, and I said, "How the hell could I put it in when the bloody thing was still maturing? I don't get my interest until the two years are up. I couldna put a figure in." "Oh," he says, "you should have assessed it." I said, "How the hell could I? I can't take figures out of the air." I said, "If I'd just put anything in, would you have believed it?" "Oh," he says, "probably would." "Well," I says, "what a system you buggers are working under." And I says, "How'd you get my name, anyway?" He said, "We just take a letter out of the alphabet. You happen to be in the C's and C's was picked." I said, "You've got forty people through in that room in there that could eat the alphabet six times over and spit it out again." And I said, "You catch me." I said, "Look, boy, in the first place you're not a Coaster." I said, "You're too pansied up, you've got collar and tie and all dressed up like a duke. Now that guy over there, he's a Coaster, see—open white shirt." "Yeah, well, as a matter a fact," he says, "I'm from Christchurch." Well, there's a big difference between a Coaster and a city guy. It's like the police force. They're always going to clean the Coast's drinking up, and most of the time they get shunt off cause they can't handle it. So I says, "Some of you buggers want to be shunt off too. Now, I'm going to tell you this. I'm only a working man and his savings. What sort of a bloody fisherman are you? Douglas is the Minister of Finance, he didn't mean you to catch me, sprats like me. No, you want promotion, boy, you catch a whale. You get a big guy and you'll get up that ladder of promotion, not little bugs like me, boy. It's the big bugs you want after." Boy, did I give him a licking. I couldn't tell him any plainer than that.

Oh, but he went on, deductions, why didn't you do that, why didn't you say this, he kept harping on, he was just like a bloody parrot. I said, "You want to shift the needle, mate, it's got stuck."

ALEX COUTTS

That sort of quietened him down a bit, and I said, "Well, I'll pay you the forty bucks"—what I'd worked out I owed them—"or are you going to wipe it?" "Oh," he says, "I might charge you that, and," he says, "the super tax, some other tax on top of that." I said, "That's being shitty." And I said, "If you get much cheekier to me I'll jump that bloody bench"—yeah, I threatened him. I said, "For two ticks I'd jump that bloody bench and give you a couple. And don't think because I'm seventy-six I can't." I think he was a bit scared of me alright. He said, "You lay a hand on me and you'll be in trouble." I said, "I know that, that's why I'm not coming over to you. I'm keeping that bit of wood between you and me because if you were closer I'd smack you one."

I had a real go with him, oh dear yes, so then he put me onto the Commissioner. And when the Commissioner wrote to me, they'd put it up to three hundred and forty-odd dollars I owed them. I went and seen the solicitor. I'm going to fight them right to the bloody line. But that's what I get for saving up. So you know what I'm going to do now? I'll draw the whole bloody lot out and put it in a jar. I'm not going to get any more of these taxes. This is the last, the bloody last. There won't be anything in the post office. I won't tell anybody, I'll just bury the bastard somewhere.

COURSE THERE'S lots of things in your life you'd like to correct, but you canna undo the past. The thing is to do right in the future to correct for what I did, for what I did that was wrong. Back home in Scotland, in the village, I was a proper thief. I could rob anything. I never bought anything. But when I come out here I never touched a thing, just changed straight away and I did what good that I could. I played the trumpet, you know, and I took on teaching the kids music. I taught them, yeah, I had some bloody good boys. Trombones, euphoniums, cornets—I had them going to contests anyway, that's how good they were. I was the Commissioner of School for three years too. I even brought the Canterbury Education Board over here. They thought they could do what they

liked with me. I bloody soon let them know. Yeah, I wrote to the Minister of Education, Peter Fraser in those days, and he got stuck into them. Well, then they all come over to get me.

I was working down the mine when they arrived. The clerk, the chief clerk, he telephoned underground in work time to tell me to come up. He said everything was paid for; I'd get a full shift like. "Well," I says, "what's wrong?" He says, "It's the Canterbury Education Board out to meet you." "Well, they can meet me in my own time," I says, and I stayed until the last, kept them hangin' there, hangin' around like a fart in a bottle. At knock-off I just done me old routine. Had a shave, put me boots on, and went down the pub for me usual beer and everything. Then got on my bike and come home for tea. While I'm havin' my tea, there's a knock on the door, so Mum went out and she says, "Oh, it's for you, Alex, from the school, foreman of schools." "Well," I said, "you can tell 'em I'll be along when I've had my tea." By this time it was starting to get dark, you see, and I had this all in my plan, because they'd built a brand-new school up there with not an electric light in it. Nor a hot point in it either. And I thought, the darker it gets the better. Well, when I finished my tea, got me tea down, they were waitin' outside with the car to take me up to the school. They didn't even have the guts to say, why were you so long? They just wanted to know why I'd got the minister. I said, "Why didn't you give me the grant I asked for?" They said, "We couldn't give you the grant, we didn't have the money." I said, "No, but you could give so many thousands to a college in Canterbury." That's what ruffled my feathers. Nobody does that with Couttsie. So I wrote to the minister and explained every bloody thing. I said, there's many a politician comes from a barbed-wire-fenced school—just because we're in the country, we're not bloody nitwits. I reckoned there was more education here than there was on the Board in Christchurch.

When we got up to the school, someone said, it's a bit dark in here. I said, well, you're at liberty to put the lights on. Christ, they were scrambling about there looking for the bloody switches.

ALEX COUTTS

I said, "You know, this is a bloody new school," I says, "brand new, and getting used too. And after dark the caretaker's got to go round with a bloody candle. That's your foreman of works and your bloody Board for you. You're not worth shit." Oh, I gave them the works, don't worry. By Christ, the next thing I asked for—everything I asked for after that—was prompt; it was pronto.

Anything that took my mind up I put energy into. Determination I call it, whatever—it was energy just the same. Anything I took serious, there was no monkeying about. Determination, see. I would do it or get defeated, leave it alone.

WHEN YOU get married you start having offspring, and the more offspring you have, the more keener your mind is on home. Cause you gotta provide for those bairns. You bring'm in, you're responsible. Time comes of course that they leave home—well, you know it's going to happen someday, sooner or later, so you prepare yourself for it. If you don't, you're a fool because it's going to be a loss. But then, as long as they are mobile, they can come back and see you. This is why I stay in Bottle Castle. That's what I call the old house, Bottle Castle—I won't sell it. They've been wantin' me to sell it up, go and live with them. But no, while I've got my home here, I've got a home for all of them, come what may. There's four bedrooms, there's six beds. What more do they want?

I tell ya, when they all lived here and they used to have all their cobbers coming in, this place was like a meeting house. Yeah, the family—when we all got together they were the happy times. I remember the oldest girl's wedding—the pipers, they came with their pipes and they played her into the hall. It was a beautiful day. Stinking hot. And when the old minister had had his say, I got up and I said, "Look here, you all, do what I'm doing." I took my tie off, opened up the shirt, took my jacket off and hung it over the back of the chair. I says, "You fellas do the same and youse women get your hats off and let everybody enjoy yourselves." Those were the times. And the time I got a hundred people in this room. Old Granny Ford, my old auntie and uncle on my mother's side. She

ALEX COUTTS

was seventy something, I just forget now, but I got them all down here quietly like and gave her a surprise party. Oh boy, it was great. I made every man in the room put a pound note in an envelope for her. Oh yeah, it was great—all her daughters were there and her sons and old Uncle John. By Christ, she cried, she was cracked. Oh yes, she was an auntie I always liked . . . she was always faithful. I go for these kind of people.

SOLID SERVICE

I ONLY SHIFTED once in my life, from the old country to here. Course I had my temptations, like to play football in Australia, but the wife put her foot down there. Anyway, I'm what you call stationary; I'm nae a nomad, never was.

SAILING. It can get a bit monotonous at sea, but when you get ashore, boy, it's like being reborn again. We arrived in Wellington on the twenty-fourth of May, 1926. We had to wait to catch the ferry to the South Island that night, so in the afternoon we went to the pictures. Of course at home you can smoke in the picture hall, and so out comes the brother's fags. He starts to light up, and this big commissioner comes down, "Hey, hey," he says. "Put that out or I'll put you out." And the brother, he gets up to give him one in the beak, he's gonna fight him. But then he says, "Did you just come on the home boat," and the brother says, "Yeah." "Well," he said, "it's a funny thing—all youse people from overseas start this smoking caper. You're not allowed to do that here, it's forbidden." "Oh, sorry," says the brother, and snagged his cigarette. So that was our first taste of New Zealand. We laughed like hell.

WHEN YOU get to a new place, you've got to have something to sustain yourself with. Well, the first thing you do is go to the mine. Christ, the first morning we was there, there's a knock on the door and it's One-Eyed Patterson. That's what they called him— he had one eye, and we called him One-Eyed Patterson. He came down wanting to give us a start in the gold mine at Waiuta, but

we said no, no way. We're coal miners, not quartz miners, we're goin' down to Brunner, and that was the end of it. Oh, he tried to coax us to go alright; see, they were losing that many men with the bloody silica. They were dying at the age of twenty-one—in their twenties. Their lungs was turned to stone. They coughed all their lungs out and just left stone. The cemetery's full of them. It'd pay anybody to go and have a look in that cemetery. One of the fellas dedicated his lungs to the old doctor there; he had them in a jar on his desk. The plague of Waiuta.

I was eighteen. We arrived in Dodson on my birthday, and in a week I was down the mines. That was in May, and in Decem-

ALEX COUTTS

ber, December the third, three o'clock in the morning, she went up. I lived right near, so I was one of the first there. There was three men—they'd been working in the main drive near the top, but they were outside when it took place. Christ, it would have blown them away down somewhere—anyway, that was three that got saved. Lucky, my oath—well, I'll tell you what it did, it lifted an empty truck, six hundredweight of empty coal truck, right the way down in front of the pub. Nine or ten chain to the front of the pub. And them that was down below in the mine—well, it wasn't very deep, it wasn't very well developed at the time, just two main runs. Number one depth and number two depth, and there was no other way for it to go. Just like a bloody gun barrel.

The rescue team were going down into the mine then, but all the communications were blown up and they had to put men half a chain apart down the side of the tunnel, to relay instructions. Well, I was making sure I didn't get stuck on the side. I didn't want them to put me on a perch there, I didn't want that. I couldna stand that, I wanted to go down with'm.

We got down to the bottom; we were coming down round the corner, and there he was, Eric Ashton. He was standing there with his sleeveless shirt on, just in a wee singlet, a flannel singlet. He heard us coming, and he's coming to meet us. I'm sure he couldn't see us because his eyes were all bulging. I said, "Eric's alright," but then, the poor bugger—he tripped over a bar, or a prop or something. Fella with me, he ran for it to catch him, but he just slipped right through his hands—the blisters, just water on the skin, he just skidded right through, and all the skin was hangin' off his arms. We got the stretcher and put him on it, he was singing out like hell—roaring out—"Oooooooooooh, I'm cold, I'm cold." He keep saying he was cold. Well, that was the fire, the shock. We put the blankets on to cover him, but there's no burn worse than a gas burn underground.

We took the liveliest ones first because they had the most chance. Eric was pretty lively, he kept singing out and bangin' his head on the roof. His lungs are all burnt, see. We had to stop and

ALEX COUTTS

126

tie him down—it was for his own good. It was the only way we could handle him, he was too wild. We had a job getting him to the top, but when we did the doctor had her needle ready. She gave him a jolt of that, and he quietened down. Then they were bringing up Jock Lindsay. He was tryin' to say something, and me being Scots, they said, "See what he's saying." He tried to tell me, but he couldn't get it out. It was all just a gurgle, he'd had it, and I said, he won't last long. The doctor gave him a needle, though, just the same.

We got back down there, and the next one was Bobbie Hunter. He'd got it right in the face—his lips were about two inches thick, swollen up by the fire, burnt. You could hear him sucking air in, but you didn't hear him letting it out. We said, well, he's going to die. We went up as fast as we could, but just before we got to the top he stopped breathing. Last one they got out was Richards. He was the deputy, and, do you know, he had his hand in his pocket with his shot firing key. He used to fire the shots, see. When he heard the bang he must've put his hand in his pocket—couldn't fire a shot. I've got the key.

After that we couldn't get any further. We couldn't get down to the vein, even to the first level. We couldn't get in for the fire damp—that's poisonous, you get into that, it'll drop ya. Then when we come up they said they'd have to stop off the air; there was fire down below. They had to knock off the ventilation, put in these wooden stoppings and pack them with earth to damp them off. They had to close the whole thing off so there was no oxygen and she'd burn out. The flames would go out, you see. But about three o'clock that afternoon she blew again. Twelve hours from the first explosion to the second one. It blew all the stoppings right out, and they had to put them all up again. At half-past nine that night it blew again, and that was it—they put the pumps in and flooded it with water from the river, put the fire out that way. The five men that were left down there had to stay down there. And two of them were my uncles.

Tommy Black and Jimmy Marshall, they were me uncles, and

they worked together on the coal face. Old Jimmy Marshall's been all over Canada mining, and then he comes over here. He was a beautiful euphonium player, three times Scottish champion. It's funny, his wife was a miserable old bugger—she wouldn't part with the steam off a hot dinner. She was as mean as hell. But old Jimmy, he could put his bloody sweetness into his music. I used to sit and listen—oh, he'd make you cry. I was brass too, see. "That's enough of that, Alex," he'd say, "I'll give you a bit of Scottish," and oh, he'd get into it and we'd have a great old time. Well, that night he'd left a competition in Greymouth. He cycled home from Greymouth—there were no transport, no buses, no nothing in them days. He cycled home with his euphonium on his back, he was all lather and sweat. "How'd you get on, Uncle?" I said. "Aye," he said, "I won it, laddie." But he'd promised Uncle Tom he'd be at work that night—he told them he'd be a bit late, but he went to work so as not to let his mate down. He walked right

ALEX COUTTS

128

into it. And here's a sad thing too. The night it blew up I was on afternoon shift, and Uncle Tom Black—he talked with a lisp, you know—his wife had just had twins. That was the first time he'd seen them was that day. He went down the maternity home and seen his wife and the twins. When I came out of the mine at eleven o'clock that night, I went over and I said, "You seen the twins, Uncle?" "Aye, by Christ," he said, "I've got something to work for now. I'll give up all this bloody booze and everything." You know, talking with his lisp. Jeez, he was a happy man—he loved kids. To think he went down and that was it, never seen them again. It was the first time he'd seen them and that was it. It was very sad. And you could imagine her being there in the home and the two wee twinnies. Didn't even know they had a dad.

It was about six or eight months before we started pumping it all out. They filled it up because of the fire, and they had to wait so long to make sure it was okay. Then they started repumping into the river. Of course as they were going down they started picking the bodies up. They took the caskets into the mine with them, and when they came to one of the bodies they'd take them in, put them all inside, and screw them down. They got Jimmy Marshall and they got Tommy Black, but they'd had three explosions to go through, and you could imagine how it looked after that. First they found two in the top level, Eddie Pardington and Ernie Brammer—they were mates and they got them first. Then as they went down with the water they came upon the other bodies, and they'd tell the undertaker. He'd come up with the coffins, and a party would go down—you know, rubber gloves on, Jeyes fluid, all this. You had to wash yourself in this Jeyes fluid antiseptic.

Now I'll tell you a funny part of it. There was three of them on the pumping. Three shifts keeping the pumps going. Well, it's eerie after anything like that. It's imagination—you think you hear things, you see things, you know, the mind. Down the mine, it's different from being on the surface. The least wee noise, you can hear it, like timber creaking and any noise—"What the hell's that?" You'd think there was spooks about. So anyway, there's three of

ALEX COUTTS

129

them down there. There was a pumpman, an assistant pumpman in case he needed anything, and a deputy. They were pumping both sides, see, two pumps, and the deputy says to one of them, "You'd better go and see how that other pump is." "Alright," he says, "but I'm not going on my own." See he had to walk away up this bloody coal drive, and he says to the other guy, "You comin' for a walk?" and he says, "Yes." Of course the old bugger, the deputy, he was bloody frightened too. He says, "Oh well, we'll all go for a walk." He didn't want to be left on his bloody own.

The last was Alfie Noakes. They were pumping away there, and here's wee Alfie come floating out the level, he was the last man. Yeah, he come floatin' out with the water—as the water come out the level, he come out with it. That frightened them. Course the undertaker come up with his box and his big long gloves on and took him away. But actually he was the best of the lot of them. Black and Marshall were bumped all to hell. And when it was finally pumped out and they brought some of the boys back to clean up the mine, the debris, they come across the bits and pieces. You know, bit o'leg, or a boot and the foot in it—we put everything in a sack, and they threw it in the furnace and burnt it. Burnt the bits. They werenae all in the bloody boxes, I'm sure of that.

OVER THE YEARS there were three explosions at the mine, but I was never in one—there's a lot of luck in that. We were lucky we got hit when the smallest amount was there. Nine in the mine when the first one went, only two when the second one went, and bugger all the third time. There was nobody in the mine the third time, bar the pumpman or someone like that, and it didn't affect him. He just came to the top and said, there it goes again.

Mind, I've been down there when there was an earthquake, and that was bad enough. Bloody oath it was. I was up the rise working—that's nearest to the surface—when this thing started. I got a bloody fright, I thought she'd blown again, you see. First thing I did, I grabbed me coat, I had one of those shunter's waistcoats with the sleeves in them, you know, from the railway. I grabbed that and laid down beside the drain with it over me head. And I wriggled into the water to get all the oxygen comin' off the water, see. That's the mining experience. Right away down the depth they didn't feel the shock we got, they just felt a sickness. They took to their scrapers, though. Well, you see, it was knocking timber and everything out, making the whole mine unsafe. They were running past me like whitebait. By the time I got up, I was on me own. It was frightening. Well, I'll tell you how good it was—there was one fella down there took a parcel home with him in his underpants. Yeah, he shit himself.

SOUND IS a thing to miners. Noises. A movement like timber creaking or cracking—any movement of the metal. Their ears are cocked. Their eyes are cocked. Their smell—the miners develop these things well. They listen to the trucks coming, and they're coming at a certain speed—okay, there's nothing to worry about. But the least noise that's uncommon, *swish*—there could be a race of eight or nine trucks coming towards you, a runaway, so you bloody run away too. Long as you can get round the corner, out the way. Good hearing, see. Even at the hotel, at knock off, having a beer, you can tell what the guy at the other end of the bar is saying. "What the hell you sayin' about me down there? Better keep your trap shut." Tuned in, see.

Christ, we had some toughies up in this mine. There was a boy up the back here—his name was Iggy, the man with the golden axe. If the boys wanted a few bob—well, you'd say if you wanted the first joint or the second one and lay it on the ground. One hit and off would come the finger. They were that clean, all they had to do was pull the skin together and stitch it around. Oh, they were cunning, they'd go for every penny. You know, suffered an awful lot of pain, couldn't sleep for weeks and months, this sort of thing, and we had a good lawyer too. By Jesus, he was a hard case, a cracker. We had him on retainer. Then one year Iggy got a letter from the insurance company, and he gave it to me to read.

ALEX COUTTS

131

"Go on, read it," he says, and they had offered him fifty pounds to buy his golden axe. I laughed like hell, but Iggy says, "That's an insult, fifty pounds for that axe"—he's thinking of the money part of it, see. And he said, "They've got the bloody cheek to send me a calendar and a Christmas card too."

Every three months there's a cavil. They put numbers on each section of the mine, and all the places are put in a box. Because, you see, a certain pair of miners might be on a good section where the coal is working for them. I've seen some places the coal worked itself. Like it's under heavy pressure—one blast and a bloody pile'd come out. All they have to do is keep fillin' the boxes. Easy money see, and the other poor buggers are in a place like concrete. And that's why they draw the cavil every three months—new places are drawn to give fair play to everybody. And, boy, when they come out after the draw, you see the miners. If they got a good place

ALEX COUTTS

they're jumpin' about all over. And then you see the poor buggers who got a hard place.

Of course that's your ambition, to get to the face. They took two truckers every cavil, and when it come my turn for the coal I went with a fella called Ruane. They were three brothers down the mine—Jim, Hughy was the one I went with, and Frank. They were all great miners. They used to make me cut the face down the side of the wall, trim it off. There was no necessity for that, but they were that gooda miners they made you clean it up. That's how the old miners worked. When you trim it down straight like this, there's no breakage, no spillage, just the hole. Actually it used to get on my goat. Well, it's not a bloody street you're cleaning up, is it—it's getting the bloody coal that counts. I was on the coal— what was it, now? Well, you've got to do twelve months. It's like serving your time with a certain man that takes you on. And then if you're a good worker, they'll all be divin' for ya, but if you're a lazy bugger, nobody wants ya. See you're picked by your ability, your willingness to get on. An awful lot of truckers, they'd say, no way, they'd get held back. Nobody would take them on, so they couldn't get on the coal. But I made sure it didn't get that way with me.

If i'd retired at thirty-one, after—let's see, what's that?—seventeen years in the mine, retired for life and been kept, that's the value I would put on it. But that's going back to the Ali Baba days—slaves. They never treated us the way we should have been treated. Actually we were treated better here in New Zealand than in Scotland, but it still was bad. The Grey Valley Collieries, they were misers. They gave us nothing, all they wanted was what's coming out of the ground. I thought it was a good thing when they nationalised the mines. I'll never forget Paddy Webb, Minister of Mines. He addressed us in the bath house. He said to us, "Give us time, that's all we're asking for, time. We'll give you everything you want, we'll give you your seven-hour shift." Well, we demanded that really, through not gettin' as much sunshine as

ALEX COUTTS

133

others. See, when you're down there you're not gettin' any sunshine and you're not gettin' enough light. Not like Mother Nature on the top. That's why the Labour Government retired us at sixty instead of sixty-five. We had lost that environment, so they gave it back. Well, at the wrong end of it, but that was still something. They did recognise it, and that's the good thing. The bloody Tory Government, by Christ, you'd be down to your bootstraps because they'd take your bloody boots off you.

Forty-two years solid service, that's a long time. I'm the only one that's ever held that time. Longest service at the mine. I didn't have to retire. I would have carried on till I couldn't go to work, till I dropped. But the story was someone was going to get the bullet, and that's why I chucked it in. Always wanting to play the game fair, see. Well, they were talking about having to close the mine and so I said to the boss, "You're puttin' men off." I said, "If I don't retire, which I should do, because I'm ready for the pension," I said, "somebody's going to get put off." He said, "Yeah, that's right," but he said, "Alex, you're the last one we'll put off because you've been the longest here." "Well," I says, "I can understand that, but I don't want to see one of my mates getting bowled, just because I'm holdin' onto a job."

Well, it was a week. I'd just chucked in my job a week when they stopped the mine. As soon as it came out in the paper, I got on the bike and straight up to the mine and straight in to the bloody manager. You know, straight at him about the redundancy. He said, "I told ya not to bloody retire, I told ya but no, you're a pigheaded bugger. I couldn't tell ya straight out, but we gave ya all the bloody hints in the world." "Well," I said, "I was thinking of the poor bugger you were going to sack." "Anyway," he said, "I'm for you, I reckon you're entitled." So they wrote a note to the Minister of Mines, or Undersecretary of Mines, and of course I got my redundancy money granted. Owing to the fact of forty-two years, forty-two years solid service, the longest that's ever been in the mine. They granted me my money—for service. So then I halved that with Mum—I put half in her post office and half

in mine. And I says, "Now there you are, now you've got a nest egg at your back." First time she ever had money in the bank.

So that was the money alright, that was okay. But when you lose your work, when you lose that—there's an emptiness. That comradeship, it's sort of gone. Although you still meet in the pub, it's not the same. You're not—you're not so tight to one another. See, when you work down the mine, you're brothers. Do anything to one of them and they're all after you. Same at a strike. Boy, they were strong. Too bloody right they were strong. Ha, I remember one, be about nineteen twenty-seven, twenty-eight, around about there. We were out for quite a while. We used to borrow a lorry and go up round the cow-cockies to get food and tucker, anything they could give us. Butter or mutton, anything. And this time a mate, Johnny, and I, we went up to this cocky's place and he says, "I've got the very thing for you miners, just hold

ALEX COUTTS

on a minute." So he went away into the house—it was all dark, we couldn't see him—and then he came back up the passage, up to the front door with the double barrel, a shotgun. I says, "Ho-ho-hold on, old fella, don't get yourself into trouble. You knock us down, you'll go. You're going to go too." Well, there was a great big hedge, about a seven-feet-high green hedge, and once we got round the corner of that, whooosh, we were off. I don't think his cartridges could have caught up with us. And when we were running, you know, we were slippin', and I said to Johnny, "What you skiddin' on?" He said, "Whadda you think?" Ha. Then when we got down to the lorry and told the boys, they were all wantin' to go back and burn him out. But I said to leave the old bugger alone. "We know who he is now," I said, "and he's tabooed as far as we're concerned." There was some like him in 'Fifty-one as well. You know, the waterfront dispute—the miners went out with them, in sympathy. Well, at that time they took in special police, farmers and their sons. They made them special police. A band around their arms and batons in their hands. They went in amongst the wharfies and knocked them cold, all over the place. It was a terrible fight that. One thing, we never had any scabs. No, no bloody way. They daren't. They would have got murdered, police or no police—they woulda murdered them. But the Coasters would never do that. You see, the whole coast is sort of unified. You hit one, you hit the lot.

Course it was hard on the families during those long strikes, but there was a lot of the cockies too who were good to us. There was one joker there I remember, he had a great big pig. Oh crikey, it must have gone about six or seven hundred pounds. He'd killed it and it was all dressed and hanging up in the cooler. You know, two poles and a bar across and this beast hanging there. And I'm saying to myself, surely, you know, he might give us some. And he's lecturing us about too many strikes, and what we should be doing and what we shouldn't be doing. And I'm saying, "Oh, isn't that a bonny pig. That's a broad pig you've got there, what weight does it go?" And of course I'm tryin' to skite up his meat,

ALEX COUTTS

I wouldn't let his mind off that bloody pig, I kept on and on. Finished up, he got his cleaver thing and he cut it down the middle. He gave us such a bloody lecture before we got that half-pig, but by Jesus, it was heavy, it took the two of us to carry the half we got. When we put it in the truck I asked him his name, and I never forgot that guy.

WHEN YOU'RE a miner everything is mining. You talk it, you think it, eat it, drink it, everything. How many tons did you get out? How many yards did you travel? How much did you make last pay? and all this jazz. There's work time and dust time, all these sorts of things. But when you retire—oh deary, deary. It's like smackin' you on the back of the neck. There is a hell of a lot that's gone. It's not the same comradeship, you don't talk about the same things. A piece of your life is gone, two-thirds of it, two-thirds would go. Same as if I took away something from you that you loved—there's a sort of emptiness.

ALEX COUTTS

The Cross, Kelty

PARISH OF BEATH

KELTY, K-e-l-t-y, Kelty in Fifeshire, the parish of Beath, twenty-eighth of May, 1908. My mum and dad was shiftin' from one house to another and out popped wee Alex. I was born at my uncle's place, Alex Hodge—my namesake—and my auntie Mary's. Later I went to live with them, to look after my auntie. Bandagin' her legs, rubbin' them with hot olive oil and bandage them again—I even had to take her toilet, all that. A nurse, a boy nurse I was. She was helpless without me, I was sort of her mainstayer, and that taught me a lot about how to be kind to people. But as they get older, you know, even though they love you, they get a wee bit crabby. If you don't do what they want, they get wild at you. Once she threw a walking stick at me and I got busy, I told her off. "I'm here tryin' to help you," I said, "and all you can do is sit there and growl at me. Who takes your toilet, who goes to the store, who does this, who does that? I scrub your floor, I do your washing. Don't get growling at me because I'm tryin' to do my best

ALEX COUTTS

138

for you." But it's a thing I should never have done—you see, she started cryin' and so then I apologised. "I know, Auntie," I said, "I know you're a crippled, I know you can't move, but you've got to give me a wee bit of credit too." Anyway, I said I was sorry and she took it under consideration. Mind, she was good to me. So was my uncle. He used to slip me the odd half a crown and, you know—"Don't tell your auntie." Then she would give me two bob—"Don't tell your uncle." And that was a faith I never broke. Well, if I did I was going to lose half my bloody income. No, by Jesus, that was one promise I never broke.

I WAS A DEMON at school. Ha, teachers and headmasters, boy, I "loved" them. Well, ask yourself, one hundred and forty, one hundred and fifty to a room—I wonder how the teachers would like that now. Course it had its good points and it had its bad ones. You know, I liked it but I didn't like it. I reckon it was the time—it pinned you down, and I sort of liked to be free. But it was a mining village, seventeen shafts, and you were definite, see. They knew where you were going to finish up, so they poked as much into your head as they could while you were still at school. They put it all into you. The metal works, the stratas of the stone, how it's laid down, the coal, all this jazz. It was the way of things. You were expected, see—you were expected to do it. It was something you could work at, and of course you needed the money. The first thing was down the hole and make the dough. Yeah, you had to help put the coppers in the house, the money for the family. Everything counted.

FAIR DO'S. I've always been a boy that's for fair do's. Even at school I was a defender, taking the good side of things. You know, squaring things up. If anybody was hittin' at the small kids who couldna defend themselves, I was in. And I was pretty good with the old fisties too. See, I used to go to the gym at home. My trainer, Charlie McDowell, took me down to Newcastle once; fella I was fightin' down there is a black boy. "Look, sonny," he says, "it's only the colour's the difference." And he says, "I'll tell you another thing—he can't take a punch in the tummy. You can hit'm in the head with a mash—an eight-pound hammer—but you'll never hurt'm on the head. You get down and work his waistline." See, he was taller than me and I worked under him—into him. I was a strong little bugger, and he couldna stand the pain. Yeah, I got that boy before the three rounds were up. I won a watch. It was a gold watch, and I took it home to my dad. It had a bell— you could pull a little lever and it rung the time. I gave it to my dad and I said, "This is carting gold from Newcastle." Well, I was giving a watch to a bloody watchmaker. But, oh he thought the world of that—cause I got it through my fists.

THE OLD FATHER was a jeweller. He had two shops, and he lost both of them. Gamblin' and drinkin'. He was a very dry man, the father. Had such an awful thirst that he drunk away both his shops. Mind, he was a celebrity in the village, alright. He was still a great tradesman, everybody knew him for miles around, but he fell in with a bad crowd, and that's how he got on the booze. I could always tell when he was goin' out, and so could Mum. He'd get all shaved and poshed up. He had a wee mustache; it was waxed at the sides, and you'd see him waxing this bugger up. Then he'd get his dickey on, his cheat the public. We called them "cheat the publics." You know, two white things down the middle like a dress shirt, and you could have a stripey shirt underneath and it didna matter. Then he'd come out and take a teaspoonful of butter and put it down his mouth and let it melt. And Mum would say, "He's on the whisky tonight."

I remember the day we were bankrupt. All the money, all the debts the old fella had, they had to be paid, so much in the pound. He come in, and he threw the keys on the table to Mum. He said, "There you are lass, you pick up the keys and go down to the shop, take what you want. The bailiffs will be in tomorrow." He'd lost the shops. Drunk them away and that was that. It was down the mines for him, and he was there for quite a while. He used to come home, his hands all blistered to hell, and they'd be telling him ease up, ease up, but no way. Oh Christ, the blisters on his hands. Well, ask yourself—off a bloody jeweller's bench and down to use a pick and shovel. That's hard, man, that's hard work.

He used to go on the night shift at midnight. He didn't like it at all, he'd get out of bed and growl and growl. He were never content. But you know, people were still bringing watches to him at the house. He still had his own work bench at home. He could have made a start at it again if he'd wanted to. Thing was, he couldna trust himself. He'd lost one shop and then the other, see, and he wouldn't trust himself to start again. He'd work for anyone and never spare himself, but he couldna do it for him. Whisky and gamblin', see, he knew that weakness was there. Later he got a job back in one of the shops he'd lost. Mr. Russell asked if he would like to come and work there, and really it was a godsend to him.

I was the one he talked to most. He used to say I'd got his hands. I'd sit alongside him at home, at his work bench, for hours and bloody hours, and I'd never say a word. He'd just put his fingers across his lips, "Shhhhhhhhhh, don't say nothin', I've got to concentrate." Then, when he was finished and he put the job down, then you could talk to him. I was always asking questions, and I remember one day—he's havin' a smoke—and he gives me a hairspring, a wee tiny thing, they were all steel in those days, and it was twisted. He said, "Here, straighten that out, Alex." He's havin' me on, see, a bit of fun. And there I was with two pair of tweezers, trying to take the kinks out of it. He never said anything, just kept looking at me, then he said, "You'll be there till doomsday, let me have that." And he just—*wizz*—pulled it out straight, then put it in a wee machine on his bench and wound it up, perfect. "You see, laddie, there's tricks to all trades," he said. "Ah but," I said, "I didn't know you had that wee thing." "No, well, you see, that's how you learn, boy, observation. That's the best way to teach you, is to show you." I never forgot that.

I always wanted to be a tradesman. I always wanted to—like my dad. He was teaching me alright—he built me a bench next

ALEX COUTTS

to his, and I loved it. But one day I looked through the window—we was up two stories—and the other boys were playing with a bouncer, a ninepenny ball, spongy rubber thing. Me mum, she never noticed me going out, she woulda stopped me if she'da noticed me, but I sneaked out down there and I was playing bloody football. And you know, I forgot it was my dad's half-holiday from the shop. When I came back up to go to my bench, it was gone; it wasnae there. That's when it suddenly dawned on me it was his half-holiday. I knew he'd come and caught the vacant seat, and that was it. He never said a bloody word, and Mum wouldnae say a word, and the suspense was terrific. It was worse than giving you a bloody good hiding. I'd have sooner taken a hiding and left my bench, and of course I was still waiting until he was ready to tell me off for what I had done. Mum wouldnae say a thing. Then, sitting down one night at tea, about a week after it—when he finished his tea and shifted his chair back to get up, he turned around and he said to me, "Alex, you'll rue the day I broke your bench."

He wouldnae teach me a bloody thing from there on. As soon as I got near him, he'd push me off. See, I could have been a tradesman, taught by my own father, but I blew it. Oh yeah, he was a hard man. From Rosieburn, see, in Neathwick, twenty-seven miles topside of Aberdeen. Right away up amongst the old Crofters. There was no comeback with him. I tried to coax him, but no way. "No," he said, "you had your chance, lad, and you spoiled it." Well, there was only one thing left for me after that, and that was down the mines, so I concentrated on that.

WE CALLED HIM Pitcher Mitchell for a nickname. He was always playing pitch and toss, you know, two-up. He was mad on it. He had a job over at Lassodie, a place about two and a half miles away. There's a big lake there, and they were workin' away under this lake. He said to be over there at a certain time, at the pit head when they're coming off the cage, and he said, "They'll see you're looking for work." So I went at that time, and this old guy came over, he said, "Are you looking for a job, laddie?"—he was a Sockie man. "Aye," I said. Well, he took me away to the side and had a wee natter, he felt my arms and that to see how well built I was, and he says, "What's your name?" I says, "Coutts." He said, "You're not Andrew Coutts's boy, the jeweller?" "Aye," I says, "and I know you, you're Andrew Scott—Alex Hodge is my uncle." "Och," he says, "then you know where I bide, Clarien Cottages, down Lower Oakfield." He said, "You come down after tea." So I went down, and he wanted to know everything about me, and then he said, "You come down tomorrow morning at seven o'clock. It'll take you an hour to walk to the mine; be down there at seven o'clock."

So there I went the next morning, carrying my crib tin in my hand. When we got to the pit, I was a wee bit scared of the shaft, but he says, "There's nothing to worry about." He says, "Sit on your hunkers"—you see, you crouched in case anything happened to the cage. You're all in a squat position, eight men on each side facing one another. Actually that gave me a bit of courage, and in I went. I could see the sign going, then suddenly it's going that bloody fast I couldna see at all. And then I felt I was goin' back up when I was goin' down. Half-way there you feel like you're goin' back up again, that's the sensation it gives you, you're travellin' that fast. When you got to the bottom you stripped off—you got on your working clothes and left your other clothes there for goin' home with. There were no bathrooms. No, you had to go home after work and strip off at the waist to wash in a tin bath at the fire. But you never washed your back—they reckoned that weakened it. Anyway, I got on me bowyangs and everything, all dressed like, and he gives me a shovel. He says, "Now you take that, that's your shovel," and he says, "I want you to get it red hot." Well, you're working on the pace, see, racing the coal. That was my first day, my first steps to work. Course I was there just as a boy. Do this, do that, do what you're told, and don't give any cheek or impudence, else you'll get a thick lug. Oh, they'd hit you alright, don't worry about that. See, in this country if you hit anyone down the mine it was a penalty, but over there the old buggers would give you one when you least expected it, no worries.

ALEX COUTTS

You know, people have asked me did I ever go back to the old country, and I say, don't ask me that. Why the hell did I leave it, that's the question you should ask. Twenty ton a day I was loadin' for four and sixpence. From the bottom of the shaft I had to walk two and three-quarter miles before I even saw the coal. Then you had to walk back again after you'd finished, and you did it in your own time, there was no pay for travellin'. I got an extra sixpence a shift for working up to my neck in water. If a box went off the rails you'd have to go down and feel for it. Oh no, I wouldn't go through that again for anybody. That made me very militant. You see, the capitalist people, they'll work anything until there's no profit in it, and then they just dump it. It doesn't matter to them who they hurt. And I'll tell you another thing, if you, or if your father, or any of your relations fell foul of the company, they would put a red line below your names, and you wouldn't get a start in the mines. You had to watch that. Yeah, your brothers or any of them did anything wrong to the company—refused to do a job or something—you were all marked off the employment list. That was British justice for you. Even the relations, they'd even score them off. That was to teach you you were just a bloody slave. Because that's all it was, slavery. And they say, have you ever been home? I wouldn't spend a penny going back there. Seven days I was out here in this country, and boy, I knew she was mine.

IN EVERY walk of life there are good things and bad things. Good men, bad men. Good women, bad women. There's good jobs and there's bad jobs, but once you get down a mine you're a miner, you all club together and that's it. It's binding. It goes for all of you.

I was still at school when they brought in the mounted police from London, and the miners, they started using these hand grenades on the horses. They threw them at these bloody Mounties because they were charging the people and there was no way of stoppin' them with our hands. They started using the small ones at first, and the horses were gettin' their legs all cut. I was still in school but I remember it all—the 'twenty-one strike. The police

ALEX COUTTS

144

was guardin' the mines, and the miners met secretly in fruit sheds and places like that. They took all our local policemen away, and they replaced them with London policemen, but they couldna hold us. We were making lead bullets and hittin' them with shanghais. We made the lead bullets in the clay—push a thimble in the clay and pour in the lead. Then we trimmed them up and gave them to the men. They had rubber shanghais and the rubber was as thick as your finger, one hit, one bump, and they're down, they're dropped. Knock them out. We were too bloody slick for them, they couldna handle it. You know, they'd get round the corner and we'd be gone. Well, then they brought in the Mounties, and that's when the hand grenades got used.

They gave us hacksaws, the miners—they got all us boys together and away we sneaked and sawed the bloody padlocks off the magazines. Jelly, detonators, fuse, the lot. Course the guards never saw anything, just the kids. We got it away down to the men, and they hid it in the garage there. Down in the pit underneath the cars. Then they gave us a shifting spanner each, and we had to go up on the pit head and get all the grease cups off the machinery. We got them in sugar sacks, all sizes. Some the size of two-bob bits and up to big fellas. Big number nines—they were heavy brutes. First we cleaned the buggers out and put the fuse in through the oil hole, the grease hole. Then they clamped the detonator on the fuse with wee pliers and covered it with about a quarter of a plug of jelly and filled the rest with hobnails and metal, all that stuff. Then screw the top down, and that was a hand grenade. They wouldn't let us kids touch the detonators—too dangerous. Seventy pounds pressure per square inch in one detonator—could blow your hands off. Blow'm to bits.

After that they took away the Mounties and they sent up an English regiment—see, they knew the Scot and the English don't mix. So up comes this English regiment, and they took over the mines. They took all the policemen's jobs, and when a blackleg—that's a scab—went to work, against the union, there'd be six soldiers there, three on each side with fixed bayonets marching them

ALEX COUTTS

to work. And all us kids on the side giving them arseholes. You know, booing at them and even throwing stones at them. But after the strike they were never forgotten. They were sent to Coventry. No bugger would mix with them, speak to them, do anything for them. They had to be shifted out.

I LEFT the old country when I was seventeen. It cost my brother thirteen pounds to come out, but I came out for five pounds ten. That's all I had to pay because I was underage. Mum and Dad, they had to borrow the money—well, they didn't have any money, nobody had money stacked at home, just bare living. So Mum had to borrow it off a fella she knew at school. I was goin' with a girl then too. It was funny, just bloody cheek really, how it happened. We were down at a wee village a coupla miles away. My mate Willy and I are walking up the road, and here are these two girls in front of us. She was a student at Edinburgh College, one of the big colleges, and her father was a well-known author. And of course just impudence, bloody cheek, I patted her on the bum as we walked past. "Oh," she said, and so we started talking to them. She was shorter than the other sheila, so we paired off, and I was going with her from there on. Very sincere.

Funny thing was, she'd never go dancing, or to pictures, it was all walkin'. A way out on the hills and through the glens—she was a bugger to walk. She'd walk the feet off a bloody regiment. Oh hell, she'd be hikin' and walkin' for miles and bloody miles. I was with her right until I left the old country—oh yeah. Then when I left I said I would write to her, but you know, she never ever wrote me a letter back. I used to say to the wee postie that was here, I says, "You bring a letter from that girl of mine, son, and you're on a quid." But she never wrote. I was on at the postie all the time, "I'll give you a quid if you bring it." But he says, "I think she's given you up, Alex." Well, that was hard, that hurt me bad. So then I wrote her a letter home and gave her a bloody good ticking off. And I wrote one to her father too, told him to rear a better family in the future, cause what she'd done to me was dirty. And

I never—you know—I never did touch her. I only cuddled, and a kiss—that's as far as I ever went with her. Well, I was frightened to lose her if I went too far. But then, when I came out here and she didn't write, I was sorry I didn't.

OF COURSE before you can go they check all the rules out and there's instructions what you've got to do. You've got to sit an examination—questions, they ask you questions to see what standard you're up to. It goes on numbers—IQ. That lets them know your ability upstairs, they're not taking dafties on. Then you go to the medical, and the patient gets thoroughly examined. Dentist, eyes, every bloody thing, you've got to go through the lot. Then it's Senior Sergeant of police to get a character reference from him. Then once you get all that, and it all piles up to okays, they send you your papers and tell you where you're going to leave from. I left Edinburgh with my brother Jimmy and another boy who was gettin' away from a sheila he'd put up the pud. He was running away from her, and I didn't like that. I told him too, straight out. His uncle was a lawyer and he got all his paperwork done in a week, where it took us months. See, that's the pull lawyers and them have got. Well, that's not fair—I don't believe in that, and he had no right to run away from the lassie anyway. If she was good enough to get into trouble, she was good enough for him to marry, that's my philosophy. I had a few yacks to him about that.

When we left, my mother, she said, "I'll never see you again, Alex." "Well," I said, "I don't think so." She used to write to us, but the only thing, the dad, he never wrote to me. No, he wasnae a writin' man. We used to send money home—we knew we had to pay back to Mum and Dad, and we did that for, oh, years and years. Then one time, I must've forgot or something, anyway, the old girl put it in a letter, she started to ask for money, and that's when she got the last letter. I said, "Mum, you've never had to ask for anything in your life, but when you start askin', that's when I stop. You're finished. I've paid you back more than we've ever borrowed, three times over or more, but when you start askin'

ALEX COUTTS

147

for money, that's it." I never wrote her another bloody letter from there on. Never sent her another shilling nor nothing. Well, I used to send her a present now and again, but when they start askin' for it, that's bad. That's gettin' hungry. So I said, no way, I'm not built like that, that's the finish. Don't write to me no more, because if you do, it's only going to give you heart griefs. And that was it. That was the end.

LAST WORD

RIGHT FROM THE DAY you're born, that's the challenge, right from there. You want to crawl back, but no, it's another mouth to feed and to guide through this rotten world we've got. The maker up there, he made it right, how it should be, but we've gone and spoilt it. Now, this baby, he grows up, and when he dies, we cry. Well, it's when a baby's born you should cry, because he's coming into a cruel bloody world. When he dies we should rejoice. But funerals, some of them—the graveside scenes are terrible, terrible. It brings grief into people that shouldn't have it. It hurts them. There shouldn't be no need for that. As far as I'm seein' it, you go there to show your respect, but you're showing your respect to a lump of old mutton—meat and bones, that's all. You treat it with respect, but it's only the body dies. Spirit, it goes on to a better land. Now I'll tell ya, there's Kumara, down the coast there, and they were selling beer, the beer with the body in it. All the water that brewed the beer came out through the local cemetery, and that was their advert—the beer with the body in it. It was well liked, the beer, too, that's a fact; and so they used it as an advert. Well, that's the way it should be. Something you can laugh at—out loud.

ALEX COUTTS

Beatrice Collins

PEACE, THAT'S WHAT I'd like now, just peace. Just pottering around, living another day. Time though, it goes faster. And the older you get, the faster it goes. I seem to do less and less—the attacks I have, every attack seems to make me go slower and slower. Never mind, I'm living on borrowed time, and I've got to enjoy it. I'd be awful if I didn't; I might not get any more. Just if I could walk and the old ticker would strengthen up a bit instead of going backwards, that would be good. You see, it depends on my heart and my leg. My heart and my leg rule what I can do in the day, and they rule my sleep too. It worries me when my leg is in a lot of pain and I can't sleep. I've started taking pills for the pain. They keep saying to me at the hospital, "Take the pills when you get the pain." "Don't suffer." "Take the pills." But of course I don't like to take them. Well, sometimes I have to take them during the night, and they do leave me nice and comfortable—I just lie there and listen to the radio. I get a few hours sleep, and I'm quite happy about that. I don't think it hurts you to stay awake as long as you're not in pain. It's the pain that really gets you down.

Most nights now my leg—ooh, it's a cruel thing, it's cruel; it really is a terrible thing to live with. That pain in there, in the hip, it goes right down the leg. But do you know, it was a strange thing. I woke up one night not very long ago and there was no pain. It was so strange. Somehow I didn't have any pain in my leg. I moved my leg and it never hurt. Ooh, it was lovely, and I thought, wouldn't it be lovely if it kept like that. It didn't of course, but never mind, it could be worse. There's other things could be worse than that. Probably I'm lucky I've got that instead of something else. That's what I say to myself. And now when I can't bear it any longer during the night I take a painkiller. It's a thing I'm not happy about, the drugs, but there you are. It does ease the pain—I do it to ease the pain, and to sleep.

WHEN I WAS younger I had dreams—nightmares—for years and years that she'd come and got me. Ooh, it was terrible, terrible. She used to love to bash me. She was always hitting me about the

BEATRICE COLLINS

face, and my mouth would be all cut open, that was the sort of thing she'd do. I was like back in the old, old—hundreds of years back where they used to get these girls to work for them—a slave. It was like that. But you know, people at the time didn't want to know about that, they'd just say, never mind. I couldn't understand—I wondered why people were so awful, and I used to think, if only Mum were alive.

But there you are; the time passes and I got over it. I'm still here. And later it made me think about my own children. That I would give them all the love I could because of what I had missed. And I said to my husband, if I die don't ever let them go to somebody that won't look after them. I always used to say that, and he said he wouldn't. I couldn't bear the thought that I'd die and leave them. I was terrified of dying when my children were young, in case they were sent somewhere horrible, you see.

I shouldn't be talking about this. I try not to. It makes me think about it all again and I shouldn't. But sometimes . . . sometimes I do. I think of the things that have happened to me, and I think, aren't I lucky the way I came out of it. You see, to tell you the truth, it's rather surprising to me that I'm still living. It amazes me sometimes how I went on living after what I've gone through. Four times I had rheumatic fever, and each time I thought it would be the end. I can't understand why I'm still living, but there you are, my time will come. We've all got a time, and when it's our time, we go. Nobody can stop it. But as for now, ha, there's still a flicker. My candle hasn't burnt out yet.

Now I just try to enjoy each day. Laughter is the big thing in life. Not to take life too seriously and to be able to have a laugh. I try to stick to that and not let things worry me now. I just say, well, it's happened, and I've got to go on living. I've got to, it's no good me laying down and saying I'm going to die. Every morning when I wake up I say, thank God for another day. I've come through the night and I'm alive again—I'm alive today. Even if I'm in pain, I think, well, it might be alright tomorrow. That's how I've lived, by saying that. And now I'm getting near the end, it

doesn't worry me in the least. I won't mind going out. The longer I live, the more I don't mind going. And that's a good way to be. It would be terrible to go worrying about death, wouldn't it? You've always got to think there's a chance there, but you know, life's a funny thing—when you're well, you're worrying about this, that, and the other, but when you're close to death, nothing worries you. Nothing. You don't give two hoots. It's queer, that.

I WAS BORN in 1899. I was the seventh child, and I've been the sick one all my life. My mother used to say, "Nothing passes you, nothing. When it comes to you, it stops." I got the rheumatic fever in 1910—that was the first time—and I was that thin. I remember they weighed me, I was 3 stone 3 pound, and you could take my skin and twist it round me. My sisters used to bring other girls home from school and show them. My mother was always trying all these cures on me. She'd come home from the lodge, and somebody would have told her of another cure, and so they'd try it on me. Oh, I had all the cures under the sun, but nothing ever did the trick. And then one day I heard the doctor talking to my mother—I was in bed, you see, I couldn't walk or anything—but I heard him say something to my mother, and she said, "Oh no," and he said, "Yes, I'm sorry." So when she came—she didn't come in for a while—but when she did come, I said, "Have you been crying, Mum?" and she said, "No." I said, "Yes you have." And she said, "No." I said, "You have, it's something the doctor said to you." And she said, "Yes," she said, "the doctor's not coming any more," and later they told me he'd just totally given up on me. That's when I said to myself, "No, I'm not going to die, I'm not going to die for him. I'm not going to die."

A few days later my mother was going up the road, and she met Nurse Maude. They'd been friends and so she told her, "Aileen"—they called me Aileen when I was young—she's got the rheumatic fever and the doctor has given her up." "Oh," says Nurse Maude, "well, we'll see about that. I'll go down to her." And of course in she comes, into my room, and—"Hello, this is

a nice cup of tea, isn't it" sort of thing. Oh yes, and up go the windows; up to the top. "Fresh air, that's what you're in need of, fresh air. Now, when did your bowels last move?" "I don't know." "Think girl, think!" "I can't remember." "Well, we'll get that fixed up." And then she calls, "Dorrie!" and my sister comes running in. "Give me half a cup of water," she says, "and a spoon," and she mixes up the licorice powder, gets it out of her little Gladstone bag and mixes it up there and then. Then she gets me and sits me on the potty and she says, "Now, stay there till you do go." Then she said to Dorrie, "I'll be down this afternoon with a chair. It'll be a

BEATRICE COLLINS

long chair," she said, "with blankets and sheets, and you've got to take her out in it, out round the block." And I said, "Oh no, people will stare at me," but she said, "What does it matter, what does it matter if they stare at you?" Well, sure enough, people looked, and I mostly pulled a sheet over my face so they wouldn't see me. But anyway, that was the start of it, and every day she came down and saw that my bowels moved and that I went out in that chair.

Later Mum used to put me outside by a camellia tree, and I would lay out there all day in the chair and watch the people passing by. Then one day I'd had enough of just sitting there. I thought to myself, I want to get out of this chair. And so I did it. I crawled out, hanging onto the big wheels it had, and I got down onto the ground. I got down and I got back, and I thought, that's good, I've done it. So from then on I tried. I persevered and persevered till I was able to stand and walk a few steps, and then when I could do that I told my mother. So that's how I got better—Nurse Maude. I owed my life to Nurse Maude. She came all the time and saw that I was alright. Oh, she was good, she was very good. But see, that doctor gave me up. That's what he told Mum, he'd given me up. I was so indignant to think he'd say that—oh, I thought, what a cheek, saying a thing like that—I hate him. I won't die for him, I'll get better, you see, I won't die for him. No—it was just will power you see, and Nurse Maude. She could see there was life in me. She determined that she'd get me right—and she got me right. Sweet Nurse Maude.

Ah, but I must've been a scraggy kid. Even my sister—just a few years ago she said, "You've never been like you belong with us." She said, "You seemed to be somebody else." Because, you see, I never played with them or anything like that. I was always too sickly and I was kind of afraid to do the things they did. Even with the dancing. See, my whole family was musical, my father was a beautiful singer and so was my mother—beautiful. So you see, the girls were taught singing and pianoforte and dancing, things like that, but not me. I would go with them to practice, to the lady who used to teach them, and I would just listen, you know, take

it all in. Then when I was on my own—so nobody knew—I used to try and do the steps. They used to say I wasn't strong enough to be taught, but later on I was told it wasn't worthwhile because they thought I would probably die.

Well, I didn't die, but my mother did. She died when I was twelve, and it was a terrible thing, terrible. You see, I was with her all the time, I idolized her. Oh, she was beautiful. She went to all the openings, the opera, everything. She dressed beautiful because my father was a tailor, and we'd see her in the beautiful frocks she had; oh look, I just worshipped her, I adored her. If she was out late I couldn't go to sleep, I'd lay awake. The others couldn't give two hoots but I . . . I was that close, closer to her than any of the others, even though I wasn't her pet. The one older than me was her pet, but I was close to her. I idolized my mother.

When she got ill she went to the hospital, but she wouldn't stay—she came out of hospital and came home. The night before she died I was sitting with her, and she said to me, "What's going to happen to all you children?" That was her one worry, what was going to happen to us. It must've been a terrible thing for her. The day she died I was in the people's house next door. They made me go in there. They didn't want to tell me because they didn't know how I'd take it. But I went home—I wanted to go home—and when I went in, I saw the nurse there and I knew something was wrong. I'll never forget it. I went up to see my mother and she was dying—it was terrible, she died, she just died. I couldn't get over it, couldn't. I never got over it for years. I kept thinking I'd seen her. I saw her for days—months—afterwards. One day I saw her in a horse and cab outside our house. "I saw her!" I yelled, "I saw her!" and I called and called and I chased after the cab trying to see her until I was puffed and had to sit down on the gutter. It was awful thinking I'd seen her like that.

ABOUT TWELVE months after my mother had died, my father married his sister-in-law, his brother's widow. She lived up in Palmerston North. The young ones they put in an orphanage, and the oldest stayed here to work. The rest of us went to Palmerston North. But at the wedding she said to me, "I'm not going to have you here, sickly kid like you, why'd you want to come up here for? The rest are alright but I'm not having you." And I started to cry. "Oh, you needn't get to howling," she said, "I'll get you away somewhere, but I'm not going to have you here." And it was her that got me with this woman in Wellington—the woman in my nightmares. You see, this woman had come up for the wedding, and she made me ask her—she said, "Go and tell her that you want to go to Wellington with her." Oh, I was frightened, but she said, "You tell her or I'll put you out on the street." Course I cried and cried, but my sisters—older than me—they said, "You better do it because she's like that, she won't have you here. You'd better ask." So I did, and I went with her to Wellington, but I wished I hadn't.

I missed my mother a lot as I grew up, but that's when I missed her the most. You see, this woman was bad, very bad, and her husband was the same. I was so shy and they were so cruel. It

was shocking—it was so shocking I wanted to die, but you've got to be brave to kill yourself. I always say that the ones who commit suicide, they're brave to be able to do it. It's got to be done on the spur of the moment, as quick as anything, so you don't think first. I didn't think quick enough.

NOWADAYS I think you've just got to wait till your time comes. But it's funny you know, just the other day I came across a letter that I'd written ten years ago to the family—put with my will— telling them that I'd just been informed I could drop dead at any time. Ha, I'm a bit used now to being told I won't come out of hospital next time. Even when I was in my fifties I had to have a big operation. When I went to see the surgeon he said, "Have you made a will?" and I said, "No." "Well," he said, "I will do my best for you, I'll do the operation, but once you're on the table you'll be in God's hands because you only have a fifty-fifty chance of living." So he said, "I want you to fix things up at home first, talk to your family, and then I'll have you in hospital." Well, I went home, and there was a man I knew from up the road, he'd come down to see me, and he said, "They tell me you're going in to hospital and you've only got a fifty-fifty chance, you must be worried sick." And do you know, the thing was, it'd never entered my head to worry about it. "Oh God," he said, "I wouldn't know which way to turn, I'd go off my head if it was me." "Well," I said, "if you're going, you're going, and nothing can stop it. But knowing about it might do me some good because you see I'll fight against it and I'll get back. I'll be back," I said—and I was. So there you are.

Ha, last time I was in hospital they said, "We've got you right now but next time it's good night to you." All my life I've heard, "She won't live long," but there you are, my candle's still burning. It might go out tomorrow, but it was here today. Oh, I know one day the old ticker will stop, the doctors have told me that, they've all told me that, but I just think, live each day as it comes, it's the best thing. It's the best thing I know to do. No use to be morbid.

They tell me in hospital it's just my spirit that keeps me going. But it's strange, you know, how you kind of get left. A mystery. I've had plenty of cobbers, but you see, they gradually die, and I can't understand why I'm left. One especially never had an illness in her life. She'd been a cobber of mine for fifty years. Well, she just got tired and she didn't want to get out of bed. She slept and slept. And she said to me, "There's only one thing I want—I don't want any pain or anything—I just want to die in my sleep. That's what I want." And she got it too. I said, "You meany, it should be me that gets that."

Even with my husband—we always thought I'd die first. He would say to me, "You'd better label that jam. I won't know what it is if you don't put a label on it." We just sort of took it for granted that I'd be going first. He was a very strong man, my husband—you know, sturdy. He worked outside nearly all his life. He never drank much, he didn't believe in drinking much, and

BEATRICE COLLINS

160

he never smoked. Never smoked in his life, and yet it didn't help him much. He still got the cancer. That was the strange thing, him being such a healthy man, never had a day's illness in his life. He'd never even had a doctor before—until that night.

It happened he was having a bath and he called out to me. Well, I thought, I put the towels in, everything's in there. Anyway, I went in, and oh gosh, he'd been bleeding, the place was blood everywhere. Cancer, you see, that's what the doctor said, and he wrote him a note for the hospital, we had to get him into hospital. Well, he had some of his bowel taken out—shortened—and he was alright for eight years. He was good for eight years. But then, you see, there must have been some left in him because he took ill again. He had these funny turns, and one day I said to the doctor, "What is the matter with him?" "Well," he said, "some of the cancer must have been left," and he said, "I'm afraid it's in the stomach and he's not got long to live." I got the shock of my life. You see, he was tough, he didn't know what it was to have a

BEATRICE COLLINS

161

doctor—he hadn't even had a headache before. I don't know . . . I always thought I'd be first to go. It was so expected for me to go.

I nursed him for six months—it was a sad time. It was hard because he was not a good patient and I hated to see him suffer. You see, he didn't understand, he didn't know what it was like to have things wrong with him. He'd never known what it was like to suffer. He said to me, "You're used to it, but I'm not." Then finally he went into the hospital again, and it was very upsetting because he didn't want to go, but after six months I knew I'd had it. He had started to fall out of bed—things like that. Really it was too much for me. Just a few days before, he'd fallen trying to get out of bed and I couldn't pick him up. He was too big. It was about three o'clock in the morning when it happened, but there was still cars going past, they go past most of the night here. First I thought I'd go out and get somebody—stop a car—but then I got the wind up and I thought no, I might get someone in here I shouldn't. I didn't know what to do. Anyway, I tried to get pillows under him and I sort of raised his head a bit, I got more pillows and cushions and tried to build it up—oh, I tried and tried—but I couldn't get him up. Then after a while I said, "Can you get your hand onto the wardrobe, can you put your hand in there?" And he said, "Yes." So he got his hand in and I said, "Now, I'll crawl under you and push, and between the two of us we should get you up." And that's how I got him back into bed. But it was a big strain. I knew then, when it was happening, that it was too much for me.

He was very sick then. The doctor came—it was on the Good Friday morning—and he said he'd have to go into the hospital. He put him in the hospital. Well, that's the one thing I regret. All the way up to the hospital in the ambulance he said to the nurse, "She's making me go to hospital, she's making me go to hospital," and of course I started crying. But the nurse said, "Don't cry, don't cry, it's the best place he could go, he should have been in the hospital long ago." But he didn't want to be there, and he died the next day. I knew he would. After I'd seen him on the Saturday I knew. I didn't want him in the hospital. The doctor put him in hospital, but you see, he didn't understand, he thought that I had. That was the most upsetting thing for me.

You know, the thing you miss most is the companionship. Not husband or lover, it's the companionship you lose most. Not being able to talk to somebody, it puts a big void in your life. For a long time you've still got that presence with you. Some little incident happens, and you think, I must tell him that. Just some little thing, and you go to tell him, but suddenly, oh no, you can't. You still want to talk with him, but gradually you learn to live with yourself. For yourself. It takes about five years, but gradually you do. You come to realise you're on your own and you've got to do for yourself. I think the longer you live together—well, we all tend to become very casual towards one another. But then, when it's not there, you find you miss that companionship and somebody to do things for. Looking after him and doing things for him, I miss that terribly. Yes, caring for somebody—you miss that.

BEATRICE COLLINS

163

SHE RAN a boarding house—this woman in Wellington—a boarding house for seamen, and I was there five years. She had a boy and girl of her own, but it was me who had to run and do everything, and it was me who always got the hidings. She just used me as a little slushy. She'd make me scrub out, say, the bathroom, and of course it wouldn't be right and she'd make me do it again and again. Just throwing her weight around. And at dinner time if somebody wanted a second helping and there was only my dinner left, they got it. That was her makeup you see, that was the sadist part in her. She had the upper hand and she knew I couldn't fight back. I think that's what it was—she had the power over me. I don't know if it still happens today or not—I think it might do occasionally. But oh, it's a sad thing when you're young.

I started working when I was thirteen. She got me a special permit, and I went to work at this chemical company. I worked, and she took the money. Every pay day she'd meet me and take my money—she'd give me sixpence. Still, I enjoyed working. People were so kind to me there, and it was lovely to mix with everyone. I hated it when Saturday and Sunday came and I couldn't go to work. And every day, from the minute I came home till about ten o'clock at night, she had work for me to do. There was always something to do. There were other people kind to me. Some of the boarders used to feel sorry for me. I'd do little things—a button would come off a shirt and I would sew it on for them—all sorts of little things like that. Course they couldn't give me any money in front of her because she would take it off me. But you know, they'd say, "Oh, there's a button off my coat, could you go up and fix it? You'll find it in the pocket." Well I'd go up there and of course it wouldn't be a button off at all, it would be a couple of bob or something like that, and I would put it in my shoe— they'd tell me to put it in my shoe—then later I'd be able to buy something, buy something to eat. But you see if anybody gave me anything and she found out, she took it off me. The girls at work all had sympathy, and they would give me things. One girl gave me some ribbons to tie my hair with, but she took them off me and she gave them to her daughter. That was what she was like. But you know, always at the back of my mind I thought I would get out of it somehow—get away. I had that, I lived for that and I thought about it always. That took a lot of the hardship off it.

I ran away once when I was fifteen. I went to the sister of a lady I'd known in Christchurch. I thought she would help me get back to Christchurch, but instead she went straight to this woman and told her, and that was that. She took me to the police station to complain, and I had to see this policeman—he had all buttons on him—he was an officer of some sort. He seemed to be very high up in the force, this man, but he was nice to me. And oh, she didn't like it, she was cross because they were nice to me. I asked him if he could put me in a Home. But he said, "I couldn't, girlie— you're not a naughty girl. If you were a naughty girl I could, but you're not a naughty girl." "It's naughty running away, isn't it?" I said—I'd have given anything not to go back, because I knew I'd get a hiding when I got home. "We couldn't put you in a Home," he said, "not for that." But he could see the type of woman she was—she was so hard. And his sympathy must have been with me because when he spoke to me—he spoke very broad—he said, "Wait, girlie, wait till you're seventeen getting on towards eigh- teen, three or four months off eighteen, then go for your life. They couldn't bring you back then." He was telling me this quietly, but he got the message through. Of course she heard it too and when we came out she had a go at me. But I said I didn't understand. I played innocent. I reckoned I never heard a thing. But I did—and I waited for that time.

Nothing was worse than where I was—all those years. My sisters in Christchurch—you know, if someone was coming up to Wellington, they'd get them to come and have a look, come and see how I was. Of course she'd tell them a lot of lies, that I was alright. And I daren't tell them otherwise cause I knew I'd get a hiding. I knew I'd have to pay. I was frightened of her. Only once I hit her back. Her husband was away, but he came home the next morning and she must've told him because he met me after work.

I was walking along with two other girls from work and he grabs hold of me, just grabbed hold of me, and punches me in the face. The next thing I was lying in the gutter. Some men rushed over and they picked me up—he went for his life. But you see, nobody wanted to interfere, if you can understand that. People were too frightened to speak up, I think.

You see, today people look on things differently, more openly. You can get assistance, you can go somewhere. But there was nowhere I could have gone in those days to have asked for help. No one took any notice of you when you were young like that. And when you're young you don't know much. You don't know what to do, but oh, I hated it there. And the husband—he was bad, that man. He was as bad as her. He was disgusting. He tried a number of times to rape me. I couldn't go to bed without the fear he'd come in and try again. And I couldn't understand why she was willing to let him do that to me. The first time it happened I heard her say, "Go on, go in and try her out." But I was waiting for him then, and I thought to myself, you don't get near me. Course he would say I was a little bitch because I would fight, you see. I'd kick and scream and go on—oh, I hated him. Lots of times he tried, and I would kick and kick and then I would get hidings for kicking him. The girls at work, they knew what was going on because I'd come in to work with cut lips or a black eye, something or other, and the chemists there would dose me up—sort of look after me. They used to tell me things to do to stop him. One thing was to roll yourself up in a blanket, but that wasn't very good because you were helpless then. Oh, I tried everything they said, but nothing worked. They just—well, they should've been hung, the two of them.

That was a terrible time in my life, but I knew I would get out. I was determined to get out, and I stuck to what I intended doing. That policeman—he gave me that advice, and I remembered it. And when it was time—when I was old enough, as old as he had said—I ran away, I got out of it. At first I didn't know what I was going to do, because I didn't have money, but my work

mates, they had a confab, and they thought the best thing they could do was to get me away out of it, get me on the boat back to Christchurch. Annie, my friend from work, took me down to the wharf, and she said, "You're not going on the ferry," on the *Maori*, because, she said, if they're looking for you they'll look on the *Maori*, and she got me to go on one of the little coastal boats, the old *Patena*. But when we got to the gate, there was a policeman standing there. I thought, oh, he's waiting for me, he'll take me back, he'll take me back. But then in the finish I got up enough courage and went into the shed and got my ticket. I got my ticket and I went straight down to my bunk. It was just a little boat, and oh gosh, it was terrible. I sat on the bunk and I was that frightened somebody was going to come and get me that I never even knew we'd sailed. I said to the stewardess that was on, "How long before we leave?" "Oh," she said, "we're at sea now." Well, I relaxed a bit then. Oh yes—thank goodness.

When I got back to Christchurch I was not well at all, and I went to the doctor. He said to me, "Every nerve in your body is unstrung, you're in a terrible state. Now," he said, "tell me all about it." So I sat and told him everything about it, and he couldn't

BEATRICE COLLINS

167

get over it. You see, she wouldn't even let me have any of my clothes back, she wouldn't let me have anything. I said to him, "I'll take up a case—they tell me I can take up a case against her." But he said, "Don't do it." He said, "Don't do it because everything will come out. The newspapers will get hold of it and it will be a stigma on you all your life. People are hard," he said. "Let her keep your things, let her keep your clothes, just wipe them out of your mind, and I'll get you right." So I didn't take the case up, I didn't sue her or anything, and looking back I'm glad I didn't. Cause you see, in those days, the scandal, it would have been terrible. Probably people would have said that it was my fault, that I led him on, or something like that. I told the doctor all sorts of things about it, and he reckoned it would all have to come out, you see. So it was through him that I didn't take the case up. He said, "All you've got to do now is get well," and he said, "Just forget about it." But I was frightened for many, many years. I was terrified, I really was—terrified of her.

Now i'm an old woman. Well, that's alright, I don't mind being old. I don't mind it. Actually it's funny, you don't always remember you are as old as you are. Mostly I just think of it as getting more illness, not being able to do what you want to do. That's the hard part of old age, knowing that you can't do those things that you would very much like to do. Well, you've just got to live with that. If you were healthy it would be nice, but if you haven't got your health, it's not too good. I like to go out and see the shops and things like every woman does, see the buildings going ahead and the progress that's being made with things. You miss all that when you can't get about. You have to resign yourself. You just take what you hear—what people tell you—and be glad if you do get an outing. That's the thing in getting old, and it's no use fighting against it, you just try and do the best you can. You do the best you can.

The thing I'd like now is to spend the rest of my time here—peacefully—here in my own home. They say I shouldn't be here

because I could die at any time. But I say, to die is alright, and it doesn't matter if I had a hundred people round me, they couldn't do anything for me. If I die on my own, it's just the same, isn't it. But you see, the family are concerned—well, they are leaving me alone about it at the moment, which is a good thing—but they want me to sell the house and go into a home. They feel it would

BEATRICE COLLINS

170

be good for me, but I dread it. It would be awful to go into a nursing home. I just hope to die here. That would be best. I don't want to be in amongst a whole lot of sick people for the final days. I've told the doctor, I'd sooner die here, be found dead here, than to be found dead in the hospital. But my son tells me he thinks the roof is going, and that'll be the finish I suppose. The lawyer says, don't do anything to the place because I'd just be throwing money down the drain. I can see there is a time coming, and it feels terrible because I do want to stay—I would like to stay until the end. I know the family is worried about me, but I've got no fear. Not as far as living here or dying here. I just want to be in my own home, and what's going to happen with that is the one thing that worries me. I've always been a fighter, you see, I've always had to battle for everything. But I don't know, somehow, I suppose, you take more from people when you get older. Old age, it sort of mellows you—I suppose it does. You can do less and less, you see. You sort of know you're getting closer to going—having to get out of your home—but it's just the thought, you know, the thought of having to go when you don't really want to.

I had so much to do with building this house and saving for it—it was me that had this house built. It was just after the depression—my husband had just got a job—but I said, right, we're going to carry on living like we have been for twelve more months and save every penny and we're going to have a new home. I drew up a plan of what I was going to have, a rough plan. I wanted a room, a sun room, on the nor'west corner—I wanted that, that was my whole thing. They all used to call it my dream room. I was going to sit in it—I used always to talk about this room that I was going to sit in. Course, everybody laughed at me—you're mad, you'll never do that. But I worked hard to get it. You see, you can't build a house without money, you've got to have money to start things off. Well, I went at it—selling cakes, washing barbers' towels, making things, doing everything like that to get that money to start this house. And then, of course, it came true. We got the loan for the house to be built, and I got my sun room. You

BEATRICE COLLINS

171

know, I think if you wish enough for anything you can make it come true.

Oh, I was so happy. Seventeen years married I was when we moved in, and do you know, I didn't know what it was to turn on a hot tap till I came to live in this house. Always I'd have to boil up the copper for the children's baths—the old tin bath—oh, it was the happiest day that I came into this new home. To turn a tap on and get hot water. Oh, it was lovely to get this house, it was marvellous. But now even the doctor has said to me, "You'll have to leave by winter—you'll have to do something by next winter. Even if you just shut up the house and go into some place for the winter." Well, I suppose that's the kind of thing that comes to anybody, not only to me, but you know, when I think of what I put into this house. I struggled for it, it was me that did it, and I think that's why I don't want to leave it somehow. It was so hard to get it, and that's why I want to get as much out of it as I can before I

BEATRICE COLLINS

172

go. You see, I know when I go it will be bulldozed over. That'll be the end of my old home and everything in it. So then I think, well, I might as well make the most of it while I'm here.

YEARS AGO there used to be a chap called Ernie who lived around the corner from here. He was a seaman, and sometimes he used to stay at that boarding house in Wellington where I was. So a year or two after I ran away, I wrote her a letter. I wrote and I asked her if she would give me my things I'd had since I was a little girl. There were a few things my mother had given me, and they were precious to me—only to me. Then, when I had written the letter, I asked Ernie if he would take the letter to her. But when he gave it to her she just laughed and threw it in the fire. She said, "She gets nothing." Well, then I did a horrible thing. I said, "She won't give me my things—well," I said, "all I wish is that she loses something that's precious to her. The things that she holds dearest to her." Because, you see, I'd lost the things I held most dear. Really that was an awful thing to say. You shouldn't wish anything on people. I didn't really mean anything to happen, but not long after that her son was killed, lost on a ship wrecked at the Pencarrow Heads. She lost her son, and they got all the bodies but his. They say she turned white-headed overnight. She sat on the wharf there for days and days hoping to see his body come in. But it never did; they never found it. I thought, now surely she knows, she must know now how I felt. You see, she took everything from me, and she lost the one thing she wanted.

IT'S THE THING you don't ever think—the hardest of all—that your children will die before you. You don't ever think it will happen to you, specially when you're getting so old. When I married I had four children, and I was determined they would have a happy childhood. I prayed only to live long enough to look after them because of what had happened to me. Now two of my sons have died, and it's a dreadful feeling. You think, why, why am I allowed

to live on and they die? It's terrible . . . a terrible, terrible feeling. There's no way I know how to describe it. You have a deep sorrow. I'll never get over it. And to think that I'd been through all those things, hospitals and everything. Everyone expected me to go first. I wish it had been me. I miss them, I really miss them. And I live in the hope that I won't lose the other two before I go.

Life, it's a queer thing. Seems you've got to have sadness and gladness, just like sunshine and rain. That's what I think now, and often the ones that come through scot free and have a wonderful life all through, there's nothing—they've got nothing—I mean, in themselves. Going through life with a rose, everything rosy for yourself, it's not good for you. It's the hardships bring out your character. They teach you more than anything in life. I was a bit soft—well, I was pampered when I was young—but when I went up to Wellington, I got a rough life. Those people, they had a bad streak in them. But you know, in a way I think it's all kind of fated

BEATRICE COLLINS

174

when I look back. Although I suffered over it, I think I was sort of hardened, it made me a bit tough, and that's probably why I've lived so long. It's a funny old world, isn't it. I had such a bad time, but that's how I think goodness has come out of bad. Life's got to go on, you've got to make it go on. And if you give in when you're old, that's the finish—you can't pull yourself up again.

It's hard now in the mornings when I wake up. I'm aching all over and I know I've got to have movement. You're in pain, so it's no good laying there. I know I've got to get out of bed and move my limbs. It takes me a long time. First I sit on the side of the bed, sit there and wiggle my legs—swing my legs to get them moving. Then usually when I get out of bed I have to use the walker to get to the bathroom. It takes me a long time, always it's an hour or more after I get out of bed before I can get to the kitchen. Well, that's if it all goes good. You see, you just don't know when it's going to come on. Mostly you lose your breath when you get out of bed, you can't get your breath. You feel something's going to happen, and before you know it, it starts up. It happens a lot now. Sometimes I'm getting dressed and it's awkward—I have a bad foot, and I have to get down to fix it and to put on my stockings. Well, you see, I've got to manoeuvre so much to get down to it— it's painful, and it holds me up. And sometimes if I get het up, or get a bit mad with myself, it can bring on an attack—an angina attack. But then another time, when I've just been laying down all night, it comes on for nothing. I think, oh gosh, what's gone wrong with my arm. It really hurts, and then the other arm starts, and I think to myself, surely it's not going to be another attack. But then before you know it, it's up in your head. It starts in your hands and runs up your arms and around your neck. Then it comes into your face. It's all over your face and head, and your jaw feels like somebody has hit you. Like you've had a big punch in the jaw. Of course it's terrible because you can't breathe, you're going for your life to get your breath at the same time. Sometimes I'm asked—people say, "How do you know if you've had an angina attack?" Well, if you ever have one, you know. You never mistake it for any other pain. It's got a pain of its own.

Even so, they're not all the same, if you can understand what I mean. You don't know when you have an attack how it's going to be. Sometimes it will be over in twenty minutes, and another time it won't be. If it's a bad one I take Anginine. That stops the pain—you dissolve it in your mouth, and it eases the pain quicker. I don't always take it, but the doctor said to me, you're a fool not to because it saves that pain. Well, it does help the pain, but it also gives me a headache, and you see, if I take too much Anginine I seem to get a buildup and it makes me sick, makes me vomit. I try not to take it unless I have to. If I just have a little turn, I kind of sit and relax until it goes off—which it does sometimes. It takes longer to go, but you have avoided taking the Anginine, you see.

Sometimes, though, it doesn't go off so quickly—it can seem like ages before it goes off. I might sit for an hour before the pain starts to go, and those are the times when I think, is this the end? Is it going to be the end? I think, will I go this time, or will I come through it? You're kind of waiting. You're thinking to yourself, is it going off, is it getting less? Will I take another Anginine? When did I take the last one? Should I take another, will I get a worse headache? You're wondering how long is it going to last this time, and you never know, you see, you never know. The thing is, these days—well, I don't get too worried over it. When you're in pain like that you just think, if I go, well, at least I'll be out of pain. I won't feel anything any more. I won't get hurt any more.

Nowadays if I go five days—don't have an attack for five days—I think, that's wonderful. That doesn't happen very often, but sometimes it does, and I get all those days without it, so there you are. Once I went ten days without it. I reckon that was marvellous. Then sometimes I get an attack in the night, and it wakes me up. You never know when it will happen. But when it does, I like to be left alone. I don't want anyone to see me. I just want to be on my own. The doctors think it's a funny thing, that, but it doesn't worry me being on my own. I'd sooner be on my own when I'm in pain than have anybody see me. I can't talk to them, there's too much pain, and I think if I can just keep still and do my moaning and groaning, it's better. But I couldn't do that if someone was there. I would have to hold on to it. It's better if you can let yourself make a noise when you're in a lot of pain—do a bit of groaning. If you're with other people you tend to hold it back, and that's not doing you any good. Really I don't know if it helps you or not, but there's something in it that makes you feel better if you can make a bit of noise.

Slowly you learn to do the things you can, instead of the things you shouldn't do, but it's very hard. As time has gone on now, I find I can do less and less. You have all these things you want to do, and you want that hour to go on and on and on. But it doesn't. Time goes too fast, and you have to learn to do just a bit at a time. It was terrible in the beginning, I used to sit and cry about it because it took me so long to do things. But I know now if I hurry I'll bring on a turn, and that leaves you a bit dopey—it kind of takes all the life out of you. If it's a real bad one, it can take me three days to come back right. I've had to adjust myself to that. I have to relax and think to myself, well, I'll start getting dressed at seven o'clock and I'm sure to be in the kitchen by half-past eight. I work it like that now.

It's taken me a long time to get like that, and it still gets me down at times. I think to myself, if only I could do like other people can—how I used to do it. You see, I like doing things for myself and I can't. I want to hurry up, but I can't hurry up at all. I'm slow and it's the only way now I can go. If I try to hurry I'll just have more pain, and it worries me hurting all the time. I get frightened because it would be awful if you were taking painkillers all the time. In the hospital they were always saying to me—drumming it into me—"Have as many as you want. Have'm whenever you like." But I'd say, "No." I'd sooner put up with the pain than go on taking them and make it a habit. You take a couple of them during the night and they leave you very dopey the next day. You're never very clear of mind the next morning. Ha, I'm afraid it might take my brain away or something. That's the real sign of old age. I've seen people who have gone like that, you know—they can't talk with anybody. That's what I call old age. They tell me, though, I've got a very alert mind, and that's something I'm very thankful for. I hope I never lose the power of reason.

EVERY NOW AND AGAIN, when I feel like it, I say my little prayer about living alone. Not that I'm a religious person, not now, not any more. I've kind of turned away from religion to a certain extent. I am a believer—I know there's something—but I don't know what it is. Life kind of goes round and picks up things that have happened in the past—things that have gone past you. Then something happens—you remember—and it alters your outlook on things. Somewhere . . . somewhere there's a pattern, and in the end it will all come out, that's what I think. I used to go to church. The children went through the Bible class and the Scouts—everything. I used to donate money every so often to the church—I did that for years. Then, when my husband died, the undertaker said to me, "You'll need a minister, who will you have?" So I told him the church. I said, "I've belonged there for years." But when he came back he said, "They won't take it—they haven't got the time." Well, that finished me. The regular minister was away overseas and there were two men filling in for him, but the undertaker said, "No, neither of them will take it." I couldn't believe it when he came back and said neither of them had the time. Well, I said, "Get anybody you like—I don't care now." I think he got somebody from this New Life Church thing. People I don't think much of. They didn't know my husband. Never mind—the man said his piece. But that's why I turned away from religion.

When the minister came back from his overseas trip, I told him what I thought of the church. He said, "Don't blame me, it wasn't my fault." But I said, "They were working for you— on behalf of you. To think they couldn't spare the time to read a service for my husband. After all the years we contributed to the church, you couldn't do that much for us." I said, "I've never

asked you for another thing. That's all I've ever asked. Well, that's finished me with religion, and it's finished me with your church. I won't contribute towards it any longer. I'll have nothing to do with you." He was pretty annoyed with me, but I didn't care. I thought to myself, if this is religion, they could have it. From now on my religion is to live a decent life, as I've always done, and to do what I can for anyone. That is what I say now. My religion is doing what I can for people—giving. Don't think of what you're going to get back, just give. At my time in life you see the values in more simple things. You come in with nothing and you go out with nothing. And if you can't do something for someone while you're living—well, it's too late when you're dead, isn't it?

I've been here a long time now and I've had a lot of experiences in my life. When you're young you think you'll be here for years and years—it would be awful to die when you're young—but now, dying, it doesn't worry me in the least. You feel pleased that you've had your day and you've seen how things have turned out. Especially if your children turn out good. To know that the work you put into bringing them up has paid off—it's a big satisfaction to know that. It's a big thing, that. Twelve months before my eldest son died, he rang me up—it was on Mother's Day—and he said, "I'm ringing to tell you that you're the best mum in the world." Well, I started to laugh, and I said, "Go on with ya, you've been on the grog." I was just joking, but he was hurt when I said that, and I was sorry later that I'd said it. But he said, "We've been around visiting friends—listening to others telling about their childhood," and he said, "Some mothers must have been awful. Some of the things they used to do. But when it came to my turn I said, you know, I've got the best mother in the world." He said, "When I look back at the things you let us do—you played with us—none of the other mothers did the same, not like you." So he said, "I've rung up to say I think you're the best mother in the world." And I thought to myself what a lovely thing, to know that they enjoyed themselves, to be told that—it was a big thing. Oh yes. I still feel good when Mother's Day comes around. I think to myself, Bob said I was the best mother in the world—so I must be.

You know, that's how I'd like to be remembered. Once when I was in hospital I read in the paper about this woman who'd died. It said, "Will be remembered as she wished, not sadly but gladly." I thought, well, that goes for me too, and I wrote it down. Not sadly but gladly. And that's why I don't cling to my children. I don't want them to say, oh, Mum was always moaning and groaning, wanting us to do this or that. I think to myself, they won't ever say that about me. You see, some people get very full of themselves when they get old, expecting a lot more than they should expect. They think the younger ones should drop everything for them. But the young ones have got their lives to live too. They've got their own things to do, and I've seen it where old people make it a burden—they make a burden of themselves, and their children resent it. I think that you should expect your children to keep in touch with you and just do what they can for you, in moderation—when they're ready to do it. It's hard sometimes when you want

181

something done, but you get it done sooner or later. I've learnt that as I've got older. You find the young ones, the grandchildren—they come over and do things when they can, but I don't expect them to drop things for me. No, they do what they can. I had a letter the other day from my great-granddaughter and she said, "My dearest, darlingest great-grandmother, I'm so sorry to know about your legs being so bad, I would hate to think you can't get around. I think about you all the time." And when I read that I thought to myself, well, that just shows, it's still in people to think of the old.

Ah, but I'm glad I was young in my time, I wouldn't like to be young now. No, they've got all the worries of the world on them now. These days I just sit back and watch the young. My life is going out and theirs is just coming on. It's funny, you know, when you're younger you think, oh, I'd hate to die. You think, I'd hate to leave this, I'd hate to leave that. Things have different values. But as you get older the value of everything seems to leave you. The things that give me most pleasure now are my plants. I've got a bit of a pash on sunflowers—I've put in some more plants this year. But it's like everything you do now—I wonder, will I see them? You wonder, will I, will I? Will I be here to see that? Last year I thought the same. Well, I did see them—and it was lovely. Now I might be able to see them again. I would like to see them flower again. Yes, I hope I do.

BEATRICE COLLINS

John and Muriel Morrison

MURIEL

IT IS A TIME of closeness. Not, of course, the only time. No, there have been others, highs and lows, on and off, but not like this. This is unique, beyond doubt a time quite different from any other. And by that I mean, this is the time, the first time, that I have really looked—and, I believe, John too—at the end of life.

It's true that as I got older I would sometimes think, oh yes, I'm going to die sooner than I was before, but it was not real. And now suddenly it is. I have been caused to look into a blackness I shan't forget, and I have seen a time when our relationship could end, the possibility of a time when we shall be no longer together. I have told myself, don't forget that, don't forget what you have seen. And now, instead of looking into the darkness, I am looking into the light because our time is still here. It is where we are now, a sort of doubling—a heightened perception—and a greater appreciation of every minute.

JOHN

THE PHONE RANG one night, and when I answered it, they said—they were fairly blunt about it—they said, "The biopsies indicate that you have cancer." That's how it came . . . over the telephone. And the image I'd had of myself till then, the image of my existence at that time, was of being physically alert, of doing things, investigating things, that was the image of the rest of my time. What they said to me on the telephone, that was a thing . . . oh gosh, it came like a smack between the eyes, a solid smack. Certainly it was the last thing I wanted to happen. Fortunately Muriel was there, and our friends the Lewises were there, and when I told them they just wrapped me up in their arms. That was marvellous. That was a beautiful thing . . . but inside myself . . . well, there was no question it was the last thing I wanted to hear.

Looking back, putting two and two together, I suppose I should have realised something. A friend of mine had had a prostate enlargement and waited two years for the operation. I suppose

JOHN AND MURIEL MORRISON

when they did my examination they must have felt the nodes and what have you. They certainly didn't waste any time, not once they knew. And when I think of it—how I stayed there longer than the other blokes, and the fact that my catheter was in longer—even then I remained in blissful ignorance of the whole business. In fact I had an enjoyable time. The nursing staff were superb, I trusted them implicitly. And the camaraderie between the other patients, wandering around with their bottles and what have you, it was great. It was interesting how much I enjoyed it there, and then finally I was able to go home and I seemed to be recovering really well. They did tell me when I left that they were taking biopsies, but I hadn't taken much notice. And then they told me. One night a while later, that's when they rang and told me.

MURIEL

I THINK PROBABLY it has done to us what nothing else could have done. Not so absolutely. To hear it at first, that John had cancer, was like a terrible blow. A dark night. This doesn't happen to us . . . well, it was happening to us. The possibility of death, our own proximity to it, was something we had known intellectually quite well. Now we knew it with our hearts. It was—it is—there for us to face together, to work at, and to share in whatever the pain or the joy will be. Now, inside me, there is the very clear realisation that I am part of what is happening. That what I do can be effective, can be life-giving—or not. And of course what happens to John is very important to me, as important to me as living. What is happening to us now is that natural process of turning to one another and binding together to face this thing. That kind of binding together that comes to human beings when disaster strikes them.

I should say that before this happened our life was much more casual, taken for granted. It was like having a basket of fruit with plenty in it and you could eat as much as you liked. Then suddenly you get to a time when there are only a few left. Suddenly each piece of fruit becomes something quite special. Before there seemed to be lots of opportunities, it didn't matter so much what you did, there were years and years ahead to grow and work things out in. That is what we had thought. It was a mistake of course, this pre-cancer assumption, a fallacy, but it was there.

JOHN

THERE IS a feeling in all of us, a certain kind of possibility within which we exist. It is the idea—a belief—that barring accidents, we have a lot of years to live. Having cancer was a time of waking up to that. Not at first of course, it was not a clear understanding in the beginning, not then. Probably it is only within the last twelve months that I have come to terms with the idea of death in the sense of dying from cancer. And the strange thing was that when I did come to terms with that, I suddenly realised I could be dying of anything. I had reached the point in time when the average span of life ends. There was suddenly this realisation that I could die within the next two or three years irrespective of having cancer or not. And the thing is that if I hadn't had cancer I might never have thought about it. It has brought very much to the forefront of my thinking this whole question of immediacy. The knowledge that the most important thing is what happens between now and then, and, more particularly, immediately. It can of course slip away on you occasionally, but it doesn't take much to bring it back again. Perhaps in a way it has always been there to some extent. I've always thought that the epitome of a relationship was really to enjoy the presence of that person. I mean, you can use words all over the place, but the best times have been those rare moments when it has just felt good to be with that person. To have that now with my wife, to be so much more aware of her in the present moment—that has been special. To have the opportunity of realising that there may not be all that much time . . . no . . . let me say it more positively than that. It has been what I'd call a solid jolting into the sure knowledge that this is all we have. Just this moment. Make the most of it. That is the real thing to emerge.

JOHN AND MURIEL MORRISON

188

JOHN

MURIEL, when I met her, was already a very confident and capable woman. She was intelligent—she had an MA degree—and she was a very able speaker. She seemed to me to be everything I wasn't— I put her on a pedestal. She was, I suppose, the first and only real girl friend I ever had. Love, you see, was not something that I knew a lot about at that time. In fact you might say that our association, the way in which we came together, was more fortuitous than contrived. Certainly nothing in my life had prepared me to relate in this way with another human being.

There had been certain feelings of course, but always I'd kept them to myself. There'd been a girl at the technical college I went to, in the sixth form—what they called the professional forms, the fifth and sixth—they had boys and girls in the same class. Probably the first venture at a coeducational school in Christchurch. But the girls were down one side and the boys down the other, even the playground had a line down the middle. The boys played on one side and the girls on the other, and pity help anybody caught talking to each other. That was how it was. Even so, there was this girl I had a very powerful attachment to. It was never expressed. I never told anyone, although somehow the other boys picked it up and at one time wrote something on her books. But I never spoke to her. I could never tell her. Earlier than that I remember a school dance—I would have been fourteen or fifteen perhaps—and all the other fellows seemed to have girl friends, so there was the feeling within me that I should too. That I should at least dance with a girl, which I did, and afterwards I took her home on the bar of my bike. But it was not good. All I can remember of it is that I felt uncomfortable—and that she had bad breath. And that, you might say, until I met Muriel, was the sum of my experience in that regard.

I met Muriel in the peace movement. We were both part of an anti-war organization called the No More War Movement. I had been made president and at the same time Muriel had been made secretary. It was not really a good thing for me because I had no confidence, but the older people in the movement wanted to bring the younger ones on, and this is the kind of thing they did. Anyway, I got to know Muriel, and to like her, but of course I never said anything. And then one night I was at the pictures—it was at the Theatre Royal—and I saw her there. I just glanced along

the row where I was sitting, and there she was, only a couple of seats away. When she looked down and saw me she smiled, and somehow that just sort of did it for me. From then on I was very friendly with Muriel and her family—she had three sisters, and I got to know them as well—but there was still never any hint of affection between us. I could never bring myself to say anything.

What capped it off in the end was something that happened one time while I was visiting her. Muriel's family lived up on the hill at Sumner, and while I was there one time we went along to help a friend who had a section further along the hill. We were moving a boulder, zigzagging it down, and I thought, oh crikey, why do it like this, why not drop it straight down? So we did, we dropped this boulder that must have weighed three or four

hundredweight, but it didn't stop on the lower path like it was supposed to. No, it headed down the hill straight for Flower's house.
He was then the bursar, I think—something like that—at the university. Of course I rushed down the hill after it, I don't know
what I thought I'd do. As it happened, there was one tree between
us and Flower's house, and the stone ran smack into it. What a
relief. In the meantime I had put my foot down a rabbit hole and
twisted it rather severely. I couldn't walk, so there was nothing
else for it—they took me back to Muriel's place and put me to bed.
I was there for three days, and I think that kind of cemented the
whole thing really. Even so, still, I couldn't express what I was
feeling, and in the end I resorted to writing her a letter. I spent
hours on that letter. I wrote it in such a way that if she wasn't
interested, she wouldn't think that I was either. Then one day a

little later I gave it to her. It was a day we had gone out together to see her brother-in-law—I was doing a few electrical repairs for him—and I remember her coming up to me, I was standing up on something in this doorway, fixing some wiring, and she came to the door and she looked at me, and she said, "Yes," she said, "yes, I care." And oh, my God, I just exploded. Inside I just exploded.

All those feelings in me that had been so repressed were suddenly triggered off. I had never before had this kind of experience, not this kind of potential intimacy. I'd had no experience with women at all. It was a hell of a time really. Certainly I became thoroughly miserable, and it must have shown, because I can remember my sister-in-law asking us, "What's the matter with you two?" Oh, it was not a good time at all. In fact, after we were engaged Muriel went to work at the Quaker school up in Wanganui, so we saw very little of each other during our engagement period. Ha, I remember I was so anxious at that time that on one occasion I actually wrote to Muriel and suggested that maybe sex was not really the best thing possible, and that perhaps we could have a platonic marriage. Anyway, fortunately for us she had this doctor friend that she went and saw, and he said something to the effect of, don't worry, he'll get over it. Well, that was true. It was my marriage in the end that brought some sort of normality to my life in that respect. Certainly it made me think about my parents—my upbringing—and the profound effects those experiences had had on my life. My marriage, you might say, began a process, and certainly now, looking back, I can see the many changes that have taken place in my life—so many changes. It would seem I have undergone what can only be described as a metamorphosis, an experience from which I have gained a fundamental belief. It is simply this—that while our beginnings are very powerful, they are not beyond the possibility of changing radically. So much so, I feel, that to look at my own life now—looking, as it were, through the eyes of my father—there is much I think he would not recognise.

JOHN AND MURIEL MORRISON

193

How do you get an attraction for a person? I don't know; it is, I should say, a mysterious thing. We did have things in common, John and I—we both of us had deep ideas in common. There was tremendous concern for peace and justice, we were strongly opposed to war and fighting—oh yes, there were a lot of things. A mutuality of interests, but goodness me, isn't that true of everyone. So, I don't know.

There did come a time of course when I became clear about the way I felt. It was, I imagine, an awareness which grew through those times of being together, of talking with each other. A feeling that from what we could see of each other, we were headed in the same direction. That our lives were in some way parallel. Yes, that was a great bond. Of course we didn't know any of the real things about relationships, we didn't know anything about the difficulties. Remember, I'm talking about forty going on fifty years ago. We didn't know anything about growing together, or openness, or any of those things. We didn't understand that at all.

John tells me there was a time at the pictures one night when he looked along a row and I smiled at him. Well, I had known him a while then and I was quite clearly fond of him, but there was an interesting thing happened after that. We lived on Scarborough Hill in those days, at Sumner, and there was a friend there we were helping one day with his land. John and he were attempting to shift this great rock, and they set it pelting down the hill. It was headed straight for old Flower's house. He was a house master at Christ College, I think—the man with a face like a happy potato, our friend always called him. Anyway, what a disaster, and John leapt down the hill to try and intercept it. Well, somehow it stopped of its own accord, but in the process John hurt his ankle, and that meant that he had to reside at our place for a while. Well, naturally we saw quite a lot of each other . . . I think we came together then . . . yes, that was an important time.

Of course, before that we had done a lot of things together. We

JOHN AND MURIEL MORRISON

194

had walked on the hill together and sat by the fire at night. Quite clearly there was a feeling between us. And I did wonder—you know, I would sort of say to myself—will he ever say anything? Well, no, he didn't. Never mind, I didn't feel broken-hearted or anything, probably I was quietly confident. But that was the thing that did it alright. Yes, after he hurt his ankle—ha, it seemed to me that things came on then. Yes, quite quaint.

Actually he wrote me a letter—it was not long after that. It could have meant anything or nothing. Well, I understood that. I also protected myself. I did it all the time by saying no, it won't happen, it will never happen—this alongside my other feelings, which were quite different of course. I expect we all protect ourselves—well, it can be a pretty devastating thing, this falling in love business. Before I met John I had fallen passionately in love with someone else, a chap I had known who was a lovely person. I'd had a good companionship with him and I thought he was

JOHN AND MURIEL MORRISON

195

beautiful, but nothing happened. Well, thank God—now I think we would have been totally unsuitable. But you see, I knew then what it was to love somebody and suddenly to feel that life was dust and ashes. Anyway, that didn't stop me from feeling very happy when I read John's letter. "My heart did leap for joy"—I'm quoting George Fox, but that is how it felt. I went straight to him, and I just said, "Yes, yes John, I do love you." Or something like that. I don't remember the exact words, but it was something very simple. It didn't take much saying.

Strangely enough, the time between then and when we were married was not all that easy. It was a hard time for both of us, due, I should say, to a kind of deprivation in our childhood. Actually we weren't that unusual; it was, I think, the kind of thing that happened to most young people in our time. But it made it harder to get towards a real relating. It had to be done gradually. I know that before my marriage there were all these doubts and difficulties—am I doing the right thing? All was uncertain. Is John really the kind of person I think he is? It was quite agonising really, going ahead with it. But then in the end being clear, coming out of that and feeling quite clear about it before we did get married.

JOHN

THERE WAS my marriage, my wife's acceptance of me, which had a profound effect on my life—for the good. And then there was also my marriage beset with difficulties, in that I knew nothing about human relationships at all. So there was struggle. There never was any sense of breaking up, we weathered it, but yes, there was struggle.

When I was young, in the early days of marriage, there were times when things were marvellous. When Muriel had a serenity about her and a grace about her that I thoroughly enjoyed. But she wasn't always like that. And I . . . how callow I was . . . I would say things to her. "If only you were always like this." And it was true, I wanted more than anything else for her never to get cross. Always to be that calm, serene, confident person. What a disaster.

JOHN AND MURIEL MORRISON

I suppose I learned through bitter experience, you can't do that. It is in the nature of things to have change. Rough patches, smooth patches, that is the way of things.

There is no question that my perception of Muriel changed radically at that time. There had been this idealistic image which I had held on to, but now I was puzzled and bewildered that she was somehow different as well. Moving forward into more recent times, I have perhaps—through work and reading—gained more of an insight into our relationship at that time. This idea of the difference between men and women, where by and large men tend to be preoccupied with their own kind of development, their own career, the relationship becoming very much a secondary matter. Well, looking back from here I can see that that was how it was for me. As far as I was concerned, it was the way things were, and it just never occurred to me that there was any other way of being. The result of that, the images that form in my mind from

JOHN AND MURIEL MORRISON

that time, are most of all personal ones. Thoughts of myself rather than the relationship so much. It shows me, of course, just how oblivious I was to the way things were for Muriel.

That my memory of our relationship in that time can be so dim must, I suppose, signify something. And yet there was also, in many ways, a closeness. A togetherness in terms of religious associations, in our conviction of pacifist ideals, of our work for the Labour Party, and so on. In all these things there can be no question of a strong union by way of our social values. Certainly there was never the feeling of my marriage having been a mistake. But of the things that made it hard for us at that time—the pre-occupation with myself—a large part of that I now understand as a dependence on Muriel.

At the time we were married, I was a jobbing electrician and I was also starting to get involved in radio repairs. Radio was in its fairly early stages then, and I had this shed out the back where I was trying to teach myself something about it. All this required a great deal of time and attention, and sometimes I would get completely wrapped up in something I was doing and not come in for meals at all. I can remember the night Muriel challenged me about it. I remember her telling me, making it very clear, that she could not or would not tolerate this. There was a realisation then of the value of the relationship to me—enough to give it up, to stop the work—and also there was the knowledge of having to consider someone else, and that was hard. It took me a long time to really understand that. You see, my mother had waited on me hand and foot, she had done everything, and like other men, I had grown up with the idea that that was the role of women in relationships. That was what they did.

MY MOTHER fulfilled the typical patriarchal counter-role of the time. My father was the head of the household; she was responsible for the house itself and the children. There was never a question of any revolt. Never. She wasn't the kind of person to take a stand against my father. Her effect on me, however, was fairly profound.

JOHN AND MURIEL MORRISON

To some degree she made me in her own image. She did it in all sorts of ways. My father was musical, my mother thought she wasn't. And whenever I tried to whistle or anything like that, she'd say, oh, you're just like your mother, tone deaf. And I would believe her. Somehow her anxiety was always transmitted to me. For as long as I can remember, she had stomach troubles, and I had stomach troubles too, which, interestingly enough, disappeared when I was married. And there was her anxiety about the future. I was always reluctant to take steps away from the home—I did do it—but never without considerable apprehension. You know, it seems to me now that all the memories of my childhood—the ones that stand out, at least—amount to an experience that involved a great deal of fear and humiliation. Extraordinary really, how the mind continues to contain them so vividly.

Toowoomba, in Australia, where I was born—that, I think, is the earliest memory. I am in a very small room in a cottage. There is my mother and some aunts, and there is my grandmother sitting in a chair dressed in black. Long black satin dresses. And there is a little cousin, perhaps a bit younger than me. He is playing a game, toddling around, putting down and picking up a toy pig from my grandmother's lap. And then, when he is behind my grandmother, when he cannot see, I go and I take the pig away. And what I remember most is being remonstrated with by my mother—the humiliation of that—and how I kind of crept back to my mother's side and stuck my head down there. I could have been eighteen months or perhaps two years old, and that was my first memory. It left a very powerful imprint. And there are many others. On a picnic with my parents in the pony and trap. Travelling along a country road and seeing an animal strung between two poles, just slaughtered, and the man who has done this walking away from the carcass carrying entrails across his arm. Things that were bewildering, things that frightened me. A friendly dog snarling at me because it had pups. Our horse rearing up in front of me and kicking out its front legs. And on the ship coming out to New Zealand, when I was about four, one of the passengers, a man, playing with me quite happily, quite friendly, and then suddenly picking me up and hanging me over the side of the ship. I was absolutely terrified.

So, those were the types of feelings from my early childhood that remain with me, and by and large it continued that way. Always there was that expectation of catastrophe, so much so that I learned to avoid encounters when I could or shrink into myself when I could not. Given that sort of history, it is not surprising that there was a constant sense of loneliness and utter inadequacy. Like my mother, I just felt no good. She never, as I knew her, felt good. There was a sense of worthlessness that she carried to the grave. Even so, for me she was a centre point. She always looked after me. Sparse in demonstration, she was at least secure to me in a material way. Everything that needed doing, she did.

JOHN AND MURIEL MORRISON

200

THE FIRST MEAL that Muriel made for me was very important to her. The whole idea of the presentation of the first meal. And in this meal were some parsnips which were quite dry, they were not that good, and I said this to her—I made all these comments about how bad they were. Well, she was very hurt. She had gone to a great deal of trouble to make it a special meal for us.

You see, I came into my marriage with a deep sense of inferiority, and I can still remember my utter amazement at the time that somebody with her competence should at all be interested in me. Later I realised there was a kind of compensatory reaching out for somebody that I saw as so superior. It wasn't long, of course, before I was taking every opportunity I could to show my own superiority. Unconsciously I began to undermine Muriel in all sorts of ways, and there were also my expectations, wishes to be met when I wanted them. And if she dug in her heels at times, I would get very fed up. Gosh, you know, I can see it so clearly now. What a pig I was. Muriel's parents came to tea with us one night. I was keen on experimenting with food at the time, and I asked her to make some potato bread rolls. Oh dear, it was terrible, they came out as hard as boards, and this is what I did—at tea, I dropped one on the floor and I said to Muriel's parents, "This is what Muriel's cooking is like." Well, how thick can you get? And she let me know about it that time. When they had gone she was very, very angry. But you know, these kind of stabs in situations like that were a very frequent occurrence with me. And later, after we left Christchurch and went to Auckland, it happened often. Even in public—well, semi-public—situations. Even then I would take advantage of her—fault finding. And there, in that way, was my father. He was a fault finder par excellence. To be fair, I think from his point of view he wanted me to do it right, whereas my own fault finding was probably a kind of ego boost more than anything. I can see what is wrong with you—so therefore I am better than you.

JOHN AND MURIEL MORRISON

My father married my mother when he was about forty. She would have been perhaps ten years younger than him. He had come from an affluent Yorkshire family—big cartage contractors and also a fertilizer company—in Newcastle upon Tyne. He was one of ten children and probably the most rebellious. By the time he was nineteen he had started to wander all over the world. He worked on the construction of telephone communications across Canada, and he was in one of the gold rushes to Alaska. He was in the army in Malta for a time, and then he moved down to the Pacific, where he worked a while on the coastal ships around New Zealand. It wasn't till he got to Australia that he met my mother. He was working for the Toowoomba Electric Light Company then, as an engineer, and he went to board with my grandmother. My mother was a complete contrast. Where he was from this upper-middle-class family and worldly-wise, she was by comparison timid, quiet, retiring . . . and also an attractive-looking woman, I think. Her background was non-intellectual—working class, I suppose you'd say—certainly culturally it was very different from my father's. But anyhow, that was the nature of my father. Restless, competent in a large way, and yet very one-eyed about many things.

It was strange, in spite of the fact that he thought a lot, read a lot—was in some ways a radical—he was still, in the very core of his being, part of the ethos from which he came. That is to say, Victorian. Mostly he was kind in his behaviour towards other people—especially to women, he was courteous and respect-ful. There was never any intimation that he played around with women, even before he was married, and certainly there was no sign of that whatsoever during my childhood. In fact he was ex-tremely . . . I can't think of the word . . . hostile—no, it was more than hostile—when he discussed what he called "womaniz-ers." And there was also a strong hatred of men who did "that," by which of course he meant homosexuals. Later on, when I was older, he used to comment on things that had happened, and the intensity of it, the hatred . . . so now I would think he was a very repressed man. Yes, the intensity of it all would seem to indicate that. As far as affection was concerned, any demonstration of affec-tion at all, that was certainly repressed. What emerged from both my parents was a non-touching, non-sexual, relationship. And the significance of that on my own particular development was quite profound.

JOHN AND MURIEL MORRISON

I was an only child until the age of eleven, when my sister was born. Even at that age I had absolutely no idea of how she came to be. There were perhaps some very subtle kinds of implications from my father, none of which I had any way of understanding at the time. My education in that regard—my sexual education—was nil. Even when still in my cot, about four years old, I suppose, I can remember him saying, "Stop it, stop doing that," and being totally bewildered. But subsequently realising what he was on about. And then later, when we used to go for walks together, I used to saunter along—you can imagine a six- or seven-year-old or whatever I was—sauntering along with my hands in my pockets. That was how young fellows got about. And him, "Take your hands out of your pockets!" And I, at the time, didn't know the connection. But I realised afterwards, the subliminal communication . . . no sex. A complete denial of the whole thing. No sign at all except for this repressive thing. I mean, I presume there must have been something behind the doors—he used to lock the door of their bedroom—but I never attached anything to it then. You know, I never saw him cuddle my mother, I'm not sure that I ever saw him kiss her. Perhaps he may have kissed her goodbye in the mornings. But the other sort of thing—no, there was an absence of that.

There was one incident that I recall vividly that showed some connection between me and my mother. It was a time when my mother was very ill, what they called then "poorly." I was quite young at the time, and it was very disturbing to me. The bewilderment I had standing beside the bed and watching her lying there so white-faced. I must have had a strong attachment to her. And then I remember my father coming home from work and wanting his hammer for something, asking where his hammer was, and getting cross about it. And so I said, "Mummy let me have it," at which point he turned and I think just pretended to growl at her. Well, I flew at him. Now, that was unusual for me, very unusual to ever show him hostility like that because he ruled by the strap. A razor strop hung beside the fireplace, and that was a threat I

lived under at all times. He could be irritable, you see, especially in his later years when he was not liking his job. He'd come home dead tired and go to sleep, and if I bumped his chair he'd be up in the air, and boy, did I get it—severely. I can remember saying to my mother one time, "I hate him." And her saying, "Oh, you mustn't say that about your father." That, I suppose, was the kind of loyalty she had for him. But anyway, that time I went for him, that memory of my mother, it's the only kind of memory I really

JOHN AND MURIEL MORRISON

have of a strong attachment to her. Did she ever nurse me, cuddle me? I don't know. I can't remember it. And certainly my father, never . . . never at all. Later, as a young man, I began to realise that I did mean something to him. Perhaps it was because I had become fairly competent in what I was doing. I had achieved some things. But there was never . . . this really hurt in later life . . . I can never ever remember him sitting me on his knee and saying, I love you. No, to do that would have been completely foreign to him.

There was only twice in my life that I ever saw my father cry. When my grandfather died he wept. He just came home and put his head on the table and he wept. And then there was my mother. She died when she was about seventy, and my father would have been eighty. She had Parkinson's disease—it took ten years—and he nursed her. Without question he nursed her, he did it until he was eighty, and then about a fortnight before she died, he just

couldn't manage any more. She had to go into hospital, and that's what broke him. That's when I saw him cry again. I still feel about when she died. When he and I went to see her in the undertaker's chapel . . . ah gosh, I feel about it. I remember how he looked down at her . . . he said, "Lovely lady." It was the first time . . . the first indication that underneath he really cared. That was the first time I'd heard it. It was a most powerful thing.

MURIEL

LOTS OF THE GIRLS, they talked all the time about boys. Naturally it was all terribly mild and harmless compared with how kids are today, but I used to think it was such rubbish. I'd say to myself, I don't need that, I'm not interested. But then inside of course I had the same deep longings that everybody has. I should say I was incredibly naive, incredibly ill-informed, and incredibly inhibited.

JOHN AND MURIEL MORRISON

Yes, I should say all of that. Growing up with three sisters, you
see, having a father who was quite inhibited—all these things, I
suppose, made it difficult for me. It was always easy getting to
know girls, no trouble at all, but, you see, I had no practice in
the other.

Later I can remember coming home from a Saturday night
hop, or the university hop perhaps, coming home with some
young fellow who would hold my arm, put his arm through mine,
something of that nature. Quite mild. But I would be acutely em-

barrassed. I remember getting to the gate one night with a chap and him saying, "I don't know your name and you don't know mine." I was terrified. I said, "I don't think it matters, does it?" and rushed up the path. Well, I mean, I was so emphatic, it would have been very off-putting for any poor fellow trying to get near me.

When did I get to the point where that actually changed? I can't remember. Probably by the time I'd got my degree. I wonder—certainly by the time I came back from teachers college. I should say I was mostly out of it by then. Yes, I can remember I got into a way of looking every place I went to, saying to myself, is there anyone here I could be interested in? A man that I would like to be my friend. I always looked around. I must have been about twenty-four, quite mature. Well, you see, it wasn't till I was about twenty-six that I met John. We became friends then, but we weren't married until I was twenty-eight. And boy, we had a great old struggle then. I mean, we both did. It was a struggle through all kinds of layers of . . . of what? Stuff from our childhood I suppose, both of us. To go from there to this, the wonderful open place we have got to—but not immediately. The beginning was difficult. Oh yes. Lots of uncertainties to start with, for me, and a great deal of agony. Is this the right thing for me to do? Do I really love John? What is the best thing? Really wrestling with this terrible uncertainty—which was all to do, I think, with a kind of inhibiting restrictive feeling. A pushing of me towards something. A kind of chaining to the female world of the time, perhaps. I don't know. Yet I knew this. I wanted a partner. I was quite determined to have some man I would love—and be loved by. That was the thing that held me through all sorts of doubts. Extraordinary how a thing like that can happen without any guidance. We were given nothing. No advice, no counsel, not a single thing. Remarkable. Out of the abyss the human creature finds its incredible way. Quite remarkable.

It was a good wedding. I can still see it very clearly, the meeting house and all the friends who go to meeting. All our very good friends in that little room. It's no longer there now, all pulled down. I came with my father and then sat beside John, and the whole meeting sat in silence. I can remember fussing about my hat—I'd decided in the end on a brown suit and a brown hat. Looking back it was a pretty awful hat—I couldn't find a decent hat. My mother had made a sort of canary-coloured blouse for me, which I thought was lovely, but you know, there was none of the usual bridal stuff. Anyhow, we sat there together in the room, and at some suitable time we stood up and held hands. Then John said, "I take this my friend, Muriel Ockenden, to be my loving and faithful wife, and to be unto her, by divine assistance, a loving and faithful husband, as long as we both on earth shall live." Something like that. And I said very similar. "I take this my friend, John Morrison, to be my loving husband," and so on. We did that standing together and holding hands, which was nice, then we sat down. That's how it's done at Quaker weddings. And then after we had sat in silence for a while, people spoke. Perhaps with a prayer or a loving thought, or maybe even a little bit of good advice. When the meeting was over we signed the register, and then everybody there signed our wedding certificate. It was beautifully written in copperplate with the words we had said at the top. My parents and John's parents and all those dear friends signed it that day—it was very special. We had afternoon tea then—no fuss, no fuss, we'd said, just sandwiches and whatnot. I don't think we had a wedding cake—no, I don't think so. Then after it was all over we went back to the little house we had bought. A quaint little place it was, in Cuffs Road, on the way to Brighton. We'd had working bees on it before our wedding—my father was a builder, and John's father was very useful—and we'd painted it up and done lots of little things to it. Quite a big piece of land went with it as well. There was a bit of wilderness around us in those days.

Our honeymoon started early the next day. We put our bicycles and packs and things on the West Coast train and off we went. We had a wonderful time, cycling and walking and seeing old friends—oh yes, it was a really wonderful honeymoon. And

JOHN AND MURIEL MORRISON

then when it was over we caught the train back home to the reality of our married life.

We were not to have long in that house together, about eighteen months in all, I think, but I have memories still of our time there. Working in the garden, our friends coming to see us, John chopping down the bush . . . of playing the piano. But mostly I remember the shock of discovering that we weren't what we thought we were. That John wasn't what I thought he was, and that I wasn't what he thought I was. There was the discovering of reality. Of having to get used to one another in a hundred different ways. They were harrowing times. Of course we also had happy times—I'm just talking about the reality of it, when we sometimes got irritated and angry. Certainly it was not always perfect bliss.

The important thing for me in our relationship today is the place we have got to now. I might have married somebody else, and it wouldn't have happened at all. They might have been lovely men, and yet it still might not have happened. The fact that John and I have been able to grow together as we have, that is the important thing. And when you think of how we started in such an unpromising place, both so narrow in our conceptions—well, perhaps not too narrow, but still we thought we knew things, the way all young people do. Goodness me, when I think then of our inability to be ourselves, to communicate with each other and of our very deep inhibitions, we were . . . well, I suppose we were children of our times.

It was extraordinary really. Had it not been for an older teaching friend telling me a few things, I would have gone into marriage completely ignorant. My parents told me nothing at all of relating, of sex. They couldn't, just couldn't. Distressing really to think two people can be set together like that with no understanding at all in terms of any real relating. That their only knowledge might be the ridiculous ideas we pick up out of the air—books and films, I suppose. Stories of the great wonderful male who performs and has an orgasm, and the woman has one too, and it's all perfectly timed and everything is beautiful. And of course if that doesn't happen, you're both dead failures kind of thing. Well, that can be a great blight. Definitely it was a shadow on my life at that time, the fact that I didn't enjoy this part as much as I should have. You terrible woman, you terrible failure, your poor husband having to put up with you kind of thing. Obviously this troubled me when we were in bed together; whether it troubled my waking hours . . . probably it did. I'm thinking now of when we were first married, the first year maybe. If it worried me then it would have been guilt, that I was not as keen on sex as I should have been. Not as keen as a "natural" woman should be. Of course there is no such woman, but this was the sort of idea in my mind. The sort of burden I placed on myself for quite some time until John and I worked it out, worked through it together. We began to find that the more we were able to talk about these things, the more we were able to rid ourselves of all the false concepts we seemed to be carrying. The exaggerated sense of importance I had placed on the idea that I was not "performing" properly. The idea that John, poor fellow, was being in some way deprived—all this type of nonsense. But eventually John got it very clear to me that he never wanted me doing anything I didn't feel perfectly comfortable with. At ease with. We began to learn then—and much more in later life—that things like orgasm were just a small part of sex and that there was a great deal more to it than that. The idea of working out what was important for the two people concerned, sensitively doing for each other what is most rewarding at the time. Making allowances for each other and having no expectation of performance, that is the thing. Of course, one of the most important parts for me was the tenderness that followed, and you don't necessarily need sex to have that. Yes, that's something you discover later on. Yes . . . anyway, that was the kind of thing we had to struggle through and out of. A difficult time. Ha, reminds me of that terrible advice, "Lie back and think of England." Well, thank God things are at least a little better these days, and there's a lot of women who aren't going to do that any more.

As well as togetherness, of course, it is also important to have

JOHN AND MURIEL MORRISON

213

some sort of space between you. Rilke, the German poet, says something like, "We must learn to love the infinite distance between us so that we can see each other clear against the sky." The idea that growth happens in the space between you. And if there isn't any space, if we squash that space out with things like jealousy or possessiveness, then I don't think we grow at all. How long does it take to grow into some awareness, some knowing of each other—I don't know. A long time, is all I can say. There are young people today who say it's good to live together first, to find out about the other person. But I would say you don't find out. You don't know until you're stuck together. Perhaps in five years you start to know something. In ten years you're getting on. And maybe by thirty years you've started to get somewhere. Relation-

JOHN AND MURIEL MORRISON

ships, I think, are a great deal about maturing. You know, there was a lovely piece in a novel that John and I once read. I can't remember the name of the novel or the phrase exactly, but it was something like, "You were a good growing ground for me." And that was an idea we both liked very much. To be a good growing ground, each for the other. That I think is what we have tried to do.

JOHN

I AM A PACIFIST. And before the war—this would be about 1935–36—I was a very vocal pacifist. I was working then for the Municipal Electricity Department, and although by and large I was pretty conformist—believing then in the authority of the firm and all that—still, I would not hesitate in arguing the pacifist point of view with anybody. I was very much a part of the anti-war movement, and I believed totally that war would not happen. When it did, when it happened, I lived in a kind of blackness. A black cloud, as if the sun had gone out. I won't forget how that felt. It was, I realise now, depression of a high order.

I applied for conscientious objector status and it was granted. One or two others from work applied as well, and they got a bad time—I think because they had not revealed themselves before—but they said, "Oh, John, we know where he is," and there was no trouble for me at all. I stayed on working at the department, and later, when I got married, they even gave me a wedding present. It was a time then when people were "manpowered"—compelled by the government to stay where you were. Or you could be placed elsewhere, made to work somewhere else if they wanted you to. The crisis for me came some time later when they started to call up men with one child. There was a chap in the testing room, quite a competent engineer, who had one child—Ted, I think his name was. And they came to me and said they wanted me to take over his job, that he was being called up. Well, I thought, hell, I can't do that. I went home and talked it over with Muriel, and I thought, I just can't do that. To take this man's job is not something that I could live with. I sweated on it for a few days and then finally I sent in a letter of resignation with what I thought was the sure knowledge that they would pick me up, and that I would be put in prison for it. Well, I was prepared for that. It was not new to me; most of my friends were in prison anyway. Still, it was for me a profound experience in that for the first time I was prepared to do something, to go to prison, for my conscience.

I was called then to face the tribunal. When I appeared before them, and to my utter surprise, I discovered that the manager for whom I worked, and with whom I had many times argued my point, had sent them a letter. He told them that while he did not agree with my stand, he nevertheless believed that I was utterly sincere in my belief. They must have asked him, you see, and that is what he said. And on the basis of this they gave me an exemption, provided I was willing to continue working in the city doing electrical repairs. It was all a big anti-climax in a way. Anyway, after about a year of this, puddling about on a bicycle doing repairs, I started to get very uncomfortable. Well, here were all these chaps going overseas, and others, my friends, in prison, while I was doing no more than odd jobs. Then one day, out of the blue really, something happened to change it all. We heard of a hostel in Auckland for psychiatrically disturbed children wanting help. And when we wrote to them we received a letter straight back asking if we would accept a position as master and matron of this place. The pay for the two of us was only ten pounds a month, but that didn't worry us. Of course we had to apply to the tribunal, but I made my case that I was only doing odd jobs, and here instead was work of some importance. Well, they must have had some feeling for this because I was given permission to go. And so that is what we did—we went up to Auckland and took this job on.

The first night—fifteen disturbed kids—the old master and matron walked out and we walked in. Ha! I was just thinking of the resilience of youth. We took this job on with very little experience. I mean, we were not completely unused to youngsters, but by gum, we were unused to these kids. We had so little psychological know-how and the job was demanding to the nth degree. Particularly with our idealism. You see, we had a sense that in caring for these kids, you gave your all, you gave everything. We sweated and slaved for those kids because we thought it was the right thing to do. I thought then that it was right that you suffered for the kids that couldn't help themselves. I remember some of the things we tolerated, like a youngster hitting me on the head with a drawer she'd pulled out of a chest, and I stood it for as long as I could. I stood it until finally it became so painful I had to stop it. But that then was what I expected I should do. That was the kind of thing that was happening. Looking back, I see a lack of understanding on my part of what human relationships were all about. Really it had little to do with love; it was more a way of thinking. I did the things I thought I should be doing. Anyhow, we survived. It was two of the toughest years I've ever spent in my life, but somehow we survived it. Hell, I even had another run-in with the tribunal. They picked me up and said that they wanted more electricians, but I told them, I said, "I'm not going to do this; I have got a job here that I am determined to do." "Well," they said, "you will be made to." "In that case," I said, "I am prepared to go to prison." Of course they knew damned well they didn't want me in prison, and in the end they let me get on with it.

I suppose it would also be true to say that our time in Auckland, at least as far as our relationship was concerned, was one of our most difficult and unhappy times together. With hindsight, of course, it's easy to see why it was so grim. The demands of the youngsters were massive, and we just became emotionally exhausted. The effect was not good at all. Fortunately one of the things we did have was some very good psychotherapy as a support for the work we were doing. That was very helpful and a growth experience for us both, I think. Even so, I was still at that time in the business of undermining Muriel, still there was that unconscious inferiority and the seizing of opportunities to right the balance. It was terrible. We'd go somewhere, visiting friends somewhere, and some conversation might take place that would

reveal a weakness of some sort, and oh, I'd be in like a shot. Then we'd come home and Muriel would say, "John, why do you do that?" And all I could answer was, "I don't know." And it was true; I did not know. Afterwards I would always feel distressed that I had done it, but that did not stop it. It was a thing that happened frequently.

The happy moments, at least for me, happened mostly in our time away from the place. Getting away, the long weekend off— those were the times. We'd practically run down the driveway,

JOHN AND MURIEL MORRISON

elated just to be on our own. Oh yes, that was good. Then, first thing, we'd head for a cake shop. We'd buy the biggest custard pie concoction with a sort of creamy blancmange—lots of sugar—and we would take this thing, cycle somewhere with it, and then we'd stop and split it in two and eat it. It was absolute delight. In a way it was a sort of ritual, part of the getting away from the place. After that we'd cycle out to one of my uncles at Bucklands Beach, or sometimes we'd go down and catch the ferry to Waiheke Island, where a friend used to lend us a cottage. That was really enjoyable there; being right away from the tension of the work, we were able to relate and enjoy each other. Living in the hostel I can't remember us having much time at all . . . not for each other. No, it was only really in the moments away that we had real time for one another. Pretty precious that time was. They were the happy moments, a contrast and a relief to what was in reality an arduous time.

From the beginning, physically and mentally, we both worked extremely hard. I had swotted up on what psychology I could at the time. We studied the children and tried to get into some sort of effective treatment with them, but after a couple of years there was the realisation that I was just not competent in what I was trying to do. I see that realisation now as the beginning of a profound change in my existence. This was at the end of the war, and there was nothing in New Zealand at that time for the training of people working with disturbed children. There was, however, a school of social work at Sydney University, which I applied for, and they accepted me. That was wonderful, but the thing was then to get there. The war had been over for a year by then, but people were still complaining about conchies like me being allowed out of the country to do such things. I think the manpower regulations were still operating at that time, but as far as registered conscientious objectors were concerned, anyway, there were limitations—school teaching and things like that were not allowed. There was a "can't let them get away with it" sort of attitude. I mean, during the war all sorts of silly things were raised, like should I as a CO be allowed membership in the St. John's Ambulance Service. Well, it went on, you see, not only through the war but after as well. Eventually, after an interview with McLagan, who was Minister of Labour at the time, I was given the okay. I got permission to go, and we went as soon as we could.

MURIEL

THERE IS A MEMORY from my school days, a sad memory, and something which at the time really hurt me. We had a headmaster, a man who is best forgotten, whom indeed shall be forgotten. A dreadful person who did a lot of strapping. And there was a boy, a boy in my class, who wasn't very bright and who one day was sent to this headmaster. His crime was to have written the heading for his homework in big letters. He simply wrote this thing in great big letters, and it took up a number of lines at the top of the page. I thought it looked quite nice, but for this he was sent to the head-master and he was strapped. Well, a bit later I saw this boy in the playground—I'd been sent on a message or something—and I saw this little boy leaning against the wall crying, crying, his hands held to him and crying. It pierced my heart. I've never forgotten that. That a child could be thus treated. When I think of it I feel terrible still. Yes, that kind of thing distressed me beyond words. I was always sensitive to it, I always used to worry about the people in the world who were suffering. We heard quite a lot about this sort of thing at the socialist Sunday school my parents sent me to, and I can remember thinking, just to myself, that one day I would go and see the King and tell him. You know, that something must be done. There was always this kind of concern.

Later on, as an adult, when the war came, there were these same sorts of feelings. John had had his appeal as a CO allowed—he'd given up his job at the department in the hope that another man could stay, but he was still working here in Christchurch doing odd electrical jobs. And so, you see, we were still together, secure. Well, I had a conscience about this. I was probably over-influenced by Ormand Burton, but, I mean, here were people we knew locked up in detention camps, in prisons, and also there were

JOHN AND MURIEL MORRISON

people dying while we were living comfortably. While we were safe. And so we had to ask ourselves, what can we do? What is the thing we can offer? Then one morning at a Quaker meeting we met a friend who had just come back from Auckland. Over lunch she told us about this man who had set up a special school and hostel for maladjusted children. She talked to us about what he was doing and how exciting it was. And afterwards we said to ourselves, perhaps that is what we could do, perhaps we could help him. So we wrote to him and a letter came back straight away:

JOHN AND MURIEL MORRISON

Why do you live so far away? Come immediately. So we did. We put a lot of our things in storage, and we went to Auckland.

Now in Auckland it was very demanding. In a way it drew us more closely together and made us more dependent on one another. We lived there in this little room, and I can remember one of the children—she could jump up high enough to see through our door—and she said, "I saw Mrs. Morrison go in and throw herself into Mr. Morrison's arms." Great fun and achievement. She saw this wonderful happening, ha! Well yes, it was quite nice, but Auckland was also a time of greater stress and, I think because of that, sharper antagonisms. There were times there when I gave myself all sorts of heartbreaks. They weren't necessary of course, but I had them just the same. Oh yes, getting insanely jealous one time, I remember that. Having to go back to Christchurch for an operation—being away for some time—and when I came back finding there was a girl that John seemed to be very fond of. He *was* quite fond of her, but he wasn't—well, he wasn't really attached to her at all. And I looked at them and I just got insanely jealous. Now, that was quite stupid, but it happened, and I suppose it does with a lot of people. I remember once too it was John's birthday and I had made him a cake—I think a chocolate cake. We were going to have it for supper—we had our other meals with the children—and as it happened some visitors came, and John was very absorbed in talking to this chap. He was really thoroughly involved, and they went on talking, and he didn't even notice that I had made him this chocolate cake. I was heartbroken. Well, we talked about that of course. Not immediately perhaps, but quite soon after. We knew what had happened. And that was, I think, typical of us. That he has loved these intellectual exchanges—they're tremendously valuable to him. He likes to think his way clearly through so many things, and I don't. I am much more of a heart person, I feel my way around, I don't want to talk endlessly. A certain amount, yes, but there is a very different approach. Perhaps it is characteristic of women and men, that—some basic difference, I don't know. But, as I say, during our time in Auckland, the strain in many ways was considerable.

Interestingly enough, it was because of the difficulty and distress we had there that a few doors began to open in our lives. There was a time there when I had begun to cry a lot, and the chap we worked for said that we both should have the sort of support we needed in a job like this. Well, there was a very lovely psychiatrist, Doctor Burrel, and he had a wonderful assistant, Miss Gow. And John and I went to see them every week for some time. I suppose it was very like having psychotherapy. I talked a great deal, and she noted things and talked to me. I don't think I saw myself properly, but yes, lights did begin to shine on my life, and, ha, what a strange person I was. Well, I was, you know, tied up in a sense.

It's funny, I have a photograph of me as a child, a plump child sitting in front of a wheelbarrow. I am about six months old, I suppose, and absolutely bursting with life and energy. A child you might say, absolutely determined to make her mark upon the world. Yes, it's a funny picture but I quite like it. I have a memory too. I am standing on a table—the kitchen table—and I am thinking that I will fly. It must be one of my very earliest memories. Then, strangely, as I got a little older, a sort of anxiety starts to creep in. Things happening, I remember, that seemed to cause me extreme embarrassment. Like my teacher, who was the infant mistress, sending me to another class—we were singing and she wanted another child. And me standing there in front of this teacher, "Please, Miss So and So, . . . please . . ." Standing there stammering and not being able to get it out. Struggling at a sentence which would ask for this child to be sent. And then in the end the infant mistress herself coming to see what was the matter. Why it happened, why it became difficult for me to ask for things, to express myself, why I should have become so hedged in by that sort of anxiety, I don't know. I was never frightened of my parents. I was never whacked, as far as I can remember. It was quite enough for my father to get cross with me, that hurt quite enough, so nothing else was needed. There was this thing of course that children of my time were much less communicative. You just did not talk about anything to do with your feelings, or anything that mattered, not with your parents or your siblings. Well, I might with one of my older sisters. Sometimes we'd have a bath together and we'd sit with our heads at each end and talk and talk. But mostly . . . yes, mostly I should say I kept my feelings and thoughts and my deep longings to myself. And I should say that that was characteristic of a good deal of my life. Yes, until I really grew up.

All in all, my family life was what I would call a secure place. There was love, but not much of what you would term affection. No, I should have to say that affection was just not expressed. It was, I think, my father mostly—he was very inhibited. Oh, there must have been some of it sometimes, but not much. Not that I can remember. An awareness of this came to me more strongly when I was older—I suppose I was about fourteen—a time when my older sister and I were staying with a friend, the way you do sometimes, just for the weekend. And her mother, whom I liked very much—a very gracious woman—went out. Well, while she was out we all got to and did the dishes. And when she came back she saw what we had done and gave us all a big hug, and she said, "Oh, you darlings, how lovely of you." And suddenly I had this pang in my heart—if only that could happen with my mother and me.

But you see, my parents were never affectionate, not even to each other. Well, perhaps they were a little later in life, but by then of course the pattern was set. What we did have, though, was a very strong family, a family very much together. It still is today, even though both our parents are gone. There has always been a sense of belonging—I knew where I belonged, and I was very attached. I think that is where the strength came from. Definitely, yes—I hated to be away from my family. I can remember being agonisingly homesick when my youngest sister was born

and we were sent to stay with friends. I never told anyone—it never entered my head that you could. I just cried a bit whenever I could hide away from everyone. I would never show it. Oh no, that sort of thing was not part of my life, and if you live in a world where a certain thing is not done, then you don't do it. But the belonging was there, you see.

Anyway, that was my childhood. I have of course long ago

JOHN AND MURIEL MORRISON

learned to show emotion and have people whom I've loved and hugged. I suppose John and I opened that world up for ourselves. It was important for us that we each of us did it in our own way. But you know, I've also learnt to appreciate that a sense of belonging is not necessarily measured by the showing of emotion. That one can be strong without the other. Anyway, to get back to our time in Auckland, the good thing was that with the help of these two marvellous people, Doctor Burrel and Miss Gow, we were both of us in that place of gaining new insights which were really invaluable. Well, we appreciated that, and we worked jolly hard at it.

JOHN

WE WENT to Sydney and I went to the university. That was the purpose of going, to get some sort of training and qualification. But there was also a course in speech therapy with a qualification which Muriel wanted to do. It was something she had all the background for, but blow me if we'd only been there a month when they moved the course to Melbourne. Muriel was then faced with the question of going to Melbourne or staying in Sydney, and somehow it seemed that it would be too much . . . well, I don't know, I doubt whether I could have stood it, and maybe she couldn't either. And so in a sense she missed out on establishing herself professionally—although of course she was a schoolteacher and all the rest of it. Still, it was a thing of mutual regret. In the end she went to work at a girls' school on the other side of Sydney. But even that was a live-in position, which meant that in our first year there we only saw each other every couple of weeks. Well, that was pretty hellish. I found that difficult. Occasionally I was able to visit her at the school, and sometimes we'd manage to spend a bit of time together. Holidays we went tramping and bush walking, and that was fun. But then I can remember one time having a blackout in the quad at the university, and of course they carted me somewhere and rang Muriel up—well, that, on reflection, was just the stress of separation. I really did find it quite intolerable. It's true that a lot of things at that time I took for granted, but there is also this remembered feeling of a longing, a looking forward to the time when we would be together.

MURIEL

IF I THINK of my life divided into periods, I should say that my time together with John could be looked at as a series of chapters, or even a number of personal adventures, into which we have wholeheartedly leapt. I mean, like our time in Auckland, in which we grew and learned a great deal. And there was another chapter when we went to Sydney, where John wanted to do his social work. I wanted really to do speech therapy but never got to it. Just after we arrived they changed the venue to Melbourne, and John's was in Sydney. We weren't really game at that stage of our lives to live in separate cities. So I went to Abbotslea, this frightfully select boarding school for girls, where I stayed for a whole year and only saw John once a fortnight. Every other weekend I was on duty as resident mistress. John had a place in Ryde that year. An awful room in which he boarded and where we lived together on my weekends off. Occasionally John came to see me at the school, but that didn't really work. So the room at Ryde was the place we saw each other. It was a lovely Irish woman who took us in there, but oh dear, it was a pretty dreadful room.

We hadn't been married for that long by then of course, perhaps five years or something, and I think the effect of being away from each other at that time . . . I think it made us more tender. Yes, I think so. And also a feeling of longing. I can remember John sending me a book of Evelyn Underhill with a lovely poem in the front of it. "Here dear Mu I give this book"—he called me "Mu"—yes, and there were one or two more bits, and then, "The paths once chosen are still ours to tread." It was really about our way of life, and time for meditation, those sorts of things. And so this book came in the post, and oh, I remember opening it, it was so thrilling. You know, I can't ever remember a time in my married life when I haven't felt in love with John. I've always looked forward to his coming, to seeing him. I would feel, that's lovely, there's John. I don't think we ever went through a stage when we were bored with one another, or fed up with one another. There were times, I suppose, when we treated each other in a callous or discourteous way, times of anger when things have been said that we didn't mean. But never a time when we didn't love each other.

Things were better the second year, when John and I both went to live in what was called the Settlement. That was in Redfern, which at that time was quite a slum area of Sydney. In those days it was felt that the university had some responsibility to the depressed areas surrounding it, and so it set up what was called the Settlement. It was not in fact a new idea but a movement that had worked elsewhere overseas. There would be a warden with perhaps some assistance, and the whole thing would be manned by student volunteers and others who gave of their time voluntarily. Sometimes there would also be student fellowships, in the sense that you had accommodation there in return for providing recreational or social work services for the local people. It certainly had a strong effect on the community, and I think on the whole was well thought of. In our second year John ran a carpentry class there, and I got a job looking after a centre for the children. This entitled us both to have a room in the settlement, which we then joined together so that we had a kind of semi-flat. As I say, it was a slum area with bedbugs and all the usual things, but we had a good life there. I remember it as a time of lovely people and many experiences. The neighbours were beautiful. All the houses were joined together of course, and you always knew what was going on. There'd be old Mr. Clancy next door, his head out the window, "Don'tcha bloody know it's half-past bloody eleven a bloody clock." Oh, we used to lie in bed and chuckle to ourselves. And once while we were in bed like this he yelled out, "Stop your bloody muttering," and we shut up like a book. Ha ha ha, the walls were so thin that it took us a while to realise he was yelling at his kids. Yes, it's not so much the stress I remember from those times—more the experiences and the lovely people. Our adven-

They had a dog, too, that excreted all over the place, and a baby that wasn't too dissimilar. They were Irish, good-hearted people, just lousy housekeepers. We had a small room there with a double bed which just about filled the whole room. And there was a little primus we used to cook our porridge on beside the bed. I can see all these things now in my mind, vivid images of all the things that happened. Muriel and I getting away when we could, climbing in the Blue Mountains, tramping together, sleeping in the little pup tent together. Oh yes, looking back at us then, our relationship then, it was right there alright, it was solid. I don't think anything could have threatened it.

A year later there were beginnings of another kind as well. An awakening to new conceptions, new awareness in terms of relationships. We were living by then in what was known as the University Settlement. Aldous Huxley was a writer very much to the fore in those days. A lot of his books were about, and I read quite a few of them. He wrote a book called *Time Must Have a Stop*, and this was a crucial point to me. It's the story of the development of a young fellow who goes through all sorts of adventures, and at one point he meets up with an old man. I don't remember if he was a monk or what he was, but quite philosophical sort of thing. And one of the things the young man asks him—and this is probably why I was so taken with the book—was the question, what is the meaning of love? Well, part of the old chap's answer was that you cannot love to order, but you can attend. And this really went home to me. You see, at that time I took a carpentry class, teaching carpentry to all these young urchins in the area where we lived. And I had one young fellow—he was a real child of the slums. His clothes didn't fit, he stank, his nose ran, and he was a thoroughly unpleasant little boy. There was nothing I could find to like about him. Even so, my idealism was high and I thought—I felt—that I should love him. That's what I felt . . . but I didn't. Somehow I couldn't love him, but at least, I thought, I will attend. And so I did. I taught him carpentry, and I listened to him, and I attended to him . . . gosh, I've got powerful feelings when I think about this.

I remember this very strongly. It was a day some time later, I was walking up a street outside the Settlement, and here was this little fellow coming down the other side. And as soon as he saw me he got excited, and his hand went up, and he yelled out so loudly, "Sir, sir, gidday sir!" and in that instant my heart turned over. I suddenly knew what I had meant to him—and that I loved him too. That had a profound effect on me, and I don't think I've ever forgotten it. It gave a new dimension, that I didn't have to struggle to love, and if I didn't love, at least I could attend.

That time for me, I think, was a pretty important period in terms of being more aware of what feelings and responses were all about. Perhaps not knowing exactly what was meant by the word "love," but maybe understanding more about the joy of being close to another human being. Yes, I think perhaps there was a maturing and a growing at that time. How old would I have been then? . . . let's see, about thirty-two, I suppose. So yes, ha, a late adolescence, you might say.

MURIEL

LATER, WHEN John had done his social work, done all his final exams, a friend of ours suggested that we go to Britain. Well, we were sort of loose, we didn't have any children or anything like that, and so we went. And that was, I suppose, the third chapter, if you like. I don't see it as a time of great growing in our relationship, but a closeness—yes, most of our lives we've been pretty close, and in Britain there were many experiences. Yes, I did so enjoy being in Britain. The country was beautiful, I loved the spring. Oh, it was all very exciting. But we were very timid, you know—we didn't go to Europe. Extraordinary really. We went to Scotland, we cycled through Wales, we travelled all over Yorkshire on our bicycles, but we did not travel to Europe. We had this idea—we've always had it—that we didn't have much money, that we'd got to be careful with our money. And that's my father talking, I can hear him now, and John's father, him as well. So

there we were, we couldn't be adventurous. Not in the way young people go off today, without even a penny in their pockets.

All the same, some rich things happened to us there. We worked mostly in a Quaker school for maladjusted children. I taught and John did a bit of teaching and various other things. We must have been there for about eighteen months, two years perhaps, in this great old castle just outside Leeds. An interesting life in a community of caring, lovely people. A life separate and different from anything else we'd experienced before. We visited other communities as well, where the way in which damaged children were cared for made an enormous and lasting impression on us.

And then coming back to New Zealand. The difficulty of getting work at that time. It was a time when things were only just slowly beginning to change. At first it seemed like there was no place here at all that was interested in the sort of skills we had by then acquired. This would have been about 1950. I remember I was giving talks at things like Bevin Brown's Psychological Society, all of which was fairly new then. Anyway, somebody suggested that we might apply for a Church of England position that was going—master and matron of one of their children's homes. A large home that was going to have boys and girls together. Well, that was a really stressful time—a lot of it was hell. When we moved in, it was more like a hospital than a home. All the beds in nice straight rows, a white quilt on every one. All the floors were highly polished, and on the wall brass plates—above the child's bed, for goodness sake—"This bed was donated in the memory of so and so." Really it was all very well-intentioned by good and kind people, but we had had other experiences and our ideas were quite different. I had already told them when we were appointed that I would not take the children to prayers every day, and the brass plates soon came off the walls and disappeared as well. We tried to create a more permissive and creative atmosphere for the children. Well, not altogether permissive, but quite a bit of responsibility was given to the young people and a certain amount of self-government. You know, I remember one little boy coming to us and saying, "I don't know why you don't give us six of the best the way they used to in Timaru." They were so used to being belted, you see. Well, we were quite rebellious in that time, the way we changed things around. At times it must have looked like it was going to get in a real mess and never be the same again. Of course we didn't want it to be the same, and probably, I think, there must have been a few people that were sorry they'd ever let the Morrisons in. Never mind, in due course it all seemed to work out.

I suppose we must have been there at the home for three or four years. In the end, however, the effect of all this—looking after forty or fifty children as well as trying to change the attitudes of the times—was to just about wear me out. Certainly we were under a lot of stress there at times. Never mind, we survived it, and later we moved into what they called a cottage home. There we only had about eleven children with us—a smallish family compared to what we had been used to. We also had a lovely young woman, whom we came to care for very much, to help us. Things at the cottage were easier than they had been in the large home, but at times of course it could still be quite stressful. There were still lots of problems with the children, as you can imagine, but it was always worthwhile. We had relationships there that stand by us now, all these years later. And naturally we had our share of antagonisms too. Looking back, it's easy to see all the terrible mistakes I made, all the things I did not know. I mean, I don't lie awake at night and think about them, but I do see them. We both do.

When we moved into the cottage home, we had a lovely room of our own, a bed sitter type of thing really, which was nice to have, a space to ourselves. Oh, funny how you remember certain things—like John and I getting away together by shutting ourselves in the bathroom. Mind you, this idea of bathing together was something that had been ours for a long time. When we were first at this school in Britain, in the castle, it was snowing, the middle of winter, and we were always frozen. We'd have supper with the staff, and then we'd go off to our room in a very remote part of this huge castle. I mean we had to walk miles just to get there. However, on the way was a terribly old-fashioned bathroom, hundreds of years old, with the water squirting out of these great big taps, but the grand thing was, it was roaring hot. Of course we would sit in this bath together and console one another and it was wonderful. Oh yes, ha, wonderful. Well, at the cottage home we sometimes reckoned that if we shut ourselves in the bathroom, and put lots of water in the bath and made a great noise with the taps running sort of thing, we wouldn't be able to hear anything. And if we couldn't hear anything, we could have a lovely time in there by ourselves. Once we came out again we were exposed to the young, and there was no let-up. Yes, you could get a bit sick of it at times. You'd get very tired, glad often to get the children away for holidays. Sometimes I used to think I was a bit inhuman in that. Well, sometimes they were happy and sometimes they weren't, but you'd get to a point when you couldn't take it any longer.

One thing I always think about when I think of that place— ha, these darn beds that someone had made for us there. They were box beds, single beds that went along each side of the wall. They looked very nice, but oh goodness, if we wanted to get into bed together, ha, we had to be in these jolly box beds, and they had a sort of ridge on the edge which was terrible. Well, it was lovely to start with but after a while it was sheer agony. Well, we didn't do too much of it, hm.

So, that was the cottage home in Champion Street. When we left there, that was the end of another chapter, I suppose. We bought a home of our own again then. The house in Judge Street. I had become really tired after so long with so many children, and I went to see my doctor. I said, "I've got an ache in my back," and he said, "You're just working too hard, that's all." And that was when we decided to make the move. We settled into a new home, and John went back into full-time social work. It was strange after all those years of moving from one institution to another—we hadn't owned our own home since all that time ago when we were first married. Ha, we were almost like private citizens again. Not quite—we took four of the children from the home with us.

The thing I remember about moving into the house in Judge Street was that it had a lovely big bedroom, and for the first time in years we had a double bed again. We bought a double base, and John made legs and a head for each end of it. It had been such a long time, and one of my sisters said, "You'll never do it. You'll never get used to sleeping together again." Ha, it didn't take us long. And we still enjoy that bed today—it's in our cottage at Le Bons. It's in the cuddy—the cuddy is for cuddling—our bedroom there, which is big enough for the bed and not much else.

Children . . . all those children. By the time we went to Britain, I should say this theme had really emerged in our lives. We had had none of our own, you see, and so I think by then we had decided to do what we could for children who were disadvantaged. I felt by then that I had accepted what was, and I didn't go on hoping and hoping type of thing. Mostly I didn't think about it—I was quite happy that it seemed we had a purpose. Yes, so you see, working with children really became the focus of quite a large part of our life.

It's interesting—there was this wonderful old doctor, Doctor Milligan, who was a great friend of my family's and a very wise man, I always thought. He used to lecture a lot at the Workers Education Association—my parents used to go to his lectures— and oh, I can remember my father coming home and telling us all about it. Things like anatomy—oh, all sorts of things, it was very exciting. Well, before John and I got married, he examined me—I'd had peritonitis in my early twenties—and although he said there was no reason why we shouldn't have children, at the same time we had a little talk, and he put this idea into my head. He said that it was a good idea, especially these days, for some people not to have children. And he quoted Helen Simpson—he said that some people could be of tremendous influence if they weren't all cluttered up with a family, so to speak. So there was a

thought there. I didn't say at the time, I won't have children, we won't have children. We didn't say that at all, but the thought was there. And so later on, when we didn't have them, that talk made a difference—I could see a purpose.

When we went to Sydney, when we lived in Redfern, I saw lots of people having babies, and sometimes I felt a little out of it. I thought, everybody seems to have a child a year here, perhaps I'll have one too. There was that feeling . . . but at the same time, I could see that what we were doing would not have been possible if we had children. The work we did in Auckland, what we were doing in Sydney, all these things were something a young couple with no encumbrances could do. Of course people do it these days with babies or not, but you didn't then. So yes, when we didn't have children I began to accept it. Well, you see, this other thread was also there. I had a very strong social concern and conscience,

JOHN AND MURIEL MORRISON

238

so quite likely half of me at least approved. Certainly the sad bit was there, but, you see, at that point I didn't allow it to surface. I wasn't aware of feeling sadness and squashing it, nothing like that. Well sometimes . . . I'm sure I did sometimes think it would be lovely. I did sometimes look at other people's babies.

You know, I can remember a girl in the sixth form at school—she was a prefect and so was I—and she longed only to get married and have children. Quite a few of us then thought, oh, how terrible. I wasn't the sort of person that longed to set up a home. And yet, as our life has progressed, I have been a home maker. Our home has been a place where people have come. They have eaten with us, shared things, enjoyed the place. There has always been a sense of home about it. Which is interesting . . . ha, the nest was there but the birds weren't hatching. A ridiculous metaphor, for goodness sakes, but that was it. There was a saying, two people tied up together make a very small parcel—I've always thought what a terrible emptiness that would be. Well, we've been lucky that we have never had that, there has always been something pretty absorbing in our lives. Ha . . . even so, there were times when I've said to John, I would like to have had children for you, I would have loved you to have children. Ha, yes, I would like to think of you having little Morrisons around.

We had an experience to do with this—much later in our lives—that meant a lot to us. Yes, it affected us a lot. John had been to a seminar in the North Island—no, it was more than a seminar, it was a marvellous workshop. And at one point they were doing role plays. They had to make themselves into family groups, and the group he was with couldn't find a mother—there was not the right number of women—and so they had to be a family without a mother. He was telling me all this when he came home. He was telling me about it, and suddenly I burst into tears. "I was that mother!" . . . it came out all in a gush. "That was my family—I didn't have them—I wasn't there." And so we shared our grief then together. It was a grief that was quite considerable and which we had never admitted before. Somehow it hadn't seemed to press on us, but it was there. For it to come out like that so sponta-neously was very moving and worthwhile. A cleansing, after all those years.

Nowadays it's not something that I feel bad about. Perhaps in one's old age it would be quite lovely to have young people who came and looked after you. On the other hand, they might be on the other side of the world, and they mightn't come back and look after you at all. I have known people whose hearts have been quite broken because of that happening. So there you are.

I THINK it was probably the years following our move to Judge Street when we once again started our serious growing, John and I. That is to say, the growing again in our relationship. It didn't hap-pen overnight of course, I'm talking here of many years, but quite clearly that was a beginning of sorts from which we have reached what we have today. It has gone on ever since.

To start with, however, it was mostly John's life. He was working for the Anglican Social Services, and he was doing mar-riage guidance work as well. What I mean to say is that we wouldn't even go on holiday if there was a marriage guidance meeting. His work came before everything. Certainly I was happy that he should be doing things, but I was coming to a realisation that in our relationship it was John's life that really mattered. In a way it was where I had put myself with John. Perhaps it was because I was not a social worker, and his world was a social work world. People came, lots of them came, but mostly they'd just talk to John. Some would come and they would say very nicely, "Do you mind if we discuss this or that?" It made a difference, to be acknowledged, but still it was John's thing. It's true at the time I had my spiritual life, my work with the Quakers, but not many people would come to our home about that, not in the same way. And I also had this feeling—and I think it was true—that if social workers came, John's eyes lit up. Because this was his life. If people came to talk to me, his eyes didn't light up. That was the differ-ence. Our life was contained in the social work world, and that of course wasn't just John. In a way I had contributed to that, I had had a share in it. I had put myself down and I had to work at getting out of that.

The children we still had were growing up then, and gradually they left. They got married or went off in one way or another. Life became less strained certainly, and there was more time for my own growth. That's when I began to restake my own claim as a person. I can remember on one occasion, a friend coming to consult us about something—but to consult John really. And I said to myself—I can remember thinking it—always John is the one they want to see. I am only on the sideline, I can make the tea sort of thing. I put myself down fairly solidly. Well, on this occasion I had something to say—we were both standing in the kitchen with this person—and I had a contribution to make, which John just brushed aside. And afterwards I said, "John, I am a person. What I say matters." And I was quite tearful and very stressed, and very emphatic. And he heard that. John has always been very good at hearing me when I have a point to make. Sooner or later he comes to it, and this time it was sooner. He sat down and he thought about that. And it seems to me that that was a time of recognition. A sort of recognition of each other as people in our own right. All sorts of things, it seemed, started to happen in those times. It was a period of struggle, but also growing, and a very clear willingness—a desire—to understand how we could best be happiest together, while at the same time recognising our own pathway. What was right for each of us. We got involved in group life laboratories, seminars, workshops of all different sorts. Many of them to do with marriage and relationships. Of course what opened the door in large measure after all those years was John's work. The experiences that John had when he went to many of these seminars and conferences always came home with him and we shared them together.

Another thing was the strong flow of the Women's Movement, which had come on by then. There were growths in that direction—John's recognition from his reading of books like

Women's Reality and also me quietly staking my claim. I didn't do it as vigorously as some women might have done, but I was quite clear, and I did what for me were some fairly drastic things. For example, John would often come to me—he would be excited about some book or something, and he would want to tell me about it, or talk about it. And one particular day I was feeling very strong about this—I was writing a letter—and I said, "John, I'm wanting to do this thing now, I don't have time to attend to you." And that was very crushing for him. It took me quite a lot to do that. Usually I would compromise, but somehow this day it mattered. It mattered to me. It was very important, and there are times when you have to sacrifice something if you are to be true to yourself. And so I did this. I did that to John, and it was very shattering to him. He came around to it in a day or two, but he was very upset at the time. But there, it had happened, and it was a turning point. And since that time there have been quite a few turning points at which I have said, "John, I am a person, I want to be this way."

Then there came a time when I was more separate, when I was very much in my world. A world where I had my own strengths and gifts and abilities. I wasn't in the least dependent, and I didn't have to be John's wife to be somebody. I don't know that I ever did actually, but certainly at that time I became much more strengthened in myself. I went to Pendle Hill about that time too. In America. It's a Quaker retreat, a study centre, and I went there for a couple of terms. That is where I really was my very own self. I had got well on in life by then—I suppose I must have been about sixty-five—but I was very much me. A wonderful time of reading and study and meditation, of recreation, lots of things, but mostly of being my own true self. It was very special. And special for John too, because we were separated like that. It was my own separate adventure, and John lived by himself and did his own separate thing. And it was very good. We each became much more our own selves. I mean, it wasn't all that long really, only three months, but it was just good.

JOHN AND MURIEL MORRISON

242

JOHN

GOING TO Great Britain—that was a deeply satisfying time. The work we did there, the things we learnt—oh, we worked in some wonderful places with very good people. We arrived just after Christmas at the school where we were to teach. A great circular drive and this grand old manor house in the falling snow, gas lamps were everywhere, it was just like the Christmas postcards we'd been brought up on. Of course food was still being rationed then after the war—this was in 1949—but we were very fit and well on top of things. We bought bicycles and used to cycle all over the place, just absorbing the local countryside—it was wonderful. And sometimes we'd go further. I have vivid recollection of lots of really marvellous things we did together. Westminster Abbey, Cleopatra's Needle, all those places that seemed to make history come alive. Or following the sound of beautiful music in Wales until we stood on the doorstep of a little chapel, and being asked to come in, and there to see this wondrous Welsh choir in full flight. There was a kind of togetherness in that . . . yes, there is some cement in that sort of thing. Shared experiences that become part of our own personal culture, you might say, something that cannot be eliminated. Intriguing though, how, for my part at any rate, it is the incidents that are still vivid in my mind. That there is a lack of any really clear perception in terms of the relationship itself. Nevertheless, there was at that time, I think, a sense of an increased competence in our relationship, a sense of togetherness that was by that time very strongly there. Yes, Great Britain was particularly fulfilling for us both, I think. And certainly by the time we came back to New Zealand we were pretty well experienced in dealing with disturbed youngsters, which of course is why we had gone away in the first place. We had gone away together to learn about this. All our experiences were focused around that, and so there was a kind of partnership there. I see all this now with hindsight of course—at the time I was conscious only of the task. The relationship—our relationship—was taken for granted.

JOHN AND MURIEL MORRISON

WHEN WE GOT back to New Zealand we were all fired up to do something. Ha, there was nothing to do. I even went to see the Minister of Education, whom Muriel had known—she'd been a student of his when she was at university. All he could say was that we had come ten years before the right time. He was right. We had come back to Christchurch, and there was nothing doing at all. And so I became a builder's labourer, which was okay—it didn't do me any harm at all.

Then the Anglicans decided to set up a family institution; they had a boys' home in Timaru and a girls' home in Christchurch, which meant that when families came into care they were being split up. Not a good thing at all, and finally they decided to bring the two together to stop this happening—make one big family home of it. Well, they were looking around for staff, and somebody heard that we were about, and they offered us the job. Oh goodness, it was a job and a half. Almost back to where we were in Auckland. On our day off we'd virtually be running down the driveway again, desperate for a break. Even then we'd know that when we got back we'd have to unravel all the problems that had taken place through our not being there. Yes, it was very demanding. Gosh, we'd crawl into bed together and I can remember saying—I think we both said it—I wish they'd give us the sack. But they never did. Anyhow we did do some interesting things there with the children, some really quite innovative stuff. Actually I didn't realise how progressive we were there until much later on in life. But there was very much a togetherness for Muriel and I in what we were doing then, although I still saw Muriel as the dominant person. That was interesting. She was extremely capable organizationally, and I was very much a supportive person. I think I was the theoretician. Trying to work out the things that we tried with the children. And yes, there was a togetherness in that. Taken for granted again, I suppose, but solid all the same.

We had this place for about four years, I suppose, and then finally we contributed to the disbandment of it. The idea was to move from the big institution into smaller family homes in various parts of the city, trying to create a more family-like social structure for the youngsters. We ran one of these homes with thirteen or so of the more difficult youngsters, but it was Muriel really that had the job. I played the role of husband and father, kind of replicating the usual family situation where one parent goes out to work. That was the time that my own work started to develop, and eventually I became a full-time social worker. "Child field officer" I think they called me at the time.

It felt good—a relief really—to get away from the whole institutional set-up into this smaller home. There was more a feeling of family with us there—the informality of our relationship with the youngsters. Of course most of these kids had one or both parents still in existence, and it was part of our policy that those links should be maintained. We were always careful not to do anything to undermine whatever relationship they had; in fact we tended in a way to limit our intimacy with the youngsters because of this. But I can remember times . . . perhaps we'd be in bed in the morning, and we'd say, gosh, wouldn't it be marvellous if these were our own kids, and they would be in here, and they would be romping about, that's the sort of feeling that would sometimes emerge. At the same time, of course, we were very clear that we did not want in any way to be seen as competition to the parents. So that was . . . well, you know, regret would occasionally be there. I'm certain that Muriel would have loved to have had children. I remember watching her with young children in the early stages and thinking, you know, that she'd make a jolly good mother.

There was an occasion once when we did think of adopting a little fellow. This was years ago in Auckland. It came to nothing in the end. And then we went off to Australia and didn't give ourselves time to regret not having children. There was so much to do that it never became an issue. In the beginning of course, when we were first married, we'd had every intention of having a family, every intention. We thought that would be a marvellous thing to do. But then there was a gradual realisation that perhaps it was not to be. We did make considerable medical efforts in that direction.

JOHN AND MURIEL MORRISON

246

Muriel, you see, had peritonitis just before we got married—in fact she nearly died. In those days the treatment was shocking, no real way of dealing with it. It was only some superb nursing that got her through. Well, later, when the children didn't arrive, we took medical advice about it and Muriel had some operations, but their knowledge of these things then was very primitive, and in the end nothing ever happened. Gradually it dawned on us that nothing would, that it was just not possible. We got to the stage

JOHN AND MURIEL MORRISON

of accepting it as our lot, we didn't sit around being regretful and hoping that things would change. We just got on with it then, plotted our own course. Yes, we came to terms with it alright, but with a denial of the disappointment that was involved with that. We denied our own grief.

Something that strikes me nowadays of course is the way we always assumed that it was Muriel who could not have children. Later on in life, when I began to deal with adoption issues in my work, I came up against this question of men who were infertile. This was a real concern for many men—it seemed to bring in this whole question of potency—and if they had not come to terms with it properly, the adopted child, as a constant reminder of their infertility, would often cop it. By and large men never wanted to admit the fact that they might have been the cause. It was always the woman, the wife, that carried the can. Now when I thought about this as regards myself—how in the hell did I know that it wasn't me? And so there was then this realisation that perhaps it was Muriel, but it might have been me.

It's interesting that a large part of our life has been involved with children. One could make the reasonable assumption that it has been, to some degree, a compensatory activity. I mean, we were up to our necks in children, all different kinds of children and their problems, so that our thinking—everything—was wrapped up in that. So absorbed in the young, so close to so many . . . strange, isn't it, how it took so long for our grief to come. Perhaps not. But it did come, it was there all the time of course, the loss of the dream that I suppose most married couples have. To have that family of your own, the chance of a certain closeness . . . twenty-five years it took to come out.

I went to a lot of seminars and workshops at that time. This was well after the family home, after the other children had left I should think. I had gone to this workshop in Hamilton and as part of what we were doing we had to set up an imaginary family. I happened to be the father of this family, and there were three other chaps representing my children. These were men in their thirties probably, but they were acting as children. And I was supposed to go out amongst the other people there and find a mother. Well, this perhaps was typical of me in that I left it too late, and there were no women left over. So I came back and said, "We haven't got a mother." And they said, "Alright, we'll be a bereaved family." So that's what we did—we got into this and dramatically expressed it and talked about it and all the rest of it. It was a good experience. But then at the end of this whole thing the leader of the group said, "Now, send your family away." And by gosh, this was a traumatic experience. One by one I had to say, go away . . . go away to these children. Finally they went, and I was devastated. I went into the corner of the room and cried. I howled and howled. That's how it suddenly hit me. And all I could think of then was that I must get home to Muriel. Often she had said to me, "Do you mind that we haven't had any children?" And I'd say, "Oh no, of course not. Look what we've been able to do without children." We'd been able to go all over the place, do things, have adventures—"No." And then suddenly I realised, crying there in the corner I realised, we had never grieved for the children we didn't have. And I could hardly wait—I got off the plane, I was bursting to get home. The first thing I just grabbed Muriel and I said, "Look, this is what's happened." And gosh we just hugged one another and wept and wept. We did our grieving. It was important, important for both of us. A very human revelation. Unfinished business that was then finished—healed.

It doesn't pay to have regrets about things you can do nothing about. I have reflected on that as part of understanding my own existence. I suspect that a lot of people find some comfort in facing their own mortality with the knowledge that there is some sort of continuity through the having of children. Having thought about that, it makes no sense to me. We all of us have to come to terms with our own mortality. The fact that you may have children makes no difference to that. There is a side issue to this as well, I think, and that is the nuclear issue. The enormity of a situation in which all that potential for human life is suddenly destroyed for ever—that . . . that is an enormity of the highest possible order. I feel very powerfully about that. It's not my own continuity that's concerned here, it's the continuity of more than the human race even. What is in danger is the marvellous mystery of existence itself. The destruction of that I find hard to contemplate, and I live in hope that it will never happen. But in getting back to the personal, I would say that by now circumstances have detached me from the kind of longing that says, I wish I had someone to carry "me" on. What I shall be happy with is the on-going existence of all life on earth.

IT HAD BEEN something of a relief to get away from the institution and into the smaller group home, but after some years it got to the point, I think, where Muriel was emotionally exhausted. My job by then was very full too; both of us had very demanding responsibilities. In a sense we needed one another, and so a little while later, when the opportunity arose, we jumped. It was a time when a number of the kids we had were taken over by their parents—we were down to four children—so it seemed a good time to resign. We told the four that were left we were going, but if they wanted to come with us that would be okay. Well, no question, they all came. I don't suppose many people would wish to have four adolescents to cope with, but for us, having a home of our own and no committee sitting on our shoulder, it was pure joy. Gradually of course the children grew up and left home; but oh gosh, having our own home again after all that time, that was good. We got down to doing our nesting, if you like, whatever that was. But yes, it was a tremendous feeling to have our own piece of dirt again.

AS FAR AS my profession was concerned, I think it is probably true that my work over the years, my involvement with social work, opened an aperture into life and thinking I might not otherwise have had. The philosophy, meditation, therapy, workshops, and what have you—all those things have been relevant to the way in which I've lived, and to the things I've come to understand. It has,

I would say, made a profound difference—but not of course all at once. Nor would I ever presume to have all the answers. What perhaps I have done is to have understood something from my own experience along the way.

I suppose I could say that by the time I was about forty-five there had been some quite significant changes in my own self-esteem. I had been training marriage guidance counsellors for a few years by then and was well into building up the Anglican Social Services. I'd spent some time working in the new therapies, Gestalt and what have you, by then, and there had been some quite profound changes in the way I looked at life. My attitude was that everybody needs to feel worthwhile in themselves, needs to feel competent. The focus of the work was to enable people to feel good about themselves, and to overcome the sort of thing that I had inherited—a message in your head that you're not good, you are no good. I had overcome that through workshops and good therapeutic experiences; I had to learn to put into my own mind a totally new statement. And when I was working with other people, that is what the end view was, that they have within themselves their own self-support. I have come to understand that no matter how grim your beginnings are, it doesn't have to be that way. We can change and change radically, sometimes in a very short time. It works like that for some people—they can just switch overnight. Others will say, gosh, it's been like this for donkey's years, I can't expect to change in one go. It's like living in prison, I suppose. One day you get up and you find that the door is open and the sun is coming in. Some people think, ah yes!

Other people say it shouldn't come in as quickly as that. That is the way it is for many imprisoned people. They come out into the open world, and then they go back again. It's sad . . . how often our security is determined by imprisoning ourselves in some way. The move from the known to the unknown has never been an easy one.

Ha! Talk about imprisonment—I was twenty-three years with the Anglican Social Services. Now, that was far too long. Looking back it's obvious I should not have been there so long. I remember I used to joke about this old dictum—never stay in one place more than seven years. Not if you want to keep your creativity up. In seven years you will have given all you have—time to move on to new things. And there I was, twenty-three years—ridiculous. Ha, loyalty to the firm. Probably still my father's influence—staying in one place, he was very strong with that. And yet, there he had a life where he went all over the place—ha, wretched blighter. By the time I finally resigned in 1974, everything had become habitual, the pattern of the day was repetition. It's true that over the years many good things had happened, I had learned much in my time there, but finally getting out of that job was a tremendous breakthrough. A breaking out from one of my own prisons—and there is a story as to how that happened.

Muriel and I went to a weekend led by a very fine group-worker, and during the weekend he led us in some very valuable exercises. One of the things that we had to do was select an animal that we wanted to identify with, and I chose to be a sea gull. And then in fantasy we had to be that thing we had chosen. Well, I took off and I flew up over the hills and the mountains, on and on, and then I sailed down the valleys and landed on a shingle river bed. Just to stand there looking around, pleasing myself—there was such a real, wonderful freedom in this. And then he brought us back to immediate reality, and we told each other what our experience had been. Next he said, "Go into your minds—imagine in your own minds—a room in your own home." And so I tried this, but the only room that came to mind was my office. I struggled to get a room at home but it wouldn't come, so I just thought, blow it, and I got into my office instead. I could see every little nook and cranny in the place. Every mark on the wall and desk; and also the office had a large window, which the building next door blocked out almost to the top. There was just this thin line of blue sky—it was the only thing I saw outside. And what was interesting was that from time to time a sea gull would land on that parapet, and that always delighted me, to see the sea gull. Anyhow, the next thing he said to us was to imagine a cage in our room. And so I put a cage in the corner of my office. Now he said, "Get into that cage as your animal or bird or whatever." Then he said, "Jump up and down in your cage." Well, at first when I tried to it was a kind of half-hearted, pathetic heave, but then he said, "Get out of your cage," and that's when finally I really got into it. I tore at the bars until I eventually squeezed through, and then I flew around the room, bashing myself against the window going round and round and round . . . and then he brought us back. And

JOHN AND MURIEL MORRISON

253

as I began to recount it, recount what had happened, I remember I was banging my fist on the table and saying, "I'm going to leave the bloody place!" I don't remember a lot of what else happened, but it was a dramatic time for me; and subsequently I did resign.

I moved on then into the hospital system. I was five years at Princess Margaret Hospital. In lots of ways that move was very difficult, in the sense perhaps of adjusting to a completely new environment. It took me six months, I suppose, to really get accustomed to it all. But then it seemed my world opened out—all these interdisciplinary contacts—and I never looked back. Yes, it was a wonderful experience. And then I had a couple of years at the Child Health Centre before I retired. It's called the Child and Family Guidance Centre now, and I did thoroughly enjoy those two years before I was compulsorily retired.

I don't know that this thing of retirement is easy for anybody. One reason it is not easy is that people get identified with their role, their task, and when they retire feel very bereft of it. I can remember seeing a statistic back in about 1975 or '76 about headmasters. It said that after retirement their life expectancy was twelve months. And my God, it was true. I knew a headmaster who retired from Shirley School, and he was dead in three months. And when I checked this out with other school people they said, "Oh yes, that's right." Now, that doesn't mean all of them, but a large percentage do. I thought hard about that—why it could possibly be. And then it dawned on me—I've got relatives that are schoolteachers. Two sisters-in-law are schoolteachers, a brother-in-law is a schoolteacher, and Muriel was originally a schoolteacher as well. So what do they talk about—schoolteaching. Social workers are just as bad. Get them together and what do they talk about—their profession. And the unconscious thing is, I am a teacher. I am a social worker. Their identity gets so tied up with what they do that once they retire, they don't exist any more. Somebody commented that a lot of these people die of heart failure. It's an interesting metaphor, they die broken-hearted.

That made me think. I did not want it to happen to me. The

JOHN AND MURIEL MORRISON

problem was of course that I enjoyed being a social worker. I had a designation which had a certain status about it, and for which I was paid. I was competent in what I did and recognised by other members of the profession. In fact, it was a real satisfaction to be what I was. I reflected on all that, and then I thought, to hell with it. Who wants to die twelve months after they retire. I started then to philosophically divest myself of that one identity. To look at, in fact, what I did do. That there were periods of time when I did an activity which is called social work, and when I wasn't doing that I was doing something else. I was being a husband, or a gardener, or a carpenter—lots of other activities. I really grooved that into my mind, that it was an activity that I was doing, and that I did lots of different things at different moments in time. My identity then became the whole of me, not just John Morrison social worker.

Even so, retirement was awful. I was compulsorily retired from the hospital board at age sixty-five. At a time when I was functioning very well. The unit I worked at—the Child and Family Guidance Centre—wanted to keep me on. I wanted to stay—I was thoroughly enjoying my work there. But this date, this time when I was supposed to resign or retire, it came nearer and nearer and I didn't want to go. I took it very badly indeed. The whole of my being resisted it, and it created a situation where I was just hanging on, as it were. The unit made representations to the administration, and they said, alright, you can keep him on till somebody else is found, indicating that they should advertise the position. Well, they didn't advertise, and I'm pretty sure they would have mucked around with it for quite a while sort of thing—but it was all so indefinite. It didn't feel good to be in such an uncertain position. Unreal, somehow, to stay on because people weren't doing what they were supposed to be doing. In the end I felt I had to decide. I was talking about it one day to one of the psychiatrists I knew there. He said, "What are you going to do, John?" And so I just said, "Right, I'm leaving at the end of the month." Probably the way things were, it was a good thing to have happened at that stage, to cut it off like that. Fortunately for me, I was let down fairly comfortably in that I was given a job at the Polytec, a part-time job there, and then out of the blue the university offered me another part-time job as a fieldwork student liaison officer. So that let me down very nicely. Yes, that helped me recover from it, and I got into a pattern where I started to enjoy life again.

Of course it's a fascinating thing the careers that people sometimes get into—that is, in terms of things we need to understand, to know, about ourselves. There was a point in my work when I began to look at the question of dependency, to see it as being a strong factor operating in relationships. It often seemed to be part of the reason things went bad for people. Now, I also had enough insight by then to know that the reflection of this realisation was my own dependency. Certainly I didn't try to pretend that I was any different—I was in the same boat as everybody else. However, what started to emerge at that point in some of the workshops and seminars was the idea that this dependency was a consequence of not being able to care for oneself in an emotional sense.

That goes back of course—back to the time in which I entered my adulthood. A time when the expectation was that women looked after men—in every way. It was understood that women would be the nurturers, the carers. To question that—well, you questioned the whole edifice of our very belief system. It was really a kind of quantum leap later in life to discover that you didn't have to remain with what one's early upbringing had determined. It was possible that you could learn to care for yourself emotionally. Idealistically you could get to the point where you weren't dependent on one another, where a relationship could become mutually supporting and non-possessive. That was the ideal, anyway. In truth it was probably only five or six years ago—when Muriel wanted to discover herself as herself, not as John's wife—that I really came to understand what that meant. Muriel went off to America for a period, and that was a very important time. Yes . . . a really critical thing. Of course, like most things, this dependency business was taken for granted, not really felt—experienced—until it was threatened. I was not even aware of it still being there until the threat of loss. When Muriel decided to go to America, I had about nine months notice—well, that was a hell of a time, that nine months. Fortunately I managed to keep my mouth shut—but I didn't want her to go. Anyway, she went, and slowly I started to find out I could take care of myself. It was not easy to change like that, but I wanted to. I wanted to learn to manage on my own, and with difficulty I did. In the end it became a very satisfying thing. A good experience. I think it was for both of us. Although really, my knowledge of just how Muriel perceived that time—or any other, for that matter—is pretty limited. But then I suspect that's how it is for most people. The best we can do is try to put ourselves in the other person's shoes, and people who can do that well are, I suspect, few and far between.

As for the dependency now . . . I imagine to some degree it still remains, but there would be a much greater aspect of independence than there ever was before. I am now more capable in terms of meeting my own emotional needs. That doesn't mean to say I no longer have them, but I would think there is a kind of balance now that makes life within our relationship a lot easier.

You know, it's funny when you look back on your life— where has it led you, where is it now? To call it a great life seems too superficial. To call it a miserable life—well, that's a lot of nonsense too. And to say it was deeply satisfying—that doesn't seem to fit. The term I'd use is a kind of fortuitous good fortune, and I'm not even sure about that. But that's what it's felt like. Things have dropped into place. The things we did seemed to be in preparation—seemed to lead on to the next step. There's been a kind of growth pattern in the whole of my existence which in a sense I've never felt was my doing. Things just happened. I remember hearing about a book once called *Life Is What Happens When You're Making Other Plans*. When I heard that, I thought, yes, that's right. "Life is what happens" seems to have been the theme of my life too. The plans we have made . . . well, yes, there's been a modicum of that. Now, I'd say, make plans by all means, but never assume that things are going to come out that way.

JOHN AND MURIEL MORRISON

MURIEL

As a child, old age was something I don't remember seeing at all, not then. My grandmother was quite old, but I think I thought of her as another person. Yes, quite different from me, a grown-up. She was in the world of grown-ups. Later, when I had grown up myself, when I was maybe in my twenties, I think then I had the feeling of endless life—that the future was endless. There was perhaps a stage once when I worried about death, but that's very clouded over now. Funnily enough, it was the idea of infinity that used to worry me then. The notion of infinity as being beyond, somewhere beyond. I used to think of the edge somewhere—there had to be an edge to the world, and what happened after that? For a period in my adolescence this quite worried me—what happened beyond the edge. I had this visual image which strangely enough was a horse and trap, somebody driving a horse and trap. They had driven right to the edge, the very edge, and what was to be found there—that worried me. The anxiety of darkness, the abyss, something—I don't know. It was just some dark thought, not really much to do with old age, just the idea of where does it finish? That was the nearest I came to thinking about time moving. Thinking about death was too far away; it didn't happen to me, so it was too far away to be thought about. There were old people in my environment, but I never thought of being like them. And now—well, I still don't think about being in old age, but sometimes I say to myself, you know, you're seventy-four, nearly seventy-five, so yes, you are getting on. And yet in another sense that doesn't mean a thing, because I am me, and I don't feel any different.

I will say this—that I am well, that I am quite fit and supple because I have done a lot of yoga, and really I don't have any immediate disadvantage or discomfort. I get more tired than I used to perhaps; I have more rests than I used to. Well, I enjoy different things. And the things I used to love, the dancing—the country dancing, the ballroom dancing, these lovely things—I don't care if I'm a hundred, they are still very exciting for me. Even now we still burst out. We usually have some nice music on while John does his exercises in the morning, and sometimes, certain pieces, certain movements that I've always loved, always danced, they'll have me up. I'll leap out of my chair and prance around the room. We were doing that together just the other day. The only thing now is we don't go on for so long as we used to, that's all. I love swimming too, but perhaps I don't go to the sea like before. You might say things are less vigorous . . . I just see it as a different place, a different place in the journey. I can imagine it would be a very different thing if I were not well—or if I were very poor. Yes, if I was cold and didn't have enough food—those things, I think, would make old age feel really old.

Well, I am lucky. For me being older has a richness about it. There is the richness of having known people for a long time. There's the richness of looking back, of seeing where certain things have come from. There is the richness of meeting new people all the time, which is wonderful. And there's the richness now of taking things more quietly, of enjoying things in a better way than I used to. Nowadays I don't gobble things up so much. When I was young I was always thinking about what I was achieving. I did my music exams; I got my musical degree. I went to university; I got my degree there. And I would say, well, I've done that, and what am I going to do next? Doing, doing, everything then was doing. Over time, though, things change. As the years went on I got a better balance to life, a better sense of things. And along with that perhaps a greater capacity to enjoy. Yes I think so . . . I have lived long enough to see the richness in old age. Now I see every little thing that has happened as part of the total thing—call it a fabric, if you like—into which all is woven. Nothing really has been a waste. And sometimes it's been the insignificant, the little events which have shown the way to larger things.

You know, there was never actually a time when I felt, today I have become old. One day has followed the next, and I seem

JOHN AND MURIEL MORRISON

always to be just the same as I was yesterday. And yet time has gone by. I can look back on my life and say, lucky, fortunate, what opportunities, what adventures. A life I'm happy to have had. Oh, I can look back at mistakes made along the way too. Oh dear, yes, when I think of the children—making a mess of this or that—but it's a useless thing to beat oneself over past mistakes, that would be a stupid business. Anyway, it's often from the mistakes we learn most, and all life is a learning process—multifaceted. Well, old age is no different, just part of the whole.

Sometimes I see it a bit whimsically. I mean, I'm sometimes amused by it—amused by being seen as elderly. If somebody in the bus gets up and gives me their seat I think, what a joke, I must be looking a bit decrepit or something, ha ha ha! Yes, but I don't ever think of *myself* like that. So I smile a bit, you know. I mean, I suppose there is a certain respect or something in it, and maybe it's true that at certain places and times I have sat back and let other people do things for me because I'm older. Yes, but that often comes rather by surprise—I guess I'm amused by it as much as anything, amused by the idea of how people see me. After all, when I'm with old friends, everything is just the same as it ever was. Just the other day I was with my sisters writing a letter. Well, it might have been twenty years ago, or it might have been forty years ago, it felt just the same. I mean, we're very fortunate that the four of us are all still around. And sure, we all have our various little bits and pieces, we aren't as fit and hale as we used to be, but in relation to one another we are the same, you see. It would be dreadful if one grew old and the rest of the world didn't. But as everything seems to be going along with me, I don't feel out of place.

Another thing, I think, is that you can be more natural—yes, in just trivial things even. You can wear what you like, do what you like, more so, at least, than when you were young. Certainly I was more pushed around then by what I thought people would think of me. Of course I did it to myself, but I felt it as a great pressure from the outside. Nowadays I can sit in the gutter if I like, and I don't have this pressure of a peer group looking at me. You don't have anybody looking at you, unless you've got children of course, and then—ha, you've got to watch your *P*s and *Q*s. When you've got none of that you can be really natural. For example, there's no more of this stupid business of being in fashion. It just doesn't matter any more; at my age you can wear what you like. Well, the young do too, they're wonderful. They're a lovely example. Ha, it's probably only the middle-aged that get hung up on their clothes today.

What's underneath your clothes changes with the years as well, of course. Your body is a very essential part of you, and it's true, I think, at least to some degree, that we are reflected in our bodies. That is to say that my body is an expression of me. Sometimes I will look at the young women with their beautifully rounded arms and legs and remember when mine were like that. But goodness me, I wouldn't want them to be like that now. That would be too ridiculous. Though, having said that, I should also say there are things one does have to learn to accept. The fact that you are not as fit or as strong as you once were. The little sorrows—like the other day when I was looking at my old backpack. You know, we used to go on some wonderful adventures together, tramping into some lovely place, carrying everything on our backs—our sleeping bags and our little tent, everything we needed. Sleeping on the hard ground and washing ourselves in a creek the next morning. That was a wonderful time. But I was looking at that old pack, you see, and saying to myself, rather sadly, "You won't be needing that any more. You won't be carrying all that stuff no more." And I feel quite sorry about that. There is a grieving there, but not too much. We still go away of course, but what we're saying now is, we will go to some base and we'll do day trips. John can't do as much now, anyhow. Well, we don't mind, we'll have a slacker time of it. We'll do the walks we can do. Always walking. I think myself we must keep active. As long as we've got a muscle we should be using it. And as long as we go on using what we've got, it will be alright. Okay, the long trips, the really tremendous adventures, they're not for us any more, but there's still lots of beautiful places we can go.

It's not just the walks, though—there's plenty of things now I won't ever do. Always there is less and less time, and that's an important thing to realise. There are times when I've thought that I would like to see Britain once more, in the spring—we could both do that if we wanted to. There are lots of people our age who travel all over the world. But I don't suppose we will. Probably there's not the desire strong enough, and really I see the essence of life being just as rich here as anywhere. Perhaps it's more so. I know that the things which seem most important to me now are the immediate things. To get up in the morning and see with John one of our glorious daisies flowering in the early morning sun. That's better than any travel. No . . . I don't suppose I'll ever have time to do all the things I want to do, but the immediate things . . . well, ha ha, one immediate thing I want to do is to mow the back lawn. I expect I'll have time for that. Yes, and watching things grow. Actually I'm thinking of the things we've planted around the cottage at Le Bons Bay; it would be lovely to have another five years, to be around then and see all those trees growing up. Working in the soil, it keeps me attached, keeps you close to it, close to life. I mean, we all know it's going to stop one of these days and we won't be here any more. That's all. But while you're here, while you're doing something, there's no need to worry or think about that. There's too much life; too much going onwards to start thinking backwards. To be expectant of strength and life and joy, that's the thing. What you expect of life can be very in-fluential, very powerful. If I go into old age with the idea that I'm pretty sound, I'll be a lot better off than if I were to think I was going to crumple up at any minute. Attitude and expectations are important things. Worry, that's no use to anyone.

SOMETHING ELSE that changed as we got older and which I think was important to us was the way in which we related together

JOHN AND MURIEL MORRISON

physically, the whole sexual thing. In the beginning, as I've said before, we were children of our time . . . "inhibited" would be the word. Certainly we were not used to talking about such things, and so for a while it made that part of our lives more difficult. Well, naturally that changed quickly enough, and then in later years it changed again. Now, that was not just a physical thing; it had also to do with us understanding things in terms of the feminist philosophy—the way in which women, and some men, were starting to perceive things then. Looking at this whole question of the male penetration. That it's what the male does with his intellect and with his life, as well as with his penis—and the woman receiving. Well, that's only part of the story. There is a difference. Women, I think, are much—well, let's talk about me—happier to rest in warmth and tenderness. So there was starting to come through then the realisation that the penis and the orgasm were not the be-all and end-all of any sort of togetherness. In fact it often struck me as strange that even if you have orgasm together, it is still a completely self-centred act. What came as a tremendous new realisation at that time was the idea that loving a person didn't always mean sex, not in that manner. In a wider sense there was this greater recognition of the quality of relationships—of relating. The idea that tenderness and concern are also part—and truly part—of sex. I'm not saying of course that women don't enjoy the physicality of sex; no, the thing that was changing then was their awareness about the right to be themselves. Today it is the new woman who is going to say—who is saying—I am not here to serve your purposes. I am here as your partner, your companion, to love, to be loved, but not always just to be available when you want my body. Now, that is an awareness that's growing. That's happening. The ability to work something out that is satisfying for both of you— that is the important thing that's happening. And the amount of concern and consideration you have for one another is what makes it possible.

How you get from one place to the other—how that has happened for me personally—well, I don't think it was any great flash of understanding. No, it was more a blind going forward, discovering through books or films, perhaps, that other people were feeling similar things. And hearing the thing expressed, you were then more able to express it for yourself. Partly also it was my own growing . . . the experiences you have . . . all these things come together. Whatever it was it took place over quite a period of time. John and I talked about it a great deal of course, on and off over the years. His being involved in things like marriage guidance and counselling has, I think, made it very much more possible. So that I would talk to him and he would listen to me, sensitively. Lots of other women could talk to their husbands and it would be hopeless. Well, we've been lucky in that.

And now, as we've become older still, the sexual act itself has become very much less. I'm not saying that we shouldn't have it, nor am I speaking for anyone else here, but for myself, as I get older, that need does recede. The sexual act recedes and other things grow stronger. I don't mean there shouldn't be any bodily closeness; certainly there is a need for the physical, for touching, for kissing, hugging, all kinds of gentleness. What we have now is not less intimate, it's just different. I would not say it was a better way than others, that would be wrong. Each person and each couple must find their own way—that is important. This simply is our way, and for us it is good. At our age any sort of pressure to perform is long gone. What feels good for me now is to be relaxed, quiet, and just to enjoy this moment with John. And that is a long way from when we were young. The rush of those times, the pressure, the tension of the possibility of failure—ah, we were funny creatures. Bursting our boilers to get there, and then all the anxiety that ejaculation would come before the right time, trying to control things, orgasm—all those silly stresses that have disappeared along the way. Now there is nothing left of the struggle for oneself, no possessiveness, no urgency. What we have left is a certain peacefulness, the feeling of two bodies together in what I would call a peaceful enjoyment.

JOHN AND MURIEL MORRISON

265

THERE IS A thing that happens as you live over a long period of time, at least I feel it has happened to me, and it is simply this— you come to know yourself better. I know better what to do with myself and to myself. And I understand more about seeing my-self in others too. The woman who, let's say, talks on incessantly, who would once have annoyed me, I now see that bit of me in her. Now I would stop and think, ah ha, I am looking at myself. And here is the important thing—take her and love her. She is to be accepted, she is to be embraced, she is not to be cast aside. She is part of you, and without her you are not whole. The dark shadows we see in other people are our own dark shadows. That has been a very important bit of my life and growth—my spiritual life, which means a lot to me. You know I had a dream once— this would have been when we were at Judge Street, yes. Some-where in those years between 1960 and 1980, I suppose, and I had this fantastic dream. There was this glorious tree at Judge Street, a copper beech. It was my favourite, a great giant of a tree. Oh, we had to lop off branches, alas; otherwise it would have grown over the whole house. And in my dream there was a man standing beside the tree, and he wanted to speak to me. And so I went to the window, I opened it and looked down—the moon was shin-ing—and I could see on the trunk of the tree an upside-down G. Backwards, it was backwards, a back-to-front G. The man spoke to me then, he said something about going to the moon, and I said I wasn't interested. Then I shut the window, and suddenly I thought, I must go and shut the back door or he'll go around and get in. But as I went towards the door, in the dark passage on the way, I meet him face to face. This was a moment of horror . . . and then it was a moment of adjustment, for this was my own dark self. I had to work through this. This was the dark part of me which I was to meet, to recognise, to know, and to embrace.

I woke up then, and I woke John as well to tell him—I had to tell him. I said, "I've had a Jungian dream." An archetypal dream. Well, that dream has been significant to me for the rest of my life. This meeting of my dark self, which has gone on in all sorts of ways. The parts of me I really don't want to look at and see, or admit. The knowledge that there are parts of me I have not wanted to look at . . . well, I could go on, but you know, really it's just the learning process. The things that come to you over time. In fact probably there is no such thing as old age; there are just older people. Yes, just people getting more mature.

JOHN

SOMEBODY ONCE said that life was like jumping off a cliff seventy or eighty years high—the nearer you get to the bottom, the faster it goes. To me I suppose it has been a surprise more than anything— my God, suddenly I am in my seventies—but then really there are no great and sudden differences in that. As a young man I can remember looking forward to the time when I would be twenty-one. It was the adult age, you had the key to the door, and voting rights, and all the rest of it, and I can remember looking forward to that. But when it came it was all an anti-climax, it felt no different. And of course when I knew better—as I got a bit older and reflected on this—it was simply an illusion. And I think the same now. There is no kind of swap-over point, where beforehand you're an adult and then you're an older person. It is not like that, not a discernible change—at least not for me. Perhaps as I say, a surprise, but a surprise that's okay. Life is still enjoyable.

Changes have occurred of course—physical vigour would be one—but often these things have altered so gradually that you hardly notice them. The mountain tramping we once did, not mountain climbing, but pretty arduous stuff, that stopped a few years back. It gradually got less and less as we began to realise we didn't have what it takes any more. We wouldn't think of it now, not for the last maybe five or six years. We've done day trips, things within our capacity, but yes, that's changed. The structure of my day would be different now as well. Occasionally I'm not so good in the morning, but mostly I'm up at six o'clock and make a cup of tea. I'll meditate first, then off I go and sometimes I work pretty hard. After I've been going a couple of hours, though, it starts to taper off. Well, okay, I'll go and have a rest and a read; then after I've recovered a bit I'll get back to it. And often I'll think to myself, you know, how marvellous it is to be able to do this. I don't mind that I can't work all day as I once could. I'm content with the time that's there, and for the rest of it just to sleep or read, those sorts of things, I'm happy with that. I don't feel I'm missing anything. The only thing at the moment that's not so good is my leg, it's been giving me a bit of bother now and again. And the thought has come to me—you know, say it did hobble me, which it has been doing a little, say it got a bit worse, well, that wouldn't be too good. I wouldn't be able to get into the workshop then, or just generally get about, and that would be hard to take. I suppose I would adjust to it if I had to, just as many other people have, find ways of using the rest of myself. But at the moment—well, I don't know what's going to come of it—it doesn't worry me too much. I'm still fortunate in having good eyesight and hearing, touch, smell, all those things, so my sensual appreciation of the world is still very much alive, which is nice.

There's another thing about the physical at this age as well. I haven't yet perhaps articulated this sufficiently to myself to explain it properly, but—how can I put it? The passions of youth and the constant struggle to adjust, the overwhelming domination of the sexual interest and the coping with all the conflicts that are involved in that . . . that was a difficult aspect of one's living—with my living—and my impression is that it is the same with most people. And so there is something good about the fact that as you get older there is a certain diminution of the sexual aspect of existence. There appears naturally to be a physiological consideration to it, a certain diminishment that can, I believe, lead to a more sophisticated and sensitive companionship. That the purely erotic side of my life is practically gone, that I can now enjoy the subtleties of affection and delight in another person's presence, that I am able to touch or cuddle without the kind of sexual stimulus that was inherent in that at a younger age—that is a tremendous relief. Now, you see, that may be hard for a young person to understand. For a young man to lose his sexual powers, that would be a threat of the highest order. I know from working with younger people that this business of potency for the man was a kind of all-pervasive thing. There was this whole idea that unless they persuaded a woman to sleep with them, or maybe produced a child, then they were inadequate. It's hard for them to understand that you can enjoy relationships at my age in a way that was just never possible before.

There is, I think, a distinction between what you might call caring, and desire. And love in a sense has always been associated with desire. If you just listen to the current songs, the love songs on the radio, there's no question about it. Well, occasionally you might get an element of tenderness or caring for the other person, but by and large it's desire. This kind of sexual chemistry in relationships, a sort of conditioned response that sets people's blood pumping and all sorts of hormonal processes going, just by the sight or sound of something—that sort of thing seems to have gone haywire in our time. Well, maybe it always was. The thing I feel now is that to call desire "love," in any real sense of the word, is nonsense. Maybe a lot of people would disagree with me, but, I mean, if you stand back and take a look at it, just who are you loving in that sort of process? Certainly as far as my own youth was concerned, and with other blokes I knew and talked to, sexual gratification was the operating power behind what we called love. And the crazy thing about that of course—about all these disastrous attempts at the old ideals of sexual achievement and relationships—is that in the end it all seemed so unsatisfactory. And yet on it goes. The whole thing continues to carry on. All through my life, in the work I've been involved with, I have seen this sort of thing upsetting and dominating the lives of so many people. Well, my hope now is that a new time's coming, a time when maybe some of these misconceptions are going to disappear, and it would seem to me it is the women's movement that is showing the way in that direction.

The best that I can assume from women in the feminist move-

JOHN AND MURIEL MORRISON

269

ment is that they are absolutely sick of being used as sexual objects. That is something you hear coming through all the time. And the thing that they do value is companionship and affection. The tenderness and kindness and, you know, the respect in the sense of not assuming the use of them. That, I feel, has a high value to them. But as men, by and large, we have been pretty poor on that side of things. You have the classic thing of blokes coming home, tired maybe, and they will go off to bed and have intercourse, and then they will roll over and go to sleep. And the women are left completely and utterly frustrated. Maybe not sexually frustrated, but emotionally frustrated. Perhaps part of the answer to this is tied up in the sort of question that is often asked: "Do you love me?" And from that comes all sorts of superficial answers like "She's so wonderful," "She's just marvellous," "She's so beautiful," and all the rest of it, which can disappear very quickly and often does. Perhaps the question to ask is, "How do I love you?" To look at the way in which we demonstrate that love to another. The consideration, the supportiveness, the touching. You see, the question of "Do you love me?" or "Why do you love me?"—heaven alone knows. But "How do I love you?" "What do I do?"—you can be very clear about that.

There's one other thing I would like to say about this while I'm on it. It often seems with young people that they have a perception of old age—an assumption really—that older people are not sexually active. Now, that's not true. There is perhaps this benchmark of the young, nubile body, which is beautiful in its own way—sure. But I think it needs to be said that while one may lose the bloom of youth, that doesn't mean to say all attractiveness is gone. And one of the delights I've found in growing old is that while our physical appearance is not what it used to be, there is certainly still enjoyment between us. I mean, I might look at Muriel and think, gosh, she's getting a bit ropey around the neck, ha, but, you see, that's beside the point. We don't have to look physically beautiful to get a response of joy and pleasure in one another's company. A cuddle in the nude is still a delightful thing.

JOHN AND MURIEL MORRISON

You know, for one to reflect at this time on the question of old age is, I suppose, not a bad thing. That I should come up with an answer is something else again. And even if one were to do so, clearly such an answer would be different for each of us. There is of course a certain span of existence for all organic things. For a butterfly it might be twenty-four hours, something else a few weeks, a bird a few years. As for human beings, there are people in the world who will live to well over a hundred years. People who at that age are still agile and alive in every way. And then you think of some other cultures—my own—where people can be grey-haired and bent in their sixties. And I suppose my own image of old age—before I got there myself—was just that. One of wrinkled skin, grey hair, a sort of arthritic slowness, and the idea that life was generally hard going. Now that I have reached that point myself, the chronological age where in our society one is categorised as old, I have come to realise the implications of that view. The implication of what we call appearance. The way in which we allocate roles and positions in society in terms of people's appearance. The policeman with his uniform, the doctor with his white coat and stethoscope, the nun in her habit. And for the elderly it is their own skin which becomes their habit—their uniform. Some grey hair or a bent back, and you have the stigmata of old age. Well, it doesn't have to be that way. Everybody has more than one dimension, and certainly philosophically there can be a to-ing and fro-ing between young and old in which there is no place for such preconceptions.

For older people there can be a tremendous amount of joy and satisfaction in being with young people, if it really is being with them. Listening to what they have to say and being on the level with them, so to speak. But it's a disaster if you assume any sort of posture—you know, more wise than thou sort of business. Yes, heaven preserve us from that. Everyone likes to have a certain respect paid them of course, but I have seen older people try to maintain a status with the idea of "I've had the experience, my boy," and that, I think, is a sad sort of nonsense. Somebody once said that experience is like a bald man's comb, no damn use to anybody. Well, there's a particular truth in that. One's experience is one's experience. It is not necessarily the experience of other people.

Having said that, I now hesitate to say that at this point in my life I understand people better . . . but yes, I have the feeling that I do. Certainly I feel I know myself better, though whether that's a consequence of living a certain length of time I'm not sure. What I do have now is the kind of conceptual framework that enables me to be more conscious of who I am, and that is something I didn't have as a young man. I was rather blithely unaware of myself in those days, or my motivations. I wince a bit when I think of the early work I did with people. It was all pretty mechanical and based on the theoretical constructs of Freudianism. I made all sorts of presumptions based on my own experience, presuming that that's what other people went through too. What you might call a very great lack of understanding. Nowadays, to make any sort of assumption that I understand another person would be an anathema to me. Today I recognise what never then occurred to me—that everybody's experience is uniquely their own.

What I am happy to do now is to tell people what I've learned, and where I have got to, about things that are important for me. But with no presumption that it should be important for them. These days I'm not of a mind to give advice to anybody, but perhaps I would be betraying people if I didn't give them information.

OF COURSE with a lot of things I am now no longer in contact with the real living experience. Yes, at the end of all this it must be said that a lot of what I have talked about is simply the residue of it all. Now, that's a distinction I first came to grips with when I used to go to the pictures, the movies. I'd be sitting there in my chair, completely involved, gripping the side of my seat sort of thing, and then later I would say to myself, hey, it's acting. It's only acting. And I began to think about the fact that I was looking at something which was two-dimensional. Just a thing on a screen, and yet here were all these powerful emotions going on. There was the realisation then that I was the one supplying the emotions, I had put all that on there as it were, and that we are doing this all the time. Projecting onto the world something that is part of us. Not that this was exactly original thinking—it had been around a long time. The Gestalt school of therapy use it as one of their dictums—"all is projection." They would say that you can get some very valuable insights into your own makeup by taking anything you like and describing it, as it were—saying, "I am." And that to do this sort of thing can be a salutary experience, one in which it is possible to learn something of yourself. Of course we don't do it, we just go on with the illusion that we are seeing reality when we're not. Oh, it would be fair to assume that there is some sort of reality out there, but that is not what we are responding to. Mostly, I think, it's like the pictures—we respond to the reality we have created in our own minds.

Time itself is a bit like that. It doesn't really have any objective or substantive meaning. We say, it takes a long time; a length of time; so little time—but that's just metaphor. It gives some focus for attention. But you can't measure time in the metaphors we use. And while some people talk of time as being precious, I by and large don't see it that way. It is true that time goes on, that it is in some way moving, as all things are in movement. A flowing on in which there is sometimes a parallel contact, a touching, as things come and go. My own idea of time is that it is immediate, it is right now, and that this continuous passing moment is all we have. So what is precious to me is to wake up this morning feeling fit, to see that the sun is shining, and to have Muriel there with me— that is rich. It is not precious in that I can preserve it, but it is rich in the sense of fully living in that moment. That is what is real for me now. I don't know who said it first, but I like the idea of living from moment to moment as though it's your last day on earth, but at the same time to plan as though you've got all the time in the world. And I suppose I try to live like that as much as possible. We are developing the garden and going to plant trees and the like

JOHN AND MURIEL MORRISON

on the basis that there will be all the time needed to do it. There are trees living today of course that people planted a hundred and more years ago, and we are the inheritors of that. I am very grateful to those people, and so the idea that I should plant a tree now seems to be a good thing to do.

At the same time, I should have to say there is a qualification to this idea of living in the moment. There is a certain dimension of it that runs along the lines of "Eat, drink, and be merry, for tomorrow we die." With those people I can only take the view that there is a kind of irresponsibility about it, to themselves and to people around them. That sort of philosophy can be exploitative and damaging to others. For myself I like to think I am part of a totality. That I am part and parcel of a much wider thing than just the narrow confines of my own bodily self. Perhaps that is why, when I try to come to terms with the idea of God, I do not conceive of God as a separate, discrete being, from myself or from anybody else. To me it is more that there is no place where God is not. It is inherent in all things. In me, in you, in the tree, in a stone, in every manifestation of existence. I suppose I feel comfortable with that concept because implicit in it is the fact that we are all part and parcel, we are all connected, each of us manifesting in our own particular way.

MURIEL

THERE IS no living without the dying. Death is something natural that is going to happen, and it is important to bring it into focus with life. Of course there are also the little deaths. All through life there are the little deaths—that's part of growing old. A time for everything. The little child who skipped down the path at five no longer does that at fifteen. When the time came that John and I could no longer do the tramping, there was the little death of the physically active person. And there was also the me who once played quite beautifully on the piano but can do it no longer. Well, there is some grief in all of that—some part of me that would like

JOHN AND MURIEL MORRISON

to still. So yes, I suppose we die a little all through life—in all sorts of ways.

When we were young of course it seemed that death did not exist at all. But now we know about death, and it's no longer a thing to be kept in the dark and not mentioned. To talk about it is natural and proper and part of life. I get quite cross with people who say, "So and so passed away." I mean, for goodness sake, say, "Died," that's what's happened. Then there are people who worry a lot about what happens after they die. Well, I don't understand life after death at all. I only think this—that somewhere or other, before I was born, I was around and that I was alright. Wherever I was, I was quite safe, and maybe when I die I'll still be around. But I don't imagine myself having this type of existence or conceiving of life as it is now. There are some who say that souls already dead, relatives or whatever, will be there to greet you. I've heard people say that who really meant it. Well, I don't know whether there is a soul or not, I really have no thoughts about it, except that I think whatever it is, it will be okay. I remember the experience I had when I nearly died all those years ago. There was a feeling I had, a sort of dream, in which I felt quite safe. And that seems to me sufficient. As for right now, I think being alive is plenty enough to cope with.

DARK. DARK . . . darkness and sorrow. If you have had someone, somebody who is very close to you—if they have died, then you know the feeling of bereavement. You have felt the devastation. Well, when we first heard of John's cancer, suddenly that possibility was there for me. Outwardly I tried to be calm, I was calm, but inside I was crying. At home I cried, and sometimes, walking back from a friend's place by myself, I would cry all the way home. I cried a lot, and I think that was good. That was not the worst time, however. The terrible time was after the radiotherapy, when he had become ill the second time. John had this lump for which he went to the hospital, and they said he would have to come in for an operation. We heard on the telephone again that he would have to be admitted in a couple of days' time. We didn't really know then just how bad it was. Then when we went in we were told that this lump was a malignant growth and that they would operate the next morning.

John was very ill then, and I didn't know what was going to happen. My sister was very kind and said, "Come and stay the night with me." And somebody else asked if I would like them to come and stay with me, but I said no thank you. I just wanted to go home. That is where I could do it, you see. Home by myself was the only place I could go into this darkness, this desert, and say to myself, "This is what can happen to you. That you will be left without John. That this is a possibility in front of your life." And go through the night with that and look at it. And to say, "Yes, yes, yes, know that this is true," and not to turn away from it. And in the end I knew it would be alright—it would be terrible, but I wouldn't fall apart. After this night I knew there was a strength for me. I don't say that I had all the answers—no, nothing like that, but just deep down a certain sureness that I can cope. Yes. "The Lord is my shepherd—my soul he doth restore again." Now, I don't have an anthropomorphic God—the Lord in the sky sort of thing—or any man looking after me, but those words "The Lord is my shepherd" have a very deep, real meaning for me.

When I next went to the hospital I was much more relieved. They hadn't taken away the whole of his intestines, which was a fear; he didn't have to have a bag. And that felt such a relief. But there were other nights, nights after that, when I knew things were quite serious. Not that he was going to die then, but that it could happen in a little while. That still had to be thought of. That possibility is still there—it's there for everyone really—but now we are doing so much about healing, we are working hard at that now. And this is what we say, that even if John's life is shorter, now he is living. Now he is living with cancer. He's not dying with cancer, he's living with it. That's the difference, and that is what it really means to us. Another joint adventure, an adventure

JOHN AND MURIEL MORRISON

in healing. An adventure that has given us far greater sensitivity and awareness than ever before. Now we can say that if we only have today, then we want today to be the very best sort of day. We are concerned to make it the best day and not just one of the hundreds and thousands of days that don't really matter. No, today matters. Every day we have now, it matters. You see, we haven't always known that—we know it now.

JOHN

IT WAS THE CANCER, the onset of cancer that brought it home to me. I am going to die. The shock of being told that. The appalling impact of it. The distress. That was the first thing to register. But later, more philosophically, the idea of the importance of the continuing moment. Okay, I'm going to die, as all people will, but it's not the death that matters, it's what happens between now and then. I had thought about that for many years, but to really experience it as an on-going thing—something that happens every day, in which I pause in some moment, or wake up in the morning and say, "I'm here, I'm alive right now"—that is different. There is somehow a perception, a lucidness, which is different than before. And in our togetherness, my awareness of Muriel in the moment— that is sharper than ever before. To meet her freshly again each morning, to wake beside her and think, "Gosh, another day"— that is special.

This sort of renewal every morning, the idea of greeting one another freshly each day, is very important I think. There was a chap—George Lyward—who we met in Britain all those years ago. George ran a place in Kent where he took in all the dropouts from the public schools, young fellows of fifteen or sixteen who just didn't make it. And one of the first things he did with the boys when they came to him was to tell them that here was a place in which they would be loved. And I remember I asked him, what did he mean by this? What did he mean by "love them"? And he said that it meant to meet a youngster freshly at every encounter. Not to judge them in terms of past experience, good or bad. And that, I think, is what Muriel and I have now. A freshness for each other. Every meeting is a new one. In a sense it's very simple, but it's also very meaningful to wake up every day and have that kind of companionship. There is a certain confirmation in having that kind of closeness with another human being, the confirmation that the presence of that other person gives you, as a person in your own right. That, I think, is important, and I can well imagine that if you do not live with someone, then to have people with whom you have a special relationship is pretty important. For myself I could not conceive of it; to withdraw and be sufficient unto oneself—it would just feel like a horror.

There is no question that the way in which I behave, the things I say and do with Muriel, I would not say or do with anyone else. And there is a specialness in that. The fact that I can do things with Muriel that would be foolish with anybody else. It's part of the development, I suppose, of having been so long with another. In a way you become a part of each other. You have accepted the idiosyncrasies, the things that once irritated have become tolerable, and there is, I suppose, a certain security in the familiar—certain things that Muriel does and certain things that I do which have become part of the structure of our life as a whole. We have talked about all this, Muriel and I—what we have together—and of course at our age now we have also looked towards a time when we shall no longer have that. A time when one of us will be left alone.

There's a story about a dog we once had, a spaniel dog named Jenny. We must have had her for eleven or twelve years; she was a great companion. And then she got to the stage when she was old, and for some reason—although she was always fine with us— if there was anybody passed the gate, she was out there snapping, she'd take a piece out of them at the drop of a hat. We confined her for a while as best we could, but in the end that just didn't work, and finally it got to the point where we had to have her put down. As I say it, I still wince about that. I think it's the worst thing I have ever done in my life. And it was days and days afterwards . . . the pain of this . . . a pain from which we recovered, but by gosh, both

JOHN AND MURIEL MORRISON

of us went through hell with that. It was amazing how attached to that animal we were. Well, it was an intimation, I suppose, of the type of pain one of us will someday suffer for the closeness we now have. Of course since this thing with the cancer, Muriel has had the uncertainty of how long I have got. She has me with this, which is different from the other way—of having it. But then, you see, there is also another aspect to this. If I start to think of the age we now are—well, we're of the age when people might die at any time, and so, you see, I'm not to know that Muriel mightn't go before me. Sometimes I think to myself, it is a possibility that Muriel might die before I do.

MURIEL AND I have over the years talked quite a bit about the possibility of one of us going. And how we would cope. I am aware that if either one of us dies, it's going to be a painful experience. We have become so much a part of each other that it would be

JOHN AND MURIEL MORRISON

very foolish to assume otherwise. It is perhaps part of the nature of being human. Things that are so much a part of you—if they are taken away, it would be like a wrenching apart of one's existence. Yes, that is how I would think of it, half of one's existence gone. I think both of us have come to the conclusion it's going to hurt like hell. But also there is the feeling that it can be survived. That we will survive it.

Other people, thousands and millions of people through time, have lost each other, and it has been painful, it is a process through which—one way or another—we all must go. As for Muriel and I . . . I think we might cope with this a little better now than we might have in the past. The dependency aspect of our marriage was a lot different in those days than it is now. Such a loss then could have been a lot more frightening. Now, it would be a loss of a different kind. Not easier—just, I think, that we are more able to cope. Of course, the aftermath of the death of a spouse, that would be another dimension entirely. Who you are after the loss of your mate would, I suspect, be something quite different from who you are when your mate is still alive. Just like when we first got married—we were never the same after that. Of course there's a difficulty with speculation like this—one can only kind of sense—but those are the feelings I have. I don't think it could ever be the same again.

As for the pain of it, I suppose the worst thing for me would be the loss of the one person that I can be with in every kind of way. I imagine that that aspect would be the worst. A kind of re-treat, as it were, back into myself. Muriel would be gone and there would be nobody—not that I could be just like that with. To wake up in the morning and roll over to talk with her, and she wouldn't be there—that would be tough. I have been with people who have talked to me about that; they have told me these things, and you can feel the pain as they talk . . . and so I guess that will be my pain also . . . or Muriel's.

JOHN AND MURIEL MORRISON

Acknowledgments

As WITH MOST BOOKS of this kind, there are a large number of people who have contributed to it, not the least of whom are the many older people who gave of their time and told me the things I needed to know. To these, and to all others who helped and encouraged in different ways, I give my sincere thanks.

Peggy Koopman-Boyden of the Sociology Department of the University of Canterbury gave good and enthusiastic advice from the beginning. More than that, she found funding to keep the project going at a time when it was badly needed.

Grateful acknowledgment is also made to the Arts Council of New Zealand and to the New Zealand Literary Fund for grants that helped to support the work on this project.

Good friends—Kate De Goldi, Christina De Water, Stevan Eldred-Grigg, Bruce Foster, Peter Ireland, Mala Mayo, Philip Quirk, Jenny Rockel, and John Turner—have done more than one could ever reasonably ask. As usual, Peter Black, Bruce Connew, Mary MacPherson, and Terry O'Connor were there when the need arose.

Alan Bright is a man of generous good humour. Not only has he kept my tape recorders running for some years now; he still manages to smile whenever I land on his doorstep. Likewise, Tas Carryer and Mark Inder, who helped when I battled with other technology.

Myrna Edmunds, Joyce Woods, and Marjorie Ockenden were helpful in providing additional photographs.

Megan Jenkinson of the Elam School of Fine Arts made possible the meeting with Doug Harper, series editor for Temple University Press, who offered encouragement and, with his family, fine hospitality while I was in the United States.

Lastly, I would like to acknowledge my wife, Trish Allen. She, more than any other, has helped make this project possible.